Becoming a
Digital Library

BOOKS IN LIBRARY AND INFORMATION SCIENCE

A Series of Monographs and Textbooks

FOUNDING EDITOR

Allen Kent

School of Library and Information Science
University of Pittsburgh
Pittsburgh, Pennsylvania

Global Librarianship, *edited by Martin Kesselman and Irwin Weintraub*

Using the Mathematics Literature, edited by *Kristine K. Fowler*

Becoming a Digital Library

edited by
Susan J. Barnes
University of Washington
Seattle, Washington, U.S.A.

MARCEL DEKKER, INC.   NEW YORK · BASEL

Cover art: Mann Library, courtesy of R. J. Lambert, Jr., Professor Emeritus, College of Agriculture and Life Sciences, Cornell University.

Although great care has been taken to provide accurate and current information, neither the author(s) nor the publisher, nor anyone else associated with this publication, shall be liable for any loss, damage, or liability directly or indirectly caused or alleged to be caused by this book. The material contained herein is not intended to provide specific advice or recommendations for any specific situation.

Trademark notice: Product or corporate names may be trademarks or registered trademarks and are used only for identification and explanation without intent to infringe.

Library of Congress Cataloging-in-Publication Data
A catalog record for this book is available from the Library of Congress.

ISBN: 0-8247-0966-7

This book is printed on acid-free paper.

Headquarters
Marcel Dekker, Inc., 270 Madison Avenue, New York, NY 10016, U.S.A.
tel: 212-696-9000; fax: 212-685-4540

Distribution and Customer Service
Marcel Dekker, Inc., Cimarron Road, Monticello, New York 12701, U.S.A.
tel: 800-228-1160; fax: 845-796-1772

Eastern Hemisphere Distribution
Marcel Dekker AG, Hutgasse 4, Postfach 812, CH-4001 Basel, Switzerland
tel: 41-61-260-6300; fax: 41-61-260-6333

World Wide Web
http://www.dekker.com

The publisher offers discounts on this book when ordered in bulk quantities. For more information, write to Special Sales/Professional Marketing at the headquarters address above.

PRINTED IN THE UNITED STATES OF AMERICA

To Tom Turner (1967–2003), whose kindness, intelligence, and wit touched everyone in Mann Library.

Foreword

Cornell is a young university, chartered in 1868 through the impetus of an inventor and entrepreneur. On the university's Inauguration Day, Ezra Cornell declared: "Finally, I trust we have laid the foundation of an University—an institution where any person can find instruction in any study." Perhaps as a consequence of its youthful vitality, Cornell has prized both independence and innovation. Its mixture of Land Grant and Ivy League has created a climate that is remarkably diverse, and its relative geographic isolation has produced a culture that embraces technological change as a means of closing the physical gap. Its libraries mirror this diversity and independence, with strong collections covering a broad swath of knowledge and specialized service tailored to a particular clientele, be they veterinarians, musicologists, architects, or engineers. Mann Library, Cornell's library serving agriculture, selected social sciences, and the life sciences, is internationally renowned for its cutting-edge initiatives, the creativity of its staff, and its strong relationship with its users, including both faculty and students. Mann's excellence derives from its tradition of outstanding leadership and the commitment to excellence imbued in its entire staff. The library places a premium on professionalism, and it has built an astonishing program of digital achievements through the development of a solid team, shaped through careful recruitment and warm and judicious mentoring.

The accomplishments of the Mann Library staff in the digital arena are numerous and far-reaching in their impact. Early pioneers in digitization, Mann librarians developed the Core Historical Literature of Agriculture as part of a preservation program to identify important works in agriculture. They also conceived and implemented TEEAL (The Essential Electronic Agricultural Library), which uses CD-ROM as the medium to disseminate critical resources in agriculture to developing countries. Over a decade ago Mann—first under the brilliant direction of Jan Olsen and more recently under the inspired guidance of Janet McCue—led in a vision of the liberating and potent force that electronic resources would provide scholars and researchers. Its staff has made a concerted effort to identify and provide access to a wide variety of materials in many formats, ranging from databases to geographic information systems. Along the way they became experts in all aspects of digital library creation, producing guidelines for others to follow and contributing to the advancement of our understanding of all things digital through their command of metadata, digital imaging, and archiving. With their drive to build access to more digital resources, they quickly realized that they needed an organizing structure to provide users with a convenient way to locate materials. The Mann Gateway was born and became a household name on the Cornell campus. Throughout the emerging digital library world, the Mann Gateway served as a model for the single-point-of-entry approach, a popular method for providing organized access to electronic resources. As it matured, the Mann Gateway evolved into the Cornell Library Gateway—Cornell's own single point of entry to its digital library.

Mann's staff are doers and risk-takers, always willing to explore new territory and to share their knowledge both locally and internationally. I know I can always count on them for a polished, well-researched, and useful contribution, and I look to them for groundbreaking work. Whether MyLibrary, MyUpdates, or MyContents, a virtual library tour, digital document delivery, e-reserves, loaner laptops, workshops in manipulating digital content, or some other new manifestation of evolving technology applied to the information needs of their users, I look to Mann to spot trends and to implement services that respond to changing user needs. Without skipping a beat, Mann staff, time and again, rise to the occasion and anticipate the need almost before it is expressed. Not surprisingly, the staff is a tightly knit team, resourceful, and illuminated with the joy of doing good work. It is always a pleasure, and frequently awesome, to see the results of their endeavors.

This book is an outstanding example of Mann Library's teamwork. With chapters contributed by many current and former Mann staff, *Becoming a Digital Library* both offers practical lessons in how an organization creates a new virtual information universe and is itself an example of the fine teamwork and professional outlook that permeates this special library. Reading the various chapters is sure to benefit those seeking advice on the digital library highway, but, in a broader sense, this book is vital for anyone seeking to build a healthy, vibrant, and successful organization.

Sarah Thomas
University Librarian
Carl A. Kroch University Librarian
Cornell University
Ithaca, New York, U.S.A.

Preface

This book focuses on the development and management of a digital library. The "digital library" subject domain includes topics and technologies that change with every nanosecond, so any book on the subject is doomed to instant obsolescence. New developments explode upon the scene while authors struggle to formulate the words to describe existing services. In the face of that mutability, we have chosen to focus on the human and organizational aspects of creating and running a digital library in an academic environment. We have made an effort in this book to present concepts that will remain meaningful even after the early days of the twenty-first century have receded into the past.

Digital library territory is so vast, diverse, dispersed, interdisciplinary, and complex that there is not even a generally agreed-upon definition of "digital library," which is used in a wide variety of areas of research and practice. Here, in this book, our digital library is very specific one: the Albert R. Mann Library of Cornell University. A hybrid of virtual and physical resources, Mann's collection has been carefully chosen and organized to serve a defined user group. It is available to users in a library building on a university campus in upstate New York, as well as to the world through international computer networks. It is a production and service operation, and also the site of research projects.

This book is written by digital library practitioners—the people who do the production, provide the service, and conduct the research. It is presented in three sections, the first of which, "Vision," Chapters 1 and 2, describes our organizational culture. The chapters in the "Assets" section, Chapters 3–5, provide overviews of collection and personnel management. Finally, "Technology" emphasizes the people who build and manage systems, conduct and evaluate projects, and scout new directions.

We agreed to the publisher's request to write a book about our library because we are proud of it and the digital collections and services that have been available since before the World Wide Web was born. In addition, we believe that our ideas, experiences, and approaches to making decisions and managing change could be useful to others who are navigating through digital library territory.

ACKNOWLEDGEMENTS

We express our deep gratitude to Sharon Van De Mark, Fred Pohl, and Beryl Glitz for their contributions to this book: Sharon, with her energy and organizational skills, shepherded the chapters through formatting and proofing; Fred brought his sharp eye and high standards of quality to a careful proofreading of the text; and Beryl's experience and skill with indexing provided multiple access points to the book's contents.

We also take this opportunity to recognize the previous directors of the Albert R. Mann Library—Whiton Powell, Henry Murphy, and Jan Olsen—for their dedication, creativity, and vision. Our work would not have been possible without the foundation they built and the directions they set.

Finally, we convey our most sincere appreciation to the deans, faculty, staff, and students of Cornell's College of Human Ecology and College of Agriculture and Life Sciences for their advocacy and support, and for the high expectations they have for their library.

Susan J. Barnes
Janet McCue

Introduction

In this book we have chosen *not* to present a laundry list of digital resources, software, and hardware that we purchased or leased, nor to write about techniques for building a Web site. Our approach has been to provide an overview of our decision-making environment, rather than to discuss many technical details of equipment or software. We have presented here the human aspects of building a digital library—a digital library that we recognized from the beginning as part of our library as a whole. This is a book about managing change within the library setting, with an emphasis on digital resources as motivators for that change. Each chapter was contributed by different staff members who write from their areas of expertise. Although no comprehensive literature reviews have been attempted, the authors have brought in current references to tie our work to that done elsewhere.

This is a book written by digital library practitioners. Each author has been a contributor to building and maintaining a production digital library, whether by selecting its content, organizing and providing access to it, helping people use it, expanding it, or setting the vision for its future. The focus here is on a specific library, the Albert R. Mann Library of Cornell University, and its digital collections and services. We view the audience of this book to be librarians who would like to read about some of the organizational and personal aspects of change management—librarians from many different kinds and sizes of libraries. Mann Library is part of the Cornell University Library, a very large and complex academic research library with many physically separate units. Mann itself, with its collection comprising resources spanning life, social, and health sciences, is comparable in size to many college or community college libraries. Mann, as a land grant library, serves the general public in addition to Cornell's undergraduates, graduate students, faculty, and staff. Although our perspective is that of a science research library, we believe that our experiences are potentially applicable to any library in which groups of staff are marshaled to incorporate the new and unfamiliar into their worklives, in order to bring the very best services and collections to their users.

When we speak of our digital library we are drawing from the vision provided by our former director, Jan Olsen: "The scholar can sit at home and access electronic information through a low cost personal computer and national networks." The user enters through a gateway, which provides a single point of entry to digital resources that can be located anywhere in the world but are presented as a cohesive collection at the desktop (1). Another way of looking at what we mean by "digital library" can be found in the Digital Library Federation's working definition: "Digital libraries are organizations that provide the resources, including the specialized staff, to select, structure, offer intellectual access to, interpret, distribute, preserve the integrity of, and ensure the persistence over time of collections of digital works so that they are readily and economically available for use by a defined community or set of communities" (2). Greenstein's view provides an important addition: "The digital library service environment is not simply about access to, and use of, information. It also supports the full range of administrative, business, and curatorial functions required by the library to manage, administer, monitor engagement with, and ensure fair use of its collections whether in digital or nondigital formats, whether located locally or off site.... It is designed for the library's patrons as well as for its professional staff and with an eye on the needs and capacities of those who supply it with information content and systems." Greenstein points out that a digital library environment makes no distinctions among information formats (3). That has also been key to Olsen's vision. With print collections that are complementary to the digital, Mann is in fact a hybrid library "on the continuum between the conventional and digital library, where electronic and paper-based information sources are used alongside each other" (4).

Hybrids are results of crossbreeding, the ancient technique used to produce animals or plants that display desired traits such as improved hardiness or increased production. These characteristics are known as hybrid vigor, "the tendency of crossbreeding to produce an animal or plant with a greater hardiness and capacity for growth than either of the parents" (5). The word "hybrid" in the digital library context is likely rooted in the technological sense of the word: "utilizing or involving both analogue and digital methods" (6). However, hybrid libraries do display hybrid vigor—mainstreaming the digital with the traditional analog brings new energy and strength—so both the genetic and computer meanings of the word are fitting. Borgman points out that, "we will have hybrid libraries, archives, and other information institutions for the indefinite future. New media will continue to be invented, and will supplement, rather than supplant, the old." She further explains that all of research libraries' millions of documents will be digitized, so digital libraries must be hybrid libraries, including digital materials and pointers to other formats (7).

Mann's physical library—its walls and windows, its study and meeting spaces, its shelves with their hundreds of thousands of volumes—remains important to our users. It is a busy, crowded place. For this book, however, our attention is on our library's digital component, a defining characteristic of which is the Gateway that provides access to it. The Mann Library Gateway has been our digital library's single point of entry since 1991, when it first offered navigational assistance and transparent connection and login processes (8). Mann's was one of the earliest library gateways. Borgman has speculated that the concept of library gateways may have originated at Cornell, where she encountered the concept first with the Mann Library Gateway (9). She writes that "The gateway concept emphasizes the essential role of libraries in selecting materials from the vast universe of published and ephemeral resources. Once selected, librarians are responsible for collecting and organizing these materials in ways most usable and accessible by the university community. What is new is that the library, as gateway, is no longer confined to a physical space" (10).

Another defining characteristic of our digital library has been the continuing goal of bringing work related to digital collections to the mainstream of library operations, rather than keeping it in the hands of a select few. Although new digital initiatives at Mann have typically been started by project teams, Olsen's vision was for eventual transfer of responsibility to library staff, who would then work with the collection in all its formats. The early Mann Gateway, for example, was begun by a project team in 1989, but daily Gateway operations were mainstreamed by 1993. We view the Gateway itself as a digital library success story and as a prime example of mainstreaming, because today the Mann Library Gateway no longer exists as a separate entity. It has been mainstreamed into campuswide service, adapted for use as the Cornell University Library Gateway—the single point of entry to Cornell's digital library.

Cornell University has been one of the busiest sites of such digital library growth and change, with the computer science department's William Arms a widely recognized expert on research in this area (11), Anne Kenney and Oya Reiger providing national guidance on digitization of images and texts (12), the Cornell University Library's participation in the Digital Library Federation (see http://www.diglib.org), and Cornell's leadership role in the National Science, Technology, Engineering, and Mathematics Education Digital Library (NSDL) (see http://nsdlib.nsdl.cornell.edu/nsdl/portal), among other activities. In fact, the Association for College and Research Libraries recently honored the Cornell University Library with its 2002 Excellence in Academic Libraries Award, in part for its accomplishments in the digital arena. No effort will be made here to list all of Cornell's many digital library activities; full details can be found through the Department of Computer Science Digital Library Research Group (http://www.cs.cornell.edu/cdlrg) and the Cornell University Library Gateway (http://campusgw.library.cornell.edu), and in the recent report to the Digital Library Federation (13). (It is necessary to look in more than one place to find the complete picture of digital library work at Cornell because, within one institution, Cornell provides excellent examples of the researcher and practitioner communities that Borgman has discussed, with their symbiotic relationship—research problems arising from practice and solutions from research implemented by practitioners (7).)

Again, this book is not an overview of Cornell's digital library but, instead, an exploration of a key—and pioneering—unit of the University Library system. In recognition of its accomplishments, Mann was the first winner of the American Library Association/Meckler Publishing, Inc.'s Library of the Future Award in 1993. If Mann was the Library of the Future back in 1993, what has it done lately? Has its vision proven successful? Has it continued to bring its research and development projects into production? Is it meeting its users' needs? We intend this book to provide answers to these questions.

This book presents our experience so far with mainstreaming and hybridizing as we've been building our digital library. Our goals have been to combine the theoretical with the practical, to provide techniques, and perhaps to provoke discussion.

The chapters in the first part, "Visions," describe our organizational culture, which has been fundamental to our development as a digital library. In Chapter 1, "The Culture of Engaged Institutions," Faiks and McCue present the management philosophy underlying Mann's team- and project-based approach to change in its evolution into a hybrid digital library. Mainstreaming is defined in Chapter 2, in which Kara describes examples of this approach and its history at Mann.

The "Assets" section provides overviews of managing collections and personnel. Ochs and Saylor provide expanded views of the digital library concept in Chapter 3, "Resources for the Digital Library," followed by an examination of how the growth of Mann's digital collection has been shaped by its selection processes. In Chapter 4, Turner and Raskin discuss techniques for finding and training the right people. Philip Herold, in Chapter 5, illustrates how Mann Library organizes its people into project-based teams to bring digital resources online.

While the final section focuses on technology, its emphasis is on the people who conduct and evaluate projects, build and manage systems, and scout new directions. Building on Herold's chapter about teams (some of which work on projects), Mistlebauer presents her practical view of methods for managing the projects themselves in Chapter 7, "Project Management and Implementation." Then Barnes, McCue, Heggestad, Hyland, Paulson, and Lynch, share some of the approaches Mann has used to evaluate its digital library projects in Chapter 8, "Input and Feedback from Digital Library Users." Finally, Chiang points us beyond the horizon in Chapter 9, New Frontiers and the Scout, in which she argues that investment in exploration is extremely valuable, even in a production library where user service—rather than basic research—is primary.

Susan J. Barnes

REFERENCES

1. Olsen J. In: Dowler L, ed. Gateways to Knowledge: The role of academic libraries in teaching, learning, and research. Cambridge, MA: MIT Press, 1997.
2. Waters DL. CLIR Issues, 4, 1998. http://www.clir.org/pubs/issues/issues04. html.
3. Greenstein D. Library Trends 2000; 49(2):290–303.
4. Pinfield S, et al. D-Lib Magazine, 1998.
5. *Heterosis* < http://dictionary.oed.com/cgi/entry/00105559 > in OED Online (Oxford English Dictionary). 2d ed. Oxford, England: Oxford University Press, 1989.
6. *Hybrid* < http://dictionary.oed.com/cgi/entry/00109754/00109754se11 > in OED Online (Oxford English Dictionary). 2d ed. Oxford, England: Oxford University Press, 1989.
7. Borgman C. From Gutenberg to the Global Information Infrastructure: Access to Information in the Networked World. Cambridge, MA: MIT Press, 2000.
8. Schlabach ML, Barnes S. Public-Access Computer Systems Review 1994; 5(1):5–19.
9. Borgman C, personal communication.
10. Borgman C. J Documentation 2000; 56(4):412–430.
11. Arms WY. Digital Libraries. Cambridge, MA: MIT Press, 2000.
12. Kenney AR, Rieger O. Moving Theory into Practice: Digital Imaging for Libraries and Archives. Mountain View, CA: Research Libraries Group, 2000.
13. DLF Newsletter 2002; 3(1).

Contents

TECHNOLOGY

Contributors

Susan J. Barnes   National Network of Libraries of Medicine, Pacific Northwest Region, University of Washington, Seattle, Washington, U.S.A.

Katherine S. Chiang   Public Services, Albert R. Mann Library, Cornell University, Ithaca, New York, U.S.A.

Angi Herold Faiks   MINITEX, University of Minnesota, Minneapolis, Minnesota, U.S.A.

Martin Heggestad   Division of Rare and Manuscript Collections, Cornell University, Ithaca, New York, U.S.A.

Philip Herold   Forestry Libraries, University of Minnesota, St. Paul, Minnesota, U.S.A.

Nancy C. Hyland   Public Services, Albert R. Mann Library, Cornell University, Ithaca, New York, U.S.A.

Bill Kara   Technical Services, Albert R. Mann Library, Cornell University, Ithaca, New York, U.S.A.

Tim Lynch   Information Technology, Albert R. Mann Library, Cornell University, Ithaca, New York, U.S.A.

Janet A. McCue   Director, Albert R. Mann Library, Cornell University, Ithaca, New York, U.S.A.

Holly L. Mistlebauer   Information Technology, Albert R. Mann Library, Cornell University, Ithaca, New York, U.S.A.

Mary Anderson Ochs   Collection Development and Preservation, Albert R. Mann Library, Cornell University, Ithaca, New York, U.S.A.

Joy R. Paulson   Collection Development and Preservation, Albert R. Mann Library, Cornell University, Ithaca, New York, U.S.A.

Howard Raskin   Public Services, Albert R. Mann Library, Cornell University, Ithaca, New York, U.S.A.

John M. Saylor   Director, Engineering Library, Cornell University, Ithaca, New York, U.S.A.

Thomas P. Turner   Technical Services, Albert R. Mann Library, Cornell University, Ithaca, New York, U.S.A.

1

The Culture of Engaged Institutions

Angi Herold Faiks
MINITEX, University of Minnesota, Minneapolis, Minnesota, U.S.A.

Janet A. McCue
Cornell University, Ithaca, New York, U.S.A.

This first chapter describes the cultural characteristics of an innovative library that embraces change:

- Values of engaged institutions: responsiveness, academic neutrality, accessibility, integration, coordination, respect, and resource partnerships.
- Foster shared goals, communicated within workplace and during recruitment and training.
- Reinforce goals through teamwork, especially where digital library projects have library-wide impact.
- Staff have strong sense of responsibility accompanied by self-confidence, qualities encouraged by high expectations and trust.
- Staff members who are trusted and respected feel free to propose ideas that may lead to visionary projects.
- Shared belief that all staff are responsible for providing service.
- User feedback reminds us that "we can and must do better."

Libraries building digital collections and services have an obligation to foster engaged cultures characterized by innovation, teamwork, partnerships, trust, and a focus on customers' needs.

1. INTRODUCTION

In February 1999 the Kellogg Commission on the Future of State & Land-Grant Universities challenged these institutions to serve both local and national needs in a more coherent and effective way. The Commission called upon academic institutions to become "engaged" and to be more productively involved in their communities. According to the Commission, seven characteristics define an engaged institution: responsiveness, academic neutrality, accessibility, integration, coordination, respect for partners, and resource partnerships.

Although the Commission's report focused exclusively on universities and did not address libraries specifically, these characteristics of engagement can reflect a library's culture as well. The culture of an institution consists of the values of an organization and the management practices that reflect those values. Mann Library at Cornell University is driven by the values of a library (e.g., free and equitable access to information), by the values of a land-grant academic institution (e.g., building collections and services that support the teaching, research, and extension needs of the community), and by the values of engagement. These values are shared by the staff and are reflected in the library's mission and management practices.

This chapter highlights the digital projects and management practices that foster a creative culture. The first section reviews the principles of engagement and highlights some of the programs and services libraries have developed to become more productively involved in their communities. The second section focuses on institutional culture and the management practices that promote successful and sustainable engaged libraries.

From the implementation of Mann Library's first Web Gateway in 1995 to the growth of the library's geospatial repository in 2001, there has been a conscious decision to engage the entire institution and to mainstream digital projects into the fabric of the organization. For example, the organization relies on the skills of catalogers and the talents of programmers to develop metadata structures, while the institution depends on the vision of public services and the knowledge of selectors to create a repository of information resources. The library does not build a parallel universe to develop digital collections and services. Instead, there is a strong commitment to foster the resident talents of the staff and, when new skills are required, to embed these talents—to mainstream them—into the appropriate department. This ensures that no department languishes as a print-only service and that each unit has the talents to participate fully in the development of digital collections and services. These digital projects require coordination, teamwork, and respect for partners. They have succeeded in wearing down barriers between departments in the library and fostering the trust and shared values required in an engaged culture.

CHARACTERISTICS OF ENGAGED INSTITUTIONS

The Kellogg Commission on the Future of State and Land-Grant Universities listed seven characteristics that define an engaged institution:

Responsiveness requires that we listen to our community and regularly ask what they need. Responsiveness implies a two-way conversation and that the institution gains useful feedback in the process.

Respect for partners involves equality and a recognition that each of the players provides valuable contributions. It is characterized by mutual respect and an awareness that through lively collaboration, problems can be defined, solutions proposed, and success measured.

Academic neutrality builds on the tradition of "neutral facilitator and source of information" so that different perspectives or competing theories can be studied and discussed.

Accessibility relates to untangling the bureaucracy of our institutions so that users can negotiate the landscape and discover the resources and programs available to them.

Integration links the intellectual capital of the institution with the services and outreach mission of the university. Interdisciplinary work is encouraged, and there are incentives to reward both interdisciplinary work and the effort required to translate the work of the academy into practical knowledge for the community.

Coordination ensures that we know what is being done and by whom so that information and research can be shared and communication can be coordinated.

Resource partnerships ask whether there are sufficient resources to complete the task. "The most successful engagement efforts appear to be those associated with strong and healthy relationships with partners in government, business, and the non-profit world."

---

2. CHARACTERISTICS OF ENGAGED INSTITUTIONS

2.1. Responsiveness and Accessibility: "We Can and Must Do Better"

In an engaged institution, there is a sense that "we can and must do better" [1]. The Kellogg Commission asserts that academic institutions are confusing to outsiders. So, too, are their libraries. Key to the process of engagement is making institutions accessible and more responsive. Libraries often employ a variety of traditional techniques for reaching out to users, including publishing newsletters, developing instruction programs, and hosting tours that highlight services and resources. As the collections and services become increasingly digital, libraries are finding ways to stay "high-touch" in a high-tech world.

At the University of Pennsylvania, resident library advisors provide one-on-one help at campus residences. The library's program is part of a 24-hour academic support service offered to students when and where they need it. Whether a student is stumped by a math assignment or a research paper, the program, dubbed "The Wheel" (at http://www.Collegehouses. upenn.edu/wheel/), provides online and in-person help for writing, mathematics, information technology, and library research. Each college house has its own library advisor who provides help with networked resources, plans workshops, and hosts informal and convenient sessions with reference librarians in the evenings, when students are in their dorms.

Designing spaces—whether in the physical or digital landscape—that make the library more accessible and approachable is also important. Libraries are increasingly incorporating cafés and coffeeshops into their buildings, adding collaborative computing spaces in group study rooms, and developing interfaces that make the digital landscape more welcoming. Gateways, online tutorials, and extensive help files are now commonplace features of the digital scene. But as digital collections grow to hundreds or thousands of titles—each with its own idiosyncratic features and inscrutable title—it becomes increasingly difficult for users to navigate and make use of the resources. To address this need, several libraries have recently introduced services that allow users to create their own customized selection of resources. For example, the library at North Carolina State University created MyLibrary@NCState to provide an information system with which users can organize and collect electronic resources they frequently consult [2]. The service is dynamic, customizable, and portable. Users can create their own "collection" of electronic resources, subscribe to a current awareness service, and consult the interactive help embedded in the system. Developers also made the source code freely available to other institutions and invited programmers to help enhance the system. Services that can be personalized, technologies that are "push" instead of traditional "come-and-get-it" programs, ensure that the library is both "high-tech" and "high-touch." Users want ready access and skills to use the technology. When they need assistance, they want the responsiveness of a human being (see Chap. 7 for a description of Cornell's MyLibrary project).

Knowing your users, providing the resources to meet their needs, adapting, modifying, and abandoning old services, and developing new ones are all central to the goals of accessibility and responsiveness. Responsiveness implies listening, conversing, and discussing options. The Kellogg Commission implied that too often academic institutions do not ask the right question or truly listen to the replies of their communities. Do we offer our services when and where they are needed? At the University of Pennsylvania, the library answered that question by taking services to the campus residences—when the students were in their dorms. Do we use language and terminology that are understandable? At North Carolina State, the developers of "MyLibrary" used the well-known language of the Internet to design a service that made library resources much more accessible.

Libraries can solicit user feedback and become more responsive in a number of ways: from formal structures, such as faculty committees and user surveys, to informal input garnered from suggestion boxes, instructional classes, and departmental meetings. Libraries have utilized focus groups to help define the features of digital services, online surveys to understand how students use their services and collections, and volunteers to test-drive new services. Listening to these users can help us learn what they like, how to improve the product, and where to go next. This future direction is important to next year's student and tomorrow's faculty member. More details on listening to users are provided in Chapter 8.

2.2. Integration and Academic Neutrality

Academic library services are designed to complement the teaching, research, and outreach mission of the university, a characteristic the Kellogg Commission terms "integration." Integration ensures that institutional scholarship is connected to the service and teaching mission of the university and that the institutional climate encourages outreach activities. One of the hallmarks of the land-grant movement was taking the work of the academy and translating it for the good of the community. This translation—typically handled by cooperative extension agencies—would ensure that the research from the university could be put to practical use and that real-life problems could be solved.* The Morrill Acts of 1862 and 1890, which established land-grant institutions around the United States, were founded on the idea that a higher and broader education should be accessible to all who desire it. Land-grant

---

* Land-grant institutions, as specified in the Morrill Act, were established "in order to promote the liberal and practical education of the industrial classes in the several pursuits and professions in life." Underlying this intention was the noble pursuit expressed by Myron Clark: that land-grant institutions should be the "People's College, of the people, for the people, and sustained by the people." To this end, land and monies were allocated to establish colleges in all states that were committed to the mission of serving the educational needs of their state [3].

libraries, in turn, extend this mission by supporting the educational information needs of their statewide constituents [4].

Knowing that the audience is broader than the local university population frequently has an impact on the design of services. For example, the Mann Library's original conceptual design for its Gateway incorporated icons that reflect the accessibility of resources to different constituencies. Specific icons designate those resources restricted contractually to the university community and those available to the public. Staff created the system and collected its resources with this wider community in mind, staying true to the mission of a land-grant library. Similarly, the Geographic Information System (GIS) team developing the CUGIR (Cornell University Geospatial Information Repository, at http://cugir.mannlib.cornell.edu) site designed the system so that the general public could have access to the rich geospatial data reflecting the environmental and biological features of the state (see Chap. 7 for more information about the CUGIR system, and see Chap. 5 for a description of the team that created it).

Examples of integrating the library with the work of cooperative extension can be found around the country, from the University of Wisconsin's Steenbock Library's document delivery service and videosatellite training efforts for extension, to Michigan State University's extension distance learning initiatives. For the cooperative extension community scattered throughout New York State, the Mann Library developed an aggressive outreach program in an effort to integrate library resources and services with the work and needs of extension employees. Library programmers worked with campus technology specialists to install a proxy server that allowed extension educators to connect to licensed library resources. The library appointed an extension liaison who offered classes as part of the extension's in-service and orientation programs on campus. Her close work with campus extension led to invitations to participate in regional and statewide conferences held in rural outposts in the Adirondacks and bustling offices in urban centers. Here she taught extension educators how to connect to the library's Gateway, find full-text journals, search databases, and navigate the complex information landscape. With so much of the collection now available electronically, extension educators throughout the state can gain access to much of the same material as their campus counterparts. Outreach efforts also are leading to partnering opportunities with extension. After seeing examples of several of the information systems the library created, extension staff asked the library to provide insight into how to organize, describe, and deliver cooperative extension information. In this case, integrating the library's services into the extension culture led to a better understanding of the expertise available in the library. Librarians served as consultants and partners to those working through information organization and access issues with other digital material.

In addition to being integrated into the research and teaching mission of the institution, outreach services need to remain academically neutral. Faced with controversial issues—from genetically modified plants to sustainable agriculture—land-grant institutions and their libraries must strive to maintain academic neutrality. Although the Kellogg Commission reminded the land-grant community of the importance of academic neutrality, particularly with contentious public-policy issues, this role of neutral facilitator and provider of information is one that libraries have always taken seriously. This value is clearly stated in the Bill of Rights of the American Library Association: "Libraries should provide materials and information presenting all points of view on current and historical issues and materials should not be proscribed or removed because of partisan or doctrinal disapproval" [5].

2.3. Partnerships: "Almost as Much to Learn as We Have to Offer"

Several characteristics of the engaged institution relate to partnerships. The Kellogg Commission states that these partnerships should be characterized by mutual respect and by the realization that each partner has "almost as much to learn as we have to offer" [6]. One of the most successful partnerships that the Mann Library enjoys is a long-standing agreement with the U.S. Department of Agriculture (USDA). For the past six years, the library and the economic agencies of the USDA—the Economic Research Service, the National Agricultural Statistics Service, and the World Agricultural Outlook Board—have collaborated to make available the commodity reports and data sets published by these agencies available on the USDA Economics and Statistics System Web site. The economic agencies provide the reports while the library guarantees that they will be posted on the Internet within 10 minutes of receipt. The library also provides an e-mail subscription service, an extensive archive, help files, and an e-mail and telephone reference service to system users around the globe. Every day about 7000 users visit Mann's USDA site, where they download an average of 3700 files. Chapter 2 provides more details about this site and how it is maintained.

This partnership was recently recognized with the USDA Secretary's Honor Award. The award acknowledged the staff of the libraries and the agencies "for establishing an innovative Department of Agriculture–University partnership for cost-effective and timely delivery of important economic information" [7]. The service relies on collaboration, innovation, and trust. Throughout the year, the government information librarian works closely with the agency staff. The acquisitions staff who "check in" the electronic reports have an easy relationship with the agency personnel. The parties meet annually to discuss the service, plan new initiatives, and review any problems. "How can we do better?" is a phrase echoed in these planning meetings. In 2001, the partners planned a new enhancement to the service by designing "AgMaps," an interactive mapping utility for crop data. Each partner contributed funds, expertise, and commitment to the project. These "resource partnerships" make the collective stronger than the individual parts and help ensure that the work is coordinated.

A similar effort at collaboration is occurring at the national level in an organization called the AgNIC (Agriculture Network Information Center) Alliance. This partnership relies on the collective strength of its members to provide a free and unrestricted portal to agricultural information on the Internet (http://www.agnic.org). Each member agrees to provide content and service related to a particular aspect of agricultural information. For example, the University of Arizona provides resources on rangeland management; the University of Nebraska, water-quality resources. At the Mann Library, both the USDA Economics and Statistics System and CUGIR are AgNIC sites. In addition, the Mann Library is working with the National Agricultural Library to develop the technical infrastructure for the next generation of AgNIC. The AgNIC Alliance created a System Requirements Task Force to design the features of the service; a team of programming staff from the two institutions worked with a technical advisory group to develop it. These partnerships rely on the belief that the end product will be stronger, deeper, and more robust than the individual parts and that partners have as much to learn as they have to offer. Each of these partnerships reflects the characteristics outlined by the Kellogg Commission: coordination, integration, and respect for partners. These qualities ensure a strong communication flow between partners, resulting in more informed decisions and effective actions. Partnerships can provide lasting value to an organization and the community it serves if they are approached from the beginning as long-term commitments, both externally and internally. And, when the contributions of partners are woven into the mission and daily work of the library—when they are mainstreamed—the services and resources resulting from the collaboration can be sustained.

Becoming an engaged institution is not simply a matter of putting the seven characteristics on an organization's list of goals or five-year plan. As stated in the Kellogg Commission's report, an engaged institution "is designed locally" and "requires leadership and focus." The Commission adds, "Achieving the goals of engagement will require the best efforts of us all—and the courage, conviction, and commitment to see them through." But where do this courage, conviction, and commitment originate? Organizations that are engaged already, or are poised to be, have a culture that allows, encourages, and fosters the characteristics of engagement. In fact, many of the qualities outlined by the Kellogg Commission might be a natural outcome of certain organizational cultures [8].

3. CULTURE IN ACTION: MANAGEMENT PRACTICES AT WORK

Daniel R. Denison defines the culture of an organization as

> a code, a logic, and a system of structured behaviors and meaning that have stood the test of time and serve as a collective guide to future adaptation and survival. They can be abstract and mystical, yet concrete and immediate; impossible to change, yet rapidly changing; complex and intricate, yet grounded in very basic values; and occasionally irrelevant to business issues, yet always central to an organization's strategy and effectiveness" [9].

William Ouchi suggests that successful organizations have the characteristics of a "clan" rather than a formal bureaucracy because they are ruled "by values, beliefs, norms, and traditions" [10]. One observer of the Mann Library culture noted these mystical, clanlike characteristics. In 1996, the library organized a national conference that focused on the principles and practices related to creating the library of the 21st century. Attendees rated the conference highly successful, and at least one observer felt Ouchi's "clanlike" atmosphere. This participant noted on the conference evaluation form that there is "the impression that joining Mann Library was a bit like joining the Hare Krishna." There are no initiation rites nor any indoctrination ceremonies associated with the Mann Library culture, but there is a strong tradition of service, a commitment to innovation, and a belief in teamwork.

Cultures are nurtured through management practices. These management practices begin with a common understanding of the mission of the organization. They are reinforced by teamwork and mainstreaming and are communicated effectively through mentoring and respectful work environments.

3.1. The Common Goal

Both Denison and Ouchi agree that a clear mission, or "a shared definition of the function and purpose of an organization and its members" [11], is a major influence on the effectiveness of an organization. Such a mission communicates "why the work of an organization is important and provides clear direction" [12]. The goal or mission of the Mann Library is likely very similar to that of most libraries, especially those of land-grant institutions. Everything the library does is an attempt to support the information, teaching, and research interests of the user populations and to provide equal access to information and service to the community. This is very basic, but at the same time very powerful. If every decision made and action taken has these values as the underlying impetus, then all decisions and actions are basically worthwhile and positive. This does not mean that everything done with this goal in mind is necessarily grand or perfect. It does not even mean that every decision made or action taken is the best one. It does mean that if the organization as a whole and the individuals within do act with the goal in mind, then they are making a positive contribution to the organization and to the community.

CULTURE CURING CANCER

When questioning why a certain oncology lab has seen so many positive developments and success over the years, one may not first think about organizational culture. That is unless you ask the co-principal investigators of that lab, Bert Vogelstein and Ken Kinzer of Johns Hopkins University.

In sum, they say that their lab is successful due to the kinds of people chosen to work there and because their motivation for studying this disease is the fact that it "affects people." The lab was described by Eugene Russo in his article, "Harmony in the lab" [*The Scientist* 14(17):18–19, Sept. 4, 2000].

Five students out of 200 applicants are hired each year to be a part of this cancer research team. They are selected based not only on their competence and willingness to work, but also for their creativity and team-minded approach. New students choose their own research project, therefore cutting down on competition, resulting in a low-pressure environment. In addition, Vogelstein and Kinzer encourage a positive working atmosphere by personally paying for yacht club memberships, occasional baseball games, visits to the symphony, and retreats to the beach. They even have a rock band comprised of lab members!

Oncology students say that they "spend a lot of time around the lunch table... trying to figure out what makes this lab such a great place to work." They are likely experiencing the mystical nature of culture.

Ouchi suggests that when individuals adhere to common goals, they can naturally know how to act and make good decisions on their own. He claims that, "Those who grasp the essence of [the organization's] philosophy of values and beliefs can deduce an almost limitless number of specific rules or targets to suit changing conditions" and will more naturally derive the best solutions to deal with particular situations [13]. How, then, does this common goal become ingrained into the organization and adopted by its employees?

3.2. Communicating the Culture

Shared values and goals need to be communicated. Denison refers to this as consistency, or the "need to develop a thorough understanding of the shared values and norms that make up the core of any organization" [14]. In addition to using formal structures, such as staff meetings, mentoring, and appraisals to communicate the goals of an organization, the Mann Library employs additional practices to develop the culture. For example, the Mann management team, the Administrative Council, meets weekly for information and discussion, but it also regularly schedules retreats for strategic planning or to discuss the "monolithic hairballs," or complex organizational issues, that require untangling. These retreats, held at off-campus venues, allow the council to arrive at a common vision that each member understands and that can be articulated to the rest of the staff.

The library recognizes that sharing the values of the organization begins with recruitment. The library uses a formal structure of a search committee to orchestrate every search and to make recommendations for appointments for all positions. The search committee consists of members of the hiring department and representatives from other units. Different kinds of staff—support staff, librarians, programmers—are represented on the committee, and other staff frequently meet with the candidates in a representative group meeting. During the interview, the staff attempt to share what is considered characteristic of the Mann Library, qualities such as teamwork, respect for colleagues, a supportive and creative environment, and the expectation and encouragement of learning and development. The staff try not only to hire "the best" but also to make clear to the candidates that this is the goal. This communicates the expectation that excellence is expected from those who are hired. The library tries to recruit individuals whose personal goals mirror the organization's goals. Ouchi and Raymond Price agree that "socialization [into the organization] is possible only when new members share values quite similar to those of the organizational culture" [15].

In addition to determining the qualifications and skills of candidates, search committees try to assess the potential of each candidate to contribute effectively to the organization. Would the members of the search committee enjoy working with the candidate on a project? Does the candidate offer skills the library needs? Is the candidate able to communicate effectively? Similarly, the interview process provides the candidate with a glimpse into the culture of the library so that the applicant can ask similar questions. Would I enjoy working in the Mann Library? Do I want to work in a team, or would I prefer being able to "do it myself?" (Chapter 4 provides more details.) The intent of the interview process is to give the candidate an opportunity to understand the values of an organization and to provide the search committee with the chance to assess the candidate's strengths. That the culture of the Mann Library is tangible during the interview process is evident in this anecdote: Following an interview, a candidate contacted the library director and asked her to speak at the next meeting of the New Women's Network, a discussion group at Cornell. Although the candidate had not been offered the position, she was very impressed by the interview process and by the involvement of the staff. In an excerpt from her note to the director, she asked:

> We would like to get a speaker from Mann Library, since it appeared to me when I applied, that all of the people I spoke to were incredibly committed and enthusiastic. Since it most certainly is not high salaries, there must be something else at work, and we'd like to find out what this is. (Personal e-mail, Dec. 6, 1996)

Yet fostering and communicating the culture do not stop at the interview. A new employee will continually learn about Mann culture in both subtle and overt ways. In addition to formal orientation programs that involve each department of the library, regular staff meetings, and semi-annual all-staff meetings, new employees learn the culture from supervisors and co-workers. From stories being told of past history, to observing how projects are carried out and how issues are dealt with, one begins to capture the essence of an organization's culture. In addition, long-time employees and managers embody the culture and continually reinforce it through their actions, decisions, and words. Successful culture is not entirely dependent on leaders who embody and encourage the values of the organization. Culture, by its nature, permeates the organization and its employees, encouraging internal guidance. According to Denison, people act because of internalized values, not because of external control [16]. An organization made up of employees who embody the shared culture and values helps ensure continued success as management changes.

3.3. Teamwork and Mainstreaming

According to Ouchi and Price, "Successful organizations are characterized by having many cohesive working groups that are linked together, while unsuccessful organizations frustrate the development of such groups" [17]. Managers at Mann use teamwork and mainstreaming to develop and sustain projects. This is especially evident in digital projects since they often impact staff across the library. Staff members are encouraged to brainstorm new ideas, discuss options, and listen to disparate views and varied experiences via cross-functional teams. Whenever a project is implemented or a decision is considered, the library attempts to gather the input of those who will be impacted by the project or decision. Denison calls this behavior "involvement." Depending on the project, the involvement takes different forms, but it is always a factor. For example, in a recent grant proposal relating to digital collections, staff from cataloging, collection development, preservation, and information technology met to brainstorm and shape the project. Everyone was engaged in the discussion, and each person volunteered to write a portion of the grant proposal. Although a main author/editor was assigned, each staff member could contribute to the grant proposal using a common vision.

Involvement is even more evident, though, when new projects and grants begin. The director creates an implementation team, and the team has two goals in mind: first, a successful implementation of the project; and second, a recommendation on how the project can be mainstreamed or woven into the fabric of the organization. For example, in migrating the Mann Library Gateway from its Telnet version (introduced in 1990) to the first Web version in 1995, the team consisted of a staff member from each of the following departments: cataloging, public services, collection development, and the information technology section. The team reflected the skills needed for the project and also represented departments that would feel the impact of the new service. The team was successful on both counts for the service, and the maintenance plans have been in place for more than five years. Their mainstreaming plan ensured that Collection Development staff would continue to select new resources for the Gateway, that Cataloging staff would create descriptions and access points for the material, that Public Services staff would support the services and suggest enhancements as the system went into production, and that Information Technology staff would be able to maintain and develop the system. Chapter 5 presents more details about teamwork.

Although some may argue that involvement takes up valuable time, many believe that it is worthwhile in the end. As Denison says, "High levels of involvement and participation create a sense of ownership and responsibility" [18]. This approach not only makes people feel like they count and are being heard but also shows that exciting ideas can also emerge from the investigation or conceptualization of a new project. For example, during the Web Gateway development phase, Technical Services staff suggested adding a "New Bookshelf" to the Gateway. This would be a service comparable to the physical bookcase that highlights new acquisitions. Catalogers proposed scanning the tables of contents and cover pages of new books for a virtual

"New Bookshelf" on the Gateway. Because of their involvement in the design and creation of the Gateway, Technical Services staff members were able to envision ways to apply their skills to this new service. With this new service—so unusual in the early days of the Web—Technical Services staff became pioneers and soon received inquiries from all over the globe requesting information on how to implement a library Web "New Bookshelf." That Technical Services staff generated the idea reflects the sense of ownership that Cataloging and Acquisitions staff felt about the Gateway. Rather than solely being a Public Services project, the Gateway had become a service that required the skills and commitment of the entire staff.

This democratic and team approach to projects requires coordination and implies respect for the internal partners. Although more challenging because of different cultures, priorities, or commitments, external partnership and teamwork are essential elements for the engaged institution. The Kellogg Commission asks that organizations have respect for the skills and capacities of partners in collaborative projects. This is not always natural or easy for any organization. Even if an organization is able to achieve internal trust and respect, the partnering organizations may not have that implicit trust within the organization and therefore may not expect it from the outside, or they may simply see anything external as competition. But, when a match is made where trust is expected and encouraged, the strengths and possibilities of that partnership can be tremendous. Not only can we better understand what users need by stepping outside the immediate surroundings, but we can also better respond by tapping into external expertise via cross-functional team partnerships. Without external partnerships, the Mann Library would not have enjoyed many of its successes.

For example, the former library director, Jan Olsen, and her husband and professional colleague, Wallace, began a project more than a decade ago to bring the literature of the agricultural sciences to the developing world. Because of their vision, commitment, and persistence, they were able to persuade most of the major publishers of agricultural journals to contribute the contents of their journals. With support from The Rockefeller Foundation and a commitment from the publishing and indexing community, the Mann Library created TEEAL (The Essential Electronic Agricultural Library)—a library in a box for developing countries that contains five years' worth of more than 130 journals in the agricultural and biological sciences. Only available to the developing world at one tenth the cost of subscriptions in the developed world, the project required partnerships between the library and over 70 different publishers. Because the Olsens were able to demonstrate the extraordinary need in the developing world for the project, the publishing community agreed to give their journals to the library free of charge for scanning and repackaging into a compact disc library. The product would not have been possible without these partnerships and a sense of mutual trust.*

3.4. Trust and Concern for People

At Mann, there are high expectations, a basic trust and assumption that individuals will do their jobs and do them well and that they will act with the organization's mission in mind. This combination leads to both self-confidence and internalized responsibility, making micromanagement largely unnecessary. As Denison states, "Shared values, rather than administrative control, are the true source of coordinated behavior and social control" [20]. This is not to say that supervisors do not have to work more closely with and direct certain individuals via socialization, mentoring, and nurturing. But even these individuals benefit from the trust setting and often gradually internalize a sense of responsibility to the organization.

Trust does not just travel from the top down. The Mann Library offers a work environment where outward, professional respect among staff is not simply a suggestion. It is an obligation. This is evident, for example, in instances that call for innovation and brainstorming. Because people feel secure in the respect of their colleagues, they feel comfortable offering suggestions no matter how wild or conceivably impossible to implement they may seem. Without that security, staff might not have come forward with many of the suggestions that eventually led to visionary projects and successful changes. Trust among staff is also nurtured in the cross-functional and multilevel teams described earlier and in Chapter 5. The existence and importance of these teams relay the message that everyone's opinion matters.

Within the library, there is an appropriate level of social intimacy that Ouchi says often occurs in successful organizations [21]. The underlying trust encourages an open environment where people feel safe to discuss concerns or problems but also to share their successes and joys. Humor and

---

*In fact, this fragile trust was strained by an article on TEEAL in the *Chronicle of Higher Education*. In a letter to the editor, the director of corporate communications for one publishing house said that the *Chronicle* failed to acknowledge the contributions of the publishing community to the TEEAL project and presented them "in a negative light" [19]. The letter is an excellent example of the mutual trust that must occur in a partnership the sense that each partner brings something valuable to the table. In this case, the publishers were concerned that the library/academic community was forgetting its fundamental contribution to the TEEAL project (i.e., free reproduction rights to 5 years' worth of 130 journal titles). The Olsens had established this trust in the original negotiations. But, because of the deep-seated distrust between the library community and the publishing world over journal prices, the publisher felt that the author of the *Chronicle* article ignored its generous contribution to the TEEAL project.

lightheartedness are welcomed at work. For example, at the recent opening of the new addition to the library, a parade of kazoo-playing staff marched from the old building to the new; the university dairy store concocted a new variety of ice cream ("Manngo Mann Sorbet") for the celebration; and the college dean invited students and faculty to pull a card from an old catalog and win a door prize. Staff from each department of the library planned the event, and their energy, humor, and organizational skills fostered a lively and joyful celebration.

3.5. Motivated by the Customer

Both Denison and Ouchi discuss successful organizations as being "obsessed with the customer." These organizations are focused on their ability to adapt and respond to their customers' needs. Libraries, whose ultimate goal is service to their patrons, should continually be motivated by these patrons' needs since these "customers" are the reason libraries exist. The Kellogg Commission echoes this focus in their call for engaged activity. Engagement means becoming "even more sympathetically and productively involved with [our] communities." Land-grant universities, in particular, exist to serve society, and a commitment to the community is a clear motivation. If all libraries are motivated by the needs of their customers, all seven character-istics of an engaged institution will be evident, from responsiveness to co-ordination to integration. Just simply asking whether various plans and actions are truly in the best interest of the patron is a very powerful practice. In addition, doing so is a method of removing personal motivations from the decision-making process.

At Mann, evidence of focusing on patrons' needs can be found all around. For instance, the library offers a 24-hour response time to the grow-ing number of e-mail reference questions (over 300 per month on average) that come from around the world. Although the target is 24-hour turnaround time, staff usually respond within hours and sometimes minutes of receipt. Similarly, Technical Services staff strive for 24-hour turnaround time to re-ceive, process, and shelve serials, and when check-in time is crucial for ef-fective use of the resource, they cut that time down significantly. For instance, the USDA and subscribers around the world expect that the library will post the USDA electronic data sets and reports on the online system as soon as the agency releases the publications. The library therefore ensures Web accessi-bility within 10 minutes of receipt.

The culture and practice at the Mann Library reinforce the attitude that service is everyone's business. Management makes it clear that all staff should think of themselves as public servants, no matter in which department they work. And management practice reinforces this idea. For example, staff members across the library participate in the instruction program either as instructors, as course designers, or as teaching assistants. This allows bibliographers, catalogers, and systems analysts to view the information landscape from the user's perspective. Recently, the library's too well-worn keyboards became a major hurdle for a group of emeriti faculty in a workshop in the Microcomputer Center. Not trained as touch-typists, they were frustrated throughout the class because the letters had been worn off the keyboards. In this case, the TA for the class was the library director (who assists with this workshop each semester). Although chagrinned and embarrassed at the state of the keyboards, the administration received an excellent lesson!

Librarians, programmers, and staff from various departments also work on the reference desk and actively participate in reference staff meetings. Because of this integration, collection development specialists are able to spot new research trends and are better able to shape the collection. Cataloging staff appreciate the complexity of electronic resource aggregations and the limitations of the MARC record. Because programmers and system analysts assist in teaching classes and work at the reference desk, the technology staff have a keener understanding of the user and the challenges associated with information resources. While at the desk, they are able to talk with reference librarians about the problems and possible technical solutions. On committees or working groups, they are able to understand each other's language. There is the sense that all the library's services—from selection to cataloging—from programming to interface design—are directed at the user.

3.6. Creativity and Innovation

While the library tries to support an innovative culture, there is a constant awareness that "we can and must do better." Surveys, focus groups, and feedback from users remind us of areas that can be improved. For example, a recent student survey affirmed that the library's operating hours were adequate but told the collection development staff that students wanted even more electronic journals. An academic department survey informed us that most faculty do not know whether the key journals in their fields are in electronic form. A recent comment from a faculty member at a departmental visit reminded the director that the library was often an invisible presence on the Web. Unaware that vendors use IP checking to verify subscribers, this faculty member thought that resources, such as the Web of Science's Science Citation Index (SCI), were available freely on the Internet [22]. From his point of view, there was no indication that the library was the subscriber to this expensive and valuable tool nor that the vendor verified his Cornell affiliation. To him, the library was invisible and he wondered aloud why he should direct his students to the library (via the Gateway)—when "everything was available

on the Web." User feedback reminds us that much more can be done—
whether through user education, better services, or even simple contract
negotiations requiring vendors to highlight the library as the subscriber to an
online service. Some ways of obtaining feedback are illustrated in Chapter 8.

As the Kellogg Commission points out, "One challenge [land-grant
universities] face is growing public frustration with what is seen to be our
unresponsiveness. At the root of this criticism is a perception that we are out
of touch and out of date" [23]. The Commission asks that institutions become
more responsive to the needs of society, to adapt, as Denison suggests, instead
of falling back on what we have always done. One very effective means of
combating inertia and obsolescence and responding to patron needs is
encouraging and supporting creativity and innovation.

What might be most important about the Mann Library culture is the
drive to be creative and innovative. There is a support structure and a willingness to embrace and adapt to change and to look for new and better ways
of doing things. The library looks toward the future and tries to be inventive,
not simply reactive. For example, each time a position is open, the job description is reviewed within the department and the supervisor reviews it
with the library director. Although a periodic update occurs regularly during
performance appraisals, open positions give the library the opportunity to
completely recast a position. For example, a metadata librarian position was
created in 1997 to reflect the broader scope of the cataloging staff; an interface
designer line was advertised in 1989; and in 2000 another a staff position was
recast into a programmer/systems analyst to give additional support to the
Information Technology Section. Each open position is reviewed within the
context of the whole organizational structure, and support is shifted appro-
priately. Part of the reason this position review process is possible is that
competition among managers is actively discouraged. Decisions such as
changing staff structure can be analyzed more objectively and with the needs
of the whole organization in mind. For example, 15 years ago, there was no
Information Technology Section in the library; today, the ITS unit consists of
nine staff members—a matrix of programmers, systems analysts, network
technicians, interface designers, and database experts. Total staff size in the
library has not increased—in fact, the opposite is true—but there has been a
systematic effort to build the Information Technology staff so that the library's digital collections and services could grow and be supported.

Another factor encouraging innovation is an active grant-writing
program. The library encourages grant writing in order to jump-start an
innovation, explore a new issue, or support a major initiative. Managers
monitor calls for grant proposals and actively encourage employees to pursue
funding for creative initiatives. Grants are selected carefully to ensure that

they carry the library's mission forward. The writing involves those who will actually work on the grant so they can shape the project from the beginning. If successful, the project is then mainstreamed into the ongoing work of the library. The library has been awarded an average of 8.4 grants, totaling approximately $790,000 per year, over the past 5 years. So many of today's services at Mann began with grant funding. University grant funds supported the first iteration of the Gateway, modest investments of local "Hatch" funds (research support by the USDA to land-grant institutions) were the foundation for the identification of the core literature of agriculture, federal funds supported the development of the library's geospatial repository. New employees as well as seasoned veterans are active grant writers. Soon after staff members are hired, they are invited to participate in a college grant-writing seminar. Although junior staff members are not eligible to be principal investigators (PI) due to university policy, often they are project managers. For example, in a recent grant to develop an interactive mapping capability, an assistant librarian is the project manager, but she can rely on the guidance of her supervisor, who is the principal investigator. The PI provides active mentoring, but the project manager feels a sense of responsibility and ownership in the project. No matter how green or how seasoned the people involved are, there is a sense of equal partnership and involvement in the grant activity.

Similarly, the library encourages research and experimentation. Job descriptions for professional staff include components designated "Research & Development." Depending on the person's interests or skills, this may take different forms. For example, recently one librarian began analyzing citation trends for Web documents in undergraduate research papers while another librarian was working with a survey research class to understand how users perceive the library's digital collections. The director sets aside funds to support attendance at professional conferences and seminars. This encouragement acknowledges the value of professional development but also recognizes the importance of sharing the results of research and development. When staff members present papers or chair committees, the library provides funds to attend the conference.

Financial support for professional development comes not only from the library's coffers but also from the generosity of donors. More than 10 years ago, a donor established an endowment to encourage professional development. This donor, an emeritus faculty member, honored both his wife and the librarians when he established the endowment, stating that "wives and librarians are the two most underrated professions in the world." This endowment supports a travel award to explore new technologies or develop new skills. Each spring, the professional staff are invited to submit proposals that meet the following criteria: contribution to the library, potential for professional growth, creativity, and professional contribution. Over the past 12 years, staff have explored optical scanning, GIS, instructional facilities, and fundraising techniques. A similar endowment was recently established for support staff. The intent of this new gift is to provide funds for training and professional development, but the donor (a former Mann librarian) has specifically earmarked it for support staff.

Individuals are also encouraged to share what they have learned, both outside the library and within. The library sponsors regular "professional roundtables" where all are invited to hear a presentation by a colleague and join in a discussion with their co-workers. Recent topics have included risk management of digital files, chat reference, and genomics. In addition, supervisors encourage staff to practice presentations in front of a group of colleagues. This provides staff the opportunity to change or tweak the presentation and often provides a boost in confidence.

4. SHAPING AN ENGAGED INSTITUTION

"Culture is by definition a collectively internalized normative system that outlives any one individual" [24]. The Albert R. Mann Library reflects the culture of the institution, the traditions of librarianship, and the goals of an academic, land-grant institution. In establishing the institution that bears his name, Ezra Cornell hoped that he had "...laid the foundation of a University—an institution where any person can find instruction in any study" [Cornell's welcoming address to first class, Oct. 7, 1868]. These words, which became the Cornell motto, still inspire the trustees, faculty, staff, and students of the institution. Similarly, Cornell's designation as a land-grant institution makes it unique among the Ivies—a blend of private and state-assisted colleges with agriculture and Aristotle studied side by side. Albert Mann, an early dean of both the College of Agriculture and also the College of Human Ecology, saw the library as "the educational center" of the colleges. Its central location in the quad, its physical connection to the adjoining departments, and the breadth of its collections spanning the life and social sciences reinforce this centrality. The library's culture reflects the values of Ezra Cornell, Justin Morrill, Albert Mann, and the managers and staff of the library—both past and present. Many of the management practices follows the library—from search committees to mainstreaming—were instituted by Jan Olsen, director from 1982 to 1998. These values and management practices have been internalized by the staff so that they are now a part of the culture. Because the culture relies on involvement, socialization, and adaptability, each staff member is familiar with Cornell's mission, thrives on the innovative aspects of the job, and recognizes that teamwork and partnerships will allow the organization to be more effective. The culture at the Mann Library is marked by a balance among the needs of users, the morale of the staff, and a belief in the importance of innovation.

An engaged institution can, of course, naturally grow out of a library with an effective culture, but the literature suggests that culture can also be successfully molded and changed. A series of organizational culture change case studies done by Denison "shows quite convincingly that fundamental transformation and reorientation occurred in almost all of the organizations" [25]. Ouchi provides a set of steps in his book to guide and influence this change. But cultural transformation is never easy. As Denison points out, "An organization's capacity to adapt and change is complicated because cultures have tremendous inertia and change very slowly" [26]. Some suggest that cultural change cannot happen without a drastic change in environment, leadership, or staff [27]. Two fundamental suggestions for fostering and nurturing cultural change come through clearly in the management literature. First, the organization needs to set a clear goal or mission. Next, it must translate those goals and missions into action.

Both land-grant institutions and libraries are fortunate because they have long-standing missions that can continue to provide momentum and motivation today. Believing in this shared mission is a major factor influencing the ability of the organization to be effective. Yet, belief is not enough. The mission must be communicated, management practices must reinforce the values of the culture, and the institution must foster a sense of trust, innovation, and service. As Ouchi describes this clan culture, it relies on trust, concern for people, collective decision making, teamwork, and customer obsession. Denison's effective culture model employs the concepts of involvement, consistency, adaptability, and mission. Both of these models echo the seven characteristics of engagement outlined by the Kellogg Commission. Although the Kellogg Commission recognized that creating an engaged institution was not easy, it did recommend five strategies to encourage engagement. These included making engagement a priority of the institution, developing an engagement plan, encouraging interdisciplinary learning opportunities, providing incentives to encourage involvement, and securing stable funding to support the engagement strategy.

Culture and practice continually shape and reinforce each other. Given the importance of culture in achieving effectiveness or engagement, land-grant institutions and their libraries are not just encouraged, but *obligated* to foster an effective culture. In fact, all libraries can enjoy the benefits that an engaged culture can offer. Innovation, teamwork, partnerships, and trust, balancing the needs of external customers as well as the demands on the staff, are the foundations for developing an engaged culture and a successful library. To be effective, a culture must be adaptable. As libraries direct and harvest the technology to build digital collections and services, they have extraordinary opportunities to build libraries and partnerships that are responsive, collaborative, and well-integrated.

REFERENCES

1. Kellogg Commission on the Future of State and Land-Grant Universities. Returning to Our Roots: The Engaged Institution. Washington, DC, 1999:i.
2. Tennant R. Personalizing the digital library. Library J 1999; 124(12):36–38.
3. Ross ED. Democracy's College: The Land-Grant Movement in the Formative Stage. Ames, IA: The Iowa State College Press, 1942:26.
4. Ross ED. Democracy's College: The Land-Grant Movement in the Formative Stage. Ames, IA: The Iowa State College Press, 1942.
5. Futas E. Collection Development Policies and Procedures. 3d ed. Phoenix: Oryx Press, 1995.
6. Kellogg Commission on the Future of State and Land-Grant Universities. Returning to Our Roots: The Engaged Institution Washington, DC, 1999.
7. Friedlander B Jr. Cornell Chronicle, July 8, 1999.
8. Kellogg Commission on the Future of State and Land-Grant Universities. Returning to Our Roots: The Engaged Institution Washington, DC, 1999:1, 13.
9. Dennison DR. Corporate Culture and Organizational Effectiveness. New York: Wiley, 1990:175.
10. Ouchi WG. Theory Z: How American Business Can Meet the Japanese Challenge. Reading, MA: Addison-Wesley, 1981.
11. Dennison DR. Corporate Culture and Organizational Effectiveness. New York: Wiley, 1990:13.
12. Dennison DR. Corporate Culture and Organizational Effectiveness. New York: Wiley, 1990:13.
13. Ouchi WG. Theory Z: How American Business Can Meet the Japanese Challenge. Reading, MA: Addison-Wesley, 1981.
14. Dennison DR. Corporate Culture and Organizational Effectiveness. New York: Wiley, 1990:195.
15. Ouchi WG, Price RL. Hierarchies, Clans, and Theory Z: A New Perspective on Organization Development. Organizational Dynamics 1993; 21(4):64–65.
16. Dennison DR. Corporate Culture and Organizational Effectiveness. New York: Wiley, 1990:194.
17. Ouchi WG, Price RL. Hierarchies, Clans, and Theory Z: A New Perspective on Organization Development. Organizational Dynamics 1993; 21(4):63.
18. Dennison DR. Corporate Culture and Organizational Effectiveness. New York: Wiley, 1990:7.
19. Tagler J. Letters to the Editor. The Chronicle of Higher Education Jan. 14, 2000; 46(19):B11.
20. Dennison DR. Corporate Culture and Organizational Effectiveness. New York: Wiley, 1990:180.

21. Ouchi WG. Theory Z: How American Business Can Meet the Japanese Challenge. Reading, MA: Addison-Wesley, 1981:9.
22. Institute for Scientific Information. Web of Science: Science Citation Index, 2000.
23. Kellogg Commission on the Future of State and Land-Grant Universities. Returning to Our Roots: The Engaged Institution Washington, DC, 1999.
24. Dennison DR. Corporate Culture and Organizational Effectiveness. New York: Wiley, 1990:190.
25. Dennison DR. Corporate Culture and Organizational Effectiveness. New York: Wiley, 1990:190.
26. Dennison DR. Corporate Culture and Organizational Effectiveness. New York: Wiley, 1990:190.
27. Dennison DR. Corporate Culture and Organizational Effectiveness. New York: Wiley, 1990:190.

2

Mainstreaming

Bill Kara

Cornell University, Ithaca, New York, U.S.A.

Mainstreaming—the integration of processing, support, and service for digital publications into core functional activities—underlies all digital library development at the Mann Library at Cornell University.

- It brings flexibility by establishing a broad base of knowledge among staff.
- Electronic resources are among the most heavily used parts of the collection, and their management requires the full backing of the library organization.
- Few libraries can hire new groups of staff to process the flood of digital resources.
- Many needed digital library skills already exist in most libraries' units.
- Electronic resources, while posing different challenges from print, still require selection, acquisition, cataloging, and service.
- At the same time, specialists may be needed to oversee electronic resources' incorporation into collections and services, especially when changes are significant.

- The library must strike a balance between processes to be main-streamed and issues that require specialized attention (such as licensing and programming).

This chapter summarizes the development of the mainstreaming philosophy at Mann, with details of its implementation in various functional areas.

Although predictions of the imminent demise of the printed book were quite premature, library users have grown to expect the availability of a wide range of digital publications. Today, most libraries are hybrids, comprising well-established and still-growing print collections combined with an increasing number of electronic titles. In a hybrid, there are not two separate libraries—one digital and the other not—served by two staffs. Rather, library collections in a variety of formats, and the services provided to support their use, complement each other. For the Mann Library, relatively few of the hundreds of thousands of publications acquired over the last century are available in electronic form. Physical volumes are coupled with growing digital collections to form the whole collection. Procedures for processing materials in various formats differ, just as procedures for handling print and microform publications differed in the past. Through awareness of these differences and through training and appropriate staffing, resources in electronic formats can be added to the mix of library staff responsibilities. When mainstreamed processing and services for electronic publications are integral to staff activities throughout a library's functional units, the library benefits in many ways.

1. MAINSTREAMING DEFINED

When we speak of "mainstreaming" in a digital library context, we are talking about the integration of processing, support, and service for digital publications into the core functional activities of a library. Mainstreaming is nothing new for libraries. After all, print and microform publications—whether monographs or serials—have often been selected, ordered, and processed for a library's collection by staff who would rarely limit their work to only one format. There might have been different criteria for what to acquire in which form, how to manage shelving and circulation, and whether to provide equipment for viewing and copying, but staff would still handle both types of material. In most libraries, specialized units for particular formats have not existed.

Certainly, there have always been differences among libraries and their collections and services. In some places, the large size of microform and audiovisual collections and the special equipment needed to house and use them have led to separate physical units with specialized staffing. Electronic resources, however, now increasingly accessed remotely, usually do not need such a physically contained space, nor is one particularly advisable. Even in reference areas that feature banks of computers providing access to the library's digital publications and its online catalog, the print, electronic, and microform collections are all complementary parts of a whole, rather than collections that stand on their own. Reference staff must be flexible and versatile, prepared to work with a variety of materials—just as competent reference staff have always been. It would be very awkward to have a reference desk staffed with format specialists, some responsible only for questions answered with, say, computerized indexes, and others responsible only for questions answered with printed ones. Instead, any person on duty must be able to listen to questions and then determine the best source, regardless of format.

Although technology certainly forms the foundation for the digital library, electronic collections and services to support them—rather than hardware and software—have been the impetus for mainstreaming. Regardless of the type of electronic publication, the more successfully it can be incorporated into daily routines throughout the library, the more integral it becomes to the consciousness of staff. These staff members grow to share the vision of electronic resources as an essential part of the library's collection and its services.

2. WHY MAINSTREAM?

The integration of print and microform selection and processing, as well as the processing of other formats acquired less frequently than print (e.g., videos, sound recordings, kits), has served libraries well. Different staff members know procedures and policies for different formats, giving the library flexibility in meeting its processing and service needs. The library benefits from the broad-based knowledge of many people, rather than relying on the knowledge and skills of a select few individuals.

Where a library has set the goal of providing access to electronic content according to its users' needs, digital materials are already—or will soon be—major components of the collection. This is not a transitory format but instead has become a critical part of libraries in the beginning of the 21st century. Digital, then, is not an exception to a rule. It is part of a new normal state of affairs and should be treated as such—integrated into the library's core operations.

Certainly, over a decade ago electronic resources did not fit into any established library routines and raised numerous policy and procedural questions. Often when something is new and different in an organization, there is a need to treat it separately from the familiar. When the first few electronic serials arrived for the library collection on floppy diskettes or CD-ROM, they were clearly different from print journals, which were date-stamped, marked, and shelved. Yet these titles in electronic format still required some physical processing within the library to prepare them for use. Later, titles available on the World Wide Web that were selected for the collection involved no physical processing: There was nothing whatsoever to stamp, mark, or shelve. Even then, however, each title needed to have records created, and many would need initial or ongoing attention to their licensing and payments. When these electronic resources were first available, the expertise for handling them often resided in specialized staff or units within the library. Support for them was not integrated in the core mainstream activities. This was not an uncommon practice and is still the practice in some organizations, although increasingly less common over time. Integrating the selection, acquisition, cataloging, and technical and information support for these resources into the core of library operations has been a significant challenge and opportunity for libraries.

When the flow of new titles in varied electronic formats was a trickle, they could be treated as a special group of materials for the library's collection. For example, some of the earliest electronic resources added to the collection were bibliographic databases for direct, unmediated access by patrons. At the Mann Library, these early selections were primarily joint collection development/public services decisions. This was a monumental change for our reference services and raised numerous issues for support, selection, and funding. In addition, many publications produced by the government, available in electronic form and publicly accessible, met the selection criteria for our collections. These early groups of titles raised many selection and processing issues, yet still were few enough to be handled by staff with more specialized expertise. That "trickle" period of slow growth for the electronic collections was remarkably short-lived.

Titles now available in digital form and selected for the collection are arriving in what is more similar to a flood. This steady flow increases with occasional downpours as new, sizeable aggregations of full-text titles are added to the collection. Libraries throughout the country are experiencing a similar shift. Much of what is added to serials collections are the electronic versions of titles acquired in print, or additional serial titles that are acquired as part of a collection of full-text serial publications. The proportion of cataloging time that the serials catalogers have devoted to electronic publications has continued to increase. Since 1997 the serials catalogers at the Mann Library have cataloged more new titles in electronic formats than in print, and there is no sign that this trend will change anytime soon. Now online monographic collections are beginning to be available and acquired by the library, and the quantity of titles in some of these collections far outnumbers those in many of the serials collections.

Mann Library's initial approach was simply to assign individual staff or teams to address selection and processing questions. Now, however, electronic resources are neither few nor unusual. They are no longer marginal parts of the collection, but are often among the most heavily used resources. Bibliographic databases, numeric files, geospatial data, and full-text materials are now integral parts of many library collections and services. Building, maintaining, and servicing these collections can no longer be handled by relatively few selected staff. These activities need the full backing of the library organization to be managed and supported effectively.

There are important advantages to adopting the mainstreaming approach. Staff benefit from it. They already have many skills to bring to bear in working with digital materials, and as they learn new ones their jobs are enriched. Since, in mainstreaming, employees learn about policies and procedures in many parts of their library, communication is improved. Finally, mainstreaming is the most practical approach. Most libraries are not in a position to bring whole new groups of staff on board to select, process, and provide assistance with new formats.

Many skills needed to build a digital library already exist in most libraries' individual units. Acquisitions staff already order, pay for, and process materials in other formats, handling both monographic and serial orders. Catalogers already provide bibliographic access to a variety of materials. Public services staff have worked with print and computerized information tools for years. Imagine what a library would lose if electronic resources were not integrated into its core processing and service activities! Staff experienced with print and other established formats—and who have needed to adapt to many changes over recent years—have much to bring to the increasingly digital library. Mainstreaming allows a library to make the best use of these skills and knowledge. The "business" activities of acquisitions can be expanded to include electronic materials. Many cataloging staff members are likely to be keenly interested in the further development of standards to handle new formats. Public services will see the value of working with library users to provide broader access to digital resources.

Staff skills and dedication are important assets to any organization, and it would be foolish to disregard them. The Mann Library staff have welcomed this opportunity to participate in the evolution to an increasingly electronic library. The staff benefit, and the library does, too. Involving appropriate staff throughout the library who know its collections and existing procedures and policies helps to build a firm foundation for electronic resources. This involvement leads to greater understanding and appreciation of the issues and a broader and higher level of technical skills among the staff.

The means of effectively handling a continuous stream of new electronic acquisitions have differed among organizations, which vary considerably in size, funding, staffing, and mission. The Mann Library's policy of inclusiveness, involving staff at all levels and in all departments in digital library development, has not resulted from the administration's failure to commit financial support. The use of existing staff does not diminish the importance of electronic resources—to the contrary, it affirms the fundamental nature of digital publications. Few libraries have such an abundance of employees that they can choose to exempt many of their staff from new initiatives in library collections and services, and Mann is no exception. For example, in the Collection Development and Preservation Division, it was not only expected that bibliographers would have the subject interest and expertise for our particular collections, but also that they would learn the skills needed for evaluating and selecting materials in all formats. The rapid development of the electronic library has required flexibility within the library organization, sometimes with important influences on new hiring decisions. In Technical Services, as positions became open new catalogers were hired not only for their skills and interest in cataloging, but also for their technical expertise. In many cases, especially for the librarians in the Cataloging Unit, their primary responsibility was no longer the creation of original catalog records. In addition to AACR2 and MARC, they needed to be aware of different metadata standards and their applications. Their skills for organizing information and dealing with various standards and details have increasingly been put to use in new and different ways.

This has not created a jack-of-all-trades and master-of-none situation, but rather has helped to forge a more holistic approach by staff to our collections and services. Support for electronic collections is so integrated into mainstream library activities that employees in different departments and at different levels deal with issues and procedures for digital materials on a daily basis. In this transition period, when the digital component of our library is expanding so quickly, having such a widespread awareness and involvement with electronic publications has been critical to our ability to meet our goals.

As a result of this policy and practice, staff have truly integrated electronic resources not only into their procedures, but also into their understanding about what the core services of the library include. Staff have also developed a greater appreciation for the work, responsibilities, and issues others face in the library. Skills are not isolated in one or two people, but are shared among many. This has also offered many opportunities for collaboration between departments.

A complete understanding of the workflow of an electronic resource—from its selection to availability to use—is important. For example, a selector who understands basic workflow beyond his or her department and the potential impact of a purchase on other units is more fully aware of the issues related not only to building the collection, but also to providing access and support to it over time. Whether individually selected titles in electronic formats or aggregations of possibly hundreds of such titles, these decisions impact acquisitions, cataloging, and information technology activities. They will have a continuing impact on ongoing support, maintenance, and service.

During the past year or two there have been an increasing number of job ads for positions such as "electronic resources librarian," "electronic serials librarian," and "electronic services coordinator." This evolving type of staff position is evidence of the need for someone with a system-wide view who will shepherd electronic resources through the organization. This does not negate what has been said about the need for staff in different departments to have some level of understanding of the issues that come with electronic information resources. It merely demonstrates that some libraries feel the need for someone to oversee different aspects of incorporating electronic resources into their collections and services. Electronic resources are now so numerous and involve such a wide range of issues that there is a need for some high-level expertise or coordinating responsibility in many organizations. Although these positions point out the special nature and importance of electronic resources, such an e-resources librarian would not catalog each and every title in electronic form, would not process each invoice personally, and would not answer every question regarding the use of bibliographic databases and files. Effective mainstreaming recognizes the importance of the mix of what could and should be mainstreamed and what still needs the attention of the specialist.

Specialists have had and will continue to have important roles in libraries, including contributing to mainstreaming efforts. Specialists, in fact, are critical to the development and maintenance of electronic collections. There have always been—and always will be—activities that are less successfully integrated into the routine work and responsibilities of numerous staff. For example, in most organizations only a few designated individuals are empowered to sign license agreements. Also, higher-level programming skills needed to maintain hardware and software and do programming and scripting to support electronic collections are best left to the experts. Yet, in both cases, mainstreaming is accomplished through awareness of licensing and programming needs, for both those doing the specialized activity and those having an understanding of the role these specialists play in building the electronic collections. Identifying what truly needs to be done by a specialist is part of the planning and implementation of mainstreamed processing. The continued need for some specialized activities, residing in relatively few staff with special skills or authority, does not detract from a mainstreaming effort. And, of course, the mainstreaming philosophy still recognizes the need for division of responsibilities. Our library is still organized by traditional functional divisions such as collection development, technical services, and public services.

3. ENTERING THE MAINSTREAM

An administrative decision to mainstream electronic resources is one thing, but putting it into practice is another. This decision was not made on Tuesday and implemented on Wednesday. At the Mann Library, it was also not a philosophy or vision created in one brainstorming session. Mainstreaming has been an evolutionary process that still continues.

When integrating responsibilities for electronic resources into various library positions, managers must recognize that individuals have different skills. Staff are a critical resource, not only for maintaining day-to-day services, but also for moving the library forward. Effective use of staff members and their skills is essential to good management. Throughout the library, those employees with existing technical skills and interests were initially targeted for earliest involvement.

For employees with less advanced technical skills, the organization can use a variety of ways to further develop skills and confidence. For example, formal and informal training programs, including one-on-one mentoring, are effective in building basic skills. Staff can also attend library workshops designed specifically to provide new skills and explore other training opportunities throughout the university or from outside sources. These training opportunities are used both to build a firm foundation and to prepare staff for specific responsibilities. However, laying this foundation and building the electronic library are two very different things; the second cannot proceed effectively without the first's being established.

In addition to training, recruiting new staff with particular skills or potential has been fundamental to increasing the base technical skills of the library staff. It has been the practice at the Mann Library to examine each position's responsibilities whenever positions become vacant. This review has sometimes meant changes in positions' responsibilities. Occasionally, positions have been reassigned to a different unit that had taken on additional responsibilities, usually due to the expansion of digital collections and services. If a critical need arose for such a realignment of staffing or responsibilities before any position became vacant, library managers, in consultation with individual staff, worked out required reassignments. This has been the practice at the library for over a decade for positions at all levels. Just as typing skills were considered basic office requirements in decades past, computer skills have become requirements for positions in the library at the beginning of the 21st century.

3.1. Administrative Council

The Mann Library's director, its administrative manager, and the heads of Technical Services, Public Services, Collection Development and Preservation, and Information Technology meet regularly. Although many issues demand immediate attention, from day-to-day operations, the status of the budget, and building a new library addition, this group also serves as a think tank for the library's future. The strong leadership and foresight of this group have had a critically important impact on the development of the library and its collections and services. As part of their planning efforts, these managers examine how the mission of the library can be served by new technology and how technology can best be used to achieve the library's goals. Throughout the period of the mid-1980s until the present, it has been clear that flexibility and adaptability in the face of rapid technological changes are crucial. Planning is essential, but it is also critical to take advantage of unforeseen opportunities, and, occasionally, it is important to step out of the stream and reevaluate how things are working, just in case a course correction is needed. Administrative Council's discussions helped to formulate a philosophy of how the library could best meet the challenges and take advantage of the opportunities that new technology provided. These library managers (under the leadership of Jan Olsen, the director of the Mann Library from 1982 through 1998) observed that staff throughout the library already had many skills that could be applied to electronic formats and decided to take advantage of this resource.

3.2. Electronic Resources Committee

Developing a mechanism to communicate issues and questions effectively, through both informal and formal discussions or through committees or teams, is key to the success of mainstreaming. In the early 1990s, the library's small, but expanding, collection of electronic resources—mostly bibliographic databases from a variety of vendors and statistical publications produced by the federal government—was already raising a number of issues. Mediated searching of databases was being replaced by more direct access to several core databases, raising important bibliographic instruction and user support issues. Collection Development began a long and continuing period of wrestling with duplication issues (i.e., whether to maintain subscriptions to both print and electronic formats), budgetary concerns, and archival rights and ownership issues. Catalogers needed to adequately describe electronic versions while national standards were still under development. It was clear that electronic resources posed questions not only for the individual units, but also for the library as a whole.

Mann's Administrative Council formed the Electronic Resources Council (ERC) to handle the growing number of questions posed by the increase in electronic resources. The ERC was composed of administrators and key staff from different units of the library, representing each functional area. This was not only a forum to address the needs of individual units, but also an opportunity to learn what issues other units were tackling. The ERC played a key and active role for several years, but its goal was not to remain in business permanently. It was formed to examine issues and make decisions for a momentous change taking place in the library's collections and services. These managers understood the need for flexibility. As new technology brought new possibilities, policies and issues needed to be reevaluated. The head of Collection Development and Preservation chaired the ERC; although its membership was defined, investigation and implementation teams involving other staff were formed when a new or larger topic needed additional evaluation. These teams would report back to the ERC on their work, which included, among other topics, library support for numeric files or the impact of the explosion of full-text publications. The ERC, however, used the guiding principle that if electronic resources were to be truly part of the library's collections and services, they also needed to be part of the daily operations and consciousness of each department. In some ways it would have been easier to concentrate these activities in relatively few staff, particularly in the early phase. This is not the course our library chose, because we did not believe it would be sustainable. The deluge of new titles available in electronic formats has shown that the correct decision was made. The library was better able to handle this dramatic shift toward an increasingly electronic environment with the skills and dedication of the full staff behind it, rather than relying exclusively on only a limited number of specialists in the library.

Mann's ERC played an essential role during the 1990s, a period of much change. The library benefited not only from the foresight shown in discussions and decisions in this group, but in other ways as well. Part of a much larger library system, the Albert R. Mann Library is a medium-sized library of approximately 700,000 volumes and a staff of 50 to 60 (depending on project funding and the level of state support). The size of the library permitted a flatter hierarchy and also much more direct communication among the staff in different functional areas than might have been possible in a larger organization. The importance of ongoing consultation and communication among supervisors and staff should not be underestimated—not in the early stages of integrating electronic resources into daily routines, and not now. In a larger organization, despite having more resources and staff, the managers might have been bogged down in a maze of different political, funding, and processing needs.

As different categories of materials became available—beginning with bibliographic databases and census data on CD-ROM and publicly accessible, free resources on the Internet—procedures for them were established, and individual titles no longer needed to go through the ERC but were handled by the different departments. These electronic resources and others to follow were effectively mainstreamed. Bibliographers selected the titles, acquisitions staff ordered them and processed any payments, catalogers completed the MARC records, information technology staff ensured that hardware and software were available to support access, and the reference librarians familiarized themselves with the different resources in order to answer questions from library patrons.

Over time, the need for an Electronic Resources Committee within the Mann Library lessened, as campus-wide issues relating to electronic resources and their processing, support, and service grew in importance. With the acquisition of large aggregations of electronic journals and other full-text publications, the scope, size, and cost of Cornell University Library's electronic collections became an issue of significant importance for the larger library system. At the campus level there are now groups working on a variety of issues relating to Cornell's electronic collections, many of them, like Mann Library's ERC before, having representation from different functional areas.

Mann Library's ERC no longer exists. Just as for print publications, most procedures and policies for handling electronic resources are now established, and staff handle exceptions or changes through communication within and between staff in different departments. Certainly, there are still dramatic developments and initiatives involving technology and electronic collections and services. These are handled by project teams or through the library's existing administrational and organizational structure.

3.3. Collection Development

During the past decade in Mann, the Collection Development division has worked steadily toward involving all staff in building and preserving electronic collections. Digital materials were never considered to comprise a separate collection. Instead, they were treated as part of the whole. Electronic resources still needed to meet subject and quality criteria for selection just as publications in other formats did. Rather than concentrating the selection of these electronic resources into only one bibliographer's responsibilities, all the bibliographers were involved, to different degrees, in the efforts to build the library's digital collections. There was no one "electronic resources" bibliographer who selected titles in electronic form in all subject areas. This was a shared responsibility that raised the level of understanding of the issues among the entire collection development staff.

During this period there were staffing changes, and the variety and quantity of electronic publications increased dramatically. Bibliographers needed to understand the impact of their decisions on other departments such as information technology and public services, which needed to maintain links to resources and answer questions from library users. This balance of recognizing differences while still applying collection development standards and policies is important to mainstreaming the selection of electronic resources.

There was no master plan with dates and goals tidily set out and met precisely along the way. Several models were tried, beginning with a genre expert model (for example, specialists on numeric files or geographic information systems) and shifting to a model featuring broader subject specialists who would be responsible for the selection of resources regardless of format in their subject areas. However, throughout this period the bibliographers increasingly had a mix of print and electronic selection responsibilities. In 1994 Samuel Demas et al. wrote about the early and ultimately quite successful efforts to mainstream the selection of Internet resources at the Mann Library [1]. Since this time, integrating the selection of even more numerous electronic resources into the department's routines has been realized.

In the Mann Library, collection development and preservation reside in the same division. Changes for preservation staff have been no less noteworthy. There are certainly still concerns with acid paper and book repair. Traditional preservation projects where older or unique materials are microfilmed or reproduced on acid-free paper are still conducted. However, preservation is no longer limited to these approaches and digital imaging efforts, both to preserve content and to enable easier use and dissemination, are increasingly applied. During the last five years it has become increasingly important for preservation librarians to have an understanding of the technology for the scanning and delivery of digital images. For preservation assistants involved with such efforts, a good general understanding of computers is now expected at the point of hiring, although in-house training for specific technical skills is usually necessary. This is also a period when copyright and fair-use guidelines for electronic copies are still evolving, and this is of no minor concern to preservation librarians. Furthermore, just as print publications have needed preservation attention, digital formats present their own long-term preservation issues. This is an important consideration and challenge for the future and will require continued close collaboration with selectors, metadata librarians, and information technology staff. See Chapter 3, Resources for the Digital Library, for more detail on collection development in the digital library environment.

3.4. Technical Services

The Technical Services Division at the Albert R. Mann Library is responsible for acquiring, cataloging, and processing all titles selected for the collection, regardless of format. These responsibilities are fairly standard for library technical services operations. Although some degree of specialization among the acquisitions and cataloging staff for handling monographs or serials remains, this division of duties has been somewhat blurred by the use of technology and the acquisition, cataloging, and processing of titles in different electronic formats. Procedures for cataloging, particularly the acceptance of copy cataloging in acquisitions, have also changed, further altering the division of responsibility between the acquisitions and cataloging staff. This blurring of lines has been an effective means of adding flexibility to the unit, particularly as an increasing volume of electronic resources has been integrated into the daily operations of both the acquisitions and cataloging units.

Certainly, many aspects of processing newer formats differed, yet the procedures for processing digital resources built on existing procedures—and skills—in the division. Technical Services was not a technological backwater before publications in electronic formats became increasingly numerous and important for the collection. By 1990 much of the work in the acquisitions unit was done online, including ordering, claiming, and payment of invoices. In previous decades staff were hired for good clerical skills; by this time, basic computer skills were also considered a requirement for positions in acquisitions.

Such skills were especially valuable when acquisitions staff integrated the processing of full-text reports and data sets into their routine. In 1993 the Mann Library entered into a partnership with the U.S. Department of Agriculture (USDA) to provide online access to reports and data produced by the Economic Research Service (ERS), the National Agricultural Statistics Service (NASS) and the World Agricultural Outlook Board (WAOB). The USDA Economics and Statistics System grew out of this collaboration, through which many of the electronic publications of these agencies are available to the public through the Internet via http://usda.mannlib.cornell.edu/ [2].

This partnership necessitated the retrieval and local processing of electronic publications on an ongoing basis, with several reports requiring attention most workdays. A project team with members from technical services, public services, and collection development worked out initial policies and procedures, which were then mainstreamed into each functional area. (More information on public services' role in this service is available in the Mainstreaming Public Services sidebar.) Although the service initially included access only to data sets, when it was expanded to include full-text reports produced by the three agencies, it became desirable to have more staff involved than only the project team members.

In technical services, Mann's government information librarian, Gregory Lawrence, had an interest and facility in developing his information technology skills. This specialist worked out the details for processing electronic publications provided by the USDA. With basic procedures and policies established, he trained selected acquisitions staff to have an ongoing role. As the technical services/collection development member of the project team (and current team leader), he served as a trainer and mentor, and his leadership and skills were critical to the success of integrating this new responsibility into the daily routines of the unit. Working with the specialist, several staff members, some of whom were hired long before such electronic resources become available for any library collection, were able to handle this work quite effectively. In addition, as their confidence and skills developed, they were able to undertake more problem-solving and maintenance activities for these files. Even with staff trained to handle a wide variety of processing issues, the specialist's continued participation is critically important. He is available for questions that cannot be handled by other staff and, along with others in the library, is involved in the further development and support of this important library service.

For the USDA system new issues, updates or revisions to existing files, and new titles are now uploaded to a locally maintained server by the same acquisitions staff that process print monographs and serials. After all, these USDA files are similar to serials in their nature: They are issued periodically. Unlike earlier initiatives with electronic resources, where the acquisitions unit handled only the contracts and payments for new online collections or individual titles, the USDA system also required staff in acquisitions to develop the skills and procedures for retrieving and posting data sets and reports. These skills included a basic knowledge of UNIX to move files to appropriate directories and a familiarity with text-editing programs. This processing of full-text and numeric data is quite unusual for acquisitions staff. For most online resources, once any contractual issues are resolved and the registration or linking is done, most titles will need relatively little ongoing maintenance by the acquisitions staff. For these USDA titles, however, each new issue or file needs to be processed by the staff. Since the inception of the service in 1993, the routine receipt of these new issues has been integrated into positions that previously required no advanced computing skills. Although most libraries would not have a need to build this level of technical expertise in their acquisitions staff, it is an example of what can be effectively mainstreamed with appropriate planning and training.

Licensing electronic resources provides another good mainstreaming example, one that focuses on the specialist's role. This is one of the activities that usually continue to be in the hands of one or only a few staff. Normally, relatively few in any organization are empowered to negotiate and sign contracts, regardless of whether or not these arrangements pertain to electronic resources. With the exception of free, publicly accessible sources available through the Internet and titles received on CD-ROM from the government, most electronic resources require some sort of use agreement. These vary considerably from several-page contracts with much legal terminology to relatively brief statements available online at the publishers' Web sites.

Who in the library handles these contractual issues varies with each organization. In the early 1990s, when most of these resources were bibliographic databases, it was not uncommon for someone in public services to review and sign use agreements for the library. With titles more numerous and more varied, licensing was increasingly seen in the Mann Library as an activity related to ordering. Consequently, responsibility moved into the acquisitions unit. With the continued explosion of titles available online and with the rise of consortial licensing, there continue to be changes. In different organizations and at different times, collection development staff or library administrators have had the responsibility for licensing, depending on a variety of factors, since libraries fill their needs in different ways. However, it is clear that no matter whether the final signature comes from the acquisitions librarian or someone else in the organization, the growth of digital collections very much depends on the efforts and awareness of staff throughout the library. For example, access to the electronic versions of many journals is often tied to ongoing subscriptions to their print equivalents. When an agreement is reached with a publisher to obtain access to all of its journals electronically or only those with existing print subscriptions, there are recordkeeping and payment issues that need to be worked out in the acquisitions units and with the subscription agents who handle the original print subscriptions.

All organizations need to adapt to shifting demands. Licensing responsibilities may remain specialized, but a broad-based appreciation of licensing issues has become essential. For example, in the late 1990s the number of full-text titles increased dramatically. Part of the selection process included not only the availability and quality of access of individual titles or collections, but also their cost, future access to them, and other issues important to long-term collection building. This has led to a much greater awareness and involvement by selectors in licensing issues. Also, now that full-text materials are increasingly available electronically, public services staff are needed to respond to questions relating to their use. At Cornell, problems or questions that arise regarding the Cornell University Library's online collections are posted to a library-wide e-mail discussion list that is monitored by staff from public services, collection development, information technology, and technical services. For example, if users cannot access a previously available e-journal, staff with responsibility for investigating the problem or who have some knowledge of the situation can be reached easily. By having a sufficient number of staff from different functional areas in the library system regularly monitoring this list, the organization can more quickly respond to a vast array of issues relating to our electronic collections.

Meanwhile, in the cataloging unit, staff had also embraced technology to more efficiently process materials for the collection. By 1990 all current cataloging was done online and all of the library's holdings would soon have online records, thus enabling the library to dismantle the card catalog. The catalogers routinely cataloged materials in a variety of formats. Even with the first titles in electronic formats, catalogers began examining the numerous issues involved in providing access to them. Although they looked to the further development of national standards to describe these new formats, they also recognized that waiting was not an option and that current standards needed to be applied as best as possible to a fluid situation.

The Mann Library Gateway brought an early set of challenges to the cataloging unit. In the early 1990s, Mann began to develop the Gateway to provide access to the library's growing electronic collections. Providing bibliographic organization to these collections was an important example of mainstreaming. We decided that all electronic resources would have records available through our online catalog, even though it could not provide direct links at that time. Instead, the Gateway would provide access to the resources themselves. As a growing and important subset of our collection, the resources available through the Gateway needed to be organized. What sort of subject structure would be appropriate, and what type of information in what standard form would be necessary to aid the searching and identification of these Gateway-accessible titles? Through describing the physical aspects of materials and assigning appropriate subject terms, catalogers have long done this for materials in other formats. The Gateway collection was initially weighted toward bibliographic databases and information resources in the agricultural and biological sciences. With relatively few titles in some subject areas, the granularity of Library of Congress (LC) subject headings was not particularly appropriate for this small, but growing, collection. Using the LC subject headings as a basis, catalogers assigned broader subject categories to these titles. As the collection expanded, which it did quickly, the subject terminology assigned for the Gateway also needed to be revised to include subject headings with more specificity in areas of significant growth.

Bringing electronic journals into the library's collections provides another example of changes in cataloging and confirms mainstreaming's value. Without a unit's involvement in the process, it would be easy to overlook the myriad details that need attention to obtain and maintain access to subscriptions for electronic journals. For example, the rise of aggregations (large collections of full-text publications) posed multiple challenges. When individual titles were selected for the Gateway, it was decided that each would be cataloged separately. Titles that met the selection criteria would not merely be listed on a library Web page, but would have a complete record available through the online catalog. This policy was not shared by all libraries at Cornell and probably not by most other libraries in the early to mid-1990s, but at the Mann Library it was core to our mainstreaming efforts. An electronic resource should have the same level of bibliographic access and support as a print publication. We recognized the growing importance of a still small, but increasingly heavily used, part of our collection, and this required us to deal with the full range of issues for providing access to these titles. Merely adding a link to a reference department Web page was not considered to be an option, although many other libraries have taken this route. We believed that titles identified to be useful and appropriate for our collection deserved full access, and that included cataloging.

This policy would be sorely tested with the advent of large aggregations. Similar to large microfiche sets, which in the past often did not have analytics available, these aggregations presented problems of access. Also similar to large microfiche sets, some of these aggregations were quite expensive, and without ready information about their contents, they would be in danger of underutilization.

Creativity and flexibility were needed in establishing and adapting procedures, and they remain important. For example, the use of the same bibliographic record to list holdings for multiple versions (a policy that changed several times during the last decade) significantly eased some cataloging concerns, at least for a few of the earlier e-journal collections. Also, the increased availability of cataloging copy (combined with experience in dealing with electronic resources) permitted different solutions for different products. Changes in this area continue. This mix of approaches, although perhaps inevitable during such an evolutionary period, will have an impact on ongoing record maintenance as these collections change over time.

These early initiatives formed the basis for mainstreaming other electronic publications, yet required expansion to include different and new types of electronic resources. For example, the library undertook digital preservation projects and cooperative arrangements with state and federal agencies to provide access to files they produced. These required additional specialized skills in the cataloging unit, particularly for metadata. Metadata standards, MARC standards among them, underwent considerable change in a short period of time to meet the challenge of describing and enhancing access to electronic resources. When any of the professional cataloging positions in the unit became open, interest in and/or experience with metadata applications became an essential requirement for these positions.

3.5. Public Services

Anyone who has used libraries over the course of the last few decades would easily see considerable changes in the physical layout of their reference areas. Often there is a sea of computers, providing access not only to the online catalog, but also to the bibliographic databases that have increasingly replaced the print indexes and abstracts. Additionally, many full-text publications and collections whose print counterparts had not always been shelved in the reference area have become de facto reference works. They are now more visible, and reference librarians are usually on the frontlines when questions arise regarding the use of such electronic resources. At the same time, users can access this information from their offices and homes. Whether a library patron is sitting at a computer 20 feet from the reference desk or many miles away, reference staff still need to respond to their questions. Many of these questions from patrons outside the library now come by electronic mail in addition to the phone. Mainstreaming in the context of public services means that service for the part of the collection that is in electronic format is integrated into the services of the unit whether the user is physically in the library or at another site. There still might be staff who have more in-depth experience, training, or interest in a particular type of material—for example, geographic information systems or numeric files—but even in the pre-electronic library there needed to be a balance of different levels of expertise with a sound basic level of skills that all were expected to have. See the box on Mainstreaming Public Services for their view of this process.

MAINSTREAMING PUBLIC SERVICES

Jim Morris-Knower
Cornell University, Ithaca, New York, U.S.A.

1   Overview

In public services, our patrons have decided for us over the years which applications and services get mainstreamed (and which do not). If a part of the digital library becomes heavily trafficked, like the library Gateway or the USDA Economics & Statistics System, its support gets shifted from a specialist to all reference staff. If it stays specialized or infrequently used, like census data or geographic information systems (GIS), then support stays with the specialist who fields all the questions. "What's changed over the years isn't the policy," says Public Services head Kathy Chiang, referring to mainstreaming. "What's changed is what's in the stream."

Increasingly, what's in this stream is digital information. Chiang estimates the percentage of reference work involving electronic media is over 75% today, while the amount of paper actually touched in an hour at the reference desk is much less than it used to be. Of course, it's important to keep in mind that these are *tools* that have changed, not the actual reference skills needed for quality service. The reference interview, for example, is still as important as it once was; it's just now done more and more over the Internet and less frequently face to face [1].

As the Internet and digital information have become almost ubiquitous in the lives of reference staff in the past 15 years, there has been a subsequent increase in the need to evaluate the support of these new resources. In public services at Mann, the scenario for such evaluations is pretty consistent: A new resource or tool is "bushwhacked" first by a designated staff member, who familiarizes herself with the resource and serves as the designated support specialist (see Chapter 9, New Frontiers and the Scout). If a resource becomes widely used, its specialist will be in charge of mainstreaming its support by training the rest of the reference staff [2].

The public seems okay with this. There has never been a complaint about having to make an appointment with the GIS librarian for complex or in-depth GIS questions. Should GIS become more popular, of course, its service will be mainstreamed—more desk staff will be responsible for more GIS questions.

What follows here are three narratives of mainstreaming electronic resources at Mann. In each case, a new electronic tool was made public and its support was initially the province of a single staff member or small group. While the idea of mainstreaming is indelibly wound into Mann's culture, these services were bushwhacked first and then mainstreamed only when it became clear that they were becoming widely used.

2 Mainstreaming Public Access Computing

It's easy to forget that the public access computer is a relatively recent development in the library. Public access computing in most libraries started in the early 1980s, and at Mann it began in 1982 with one Texas Instruments machine to dial up and do mediated searches via phone line and modem. Over the years, machinery was upgraded and replaced, but there was never any need to think about mainstreaming its use. An information technology section (ITS) staff member was responsible for any problems with the machinery, and although most were expert database searchers, few if any of the reference staff knew how to troubleshoot any technical problems that arose.

This arrangement was fine until 1989, when a batch of new computers arrived to provide public access to the recently unveiled online catalog. ITS staff continued to maintain these machines, but when the printers arrived to accompany the machines, reference staff realized that patrons were going through paper and ribbons so rapidly that ITS couldn't be called fast or frequently enough. Suddenly everyone at the desk had to learn how to change ribbons on the dot-matrix printers. So they learned and taught each other—and another specialized service became mainstreamed. Now, of course, everyone on Mann's reference staff must be up to speed with the basics of troubleshooting PCs; technophobia just isn't an option. But back then, this was a major transformation.

Ironically, while printers in the reference area are a good early example of mainstreaming technical support, they are also a good example of the limits of mainstreaming such support. The first dot-matrix printers were installed in 1989 in the Mann reference room, and the last ones were removed in January 2000. The decision to remove all free local printing was partially driven by the dramatic increase in full-text electronic documents available over the Web; the library was now in a position of subsidizing what amounted to free photo-copying of journal articles [3]. But the more compelling reason was this: Ten years proved that dot-matrix printers break down a great deal, that ITS staff couldn't be called on every time they did so, and that the printers were too complex to be handled by reference staff (beyond changing their ribbons, which was pretty tough anyway). This continued problem eventually forced reference to rethink this service, and free printing via dot-matrix printers ceased.

3   Mainstreaming the Mann Gateway

Shortly after Mann unveiled its online catalog and took the new public-access IBM computers out of their boxes, library staff began a collaborative project with the division of biological sciences to offer biology undergraduates access to databases linked to the university's network. Six resources—including BIOSIS (a biology index) and AGRICOLA (an agricultural index)—were chosen to be part of the Mann Library Gateway, which offered a single point of access and a simple interface so users could easily log in and use the system. This project, which in the early 1990s was something of a novelty, proved to be so popular that by 1992 its user base had expanded from 100 biology students to the entire Cornell campus.

Marty Schlabach, the public services librarian who coordinated the project, says that the Gateway development team's intent from the beginning was to eventually scale things up to campus-wide use. They even had a strategy for ensuring broader adoption: Encourage use by faculty, who would hopefully share it with their students and a ripple effect of word of mouth would carry this out of a single class. "Our goal was to change the world of scholarship," Schlabach says, only partially in jest.

Reflecting this goal of a broad audience, the support of the Gateway was mainstreamed almost immediately after the project was launched in the spring of 1991. During the first few months, two librarians (including Schlabach) and a systems analyst handled all the phone and in-person questions. Most of these questions were from people who had simply forgotten their ID and/or password. By the fall of 1991, however, support was mainstreamed out to all reference staff as the number of users quickly expanded.

The technical issues were rather complex: While there were initially only six resources on the original Gateway, there were eight different Telnet software packages across campus that could be used to access those resources. Staff training was crucial, so everyone in reference each took one Telnet package, learned it, and then trained the rest of the group in a reference meeting. In a matter of several months all reference staff could handle the majority of patrons' questions, most of which were about problems connecting to the system. The Gateway team also provided workshops for staff training and prepared a notebook for staff use at the reference desk that contained information on basic things to remember like what the various databases contained and answers to common questions about connecting to the resources.

While Schlabach remembers that there was some initial concern among some staff about handling difficult technical questions, no exceptions were made: everyone in reference had to learn how to perform all the steps a patron would go through—how to connect, log in, and so forth. At the same time, even though anyone working the desk was expected to try to answer all incoming questions, more complex technical questions could be forwarded to Gatebugs, an e-mail discussion list of the Gateway Project team members who would field these tougher inquiries.

4   Mainstreaming the USDA Economics and Statistics System

In January 1994, a Mann project team with members from both public and technical services launched the USDA Economics and Statistics System, which provided the public with free access via the Internet to vital agricultural information published by the Department of Agriculture. (As mentioned earlier in this chapter, Gregory Lawrence was the technical services point person.) The system, which today is on the Web and has over 7000 visitors a day downloading roughly 3700 files, was originally a Gopher-based system with about 178 daily logins. Even so, by June of 1994, the site had recorded over 25,000 logins from all over the country, and its use was increasing dramatically every month.

Oya Rieger, the Mann public services librarian who coordinated the project, initially provided all the user support, while the library's technical services unit handled the logistics of acquiring and cataloging the files and ITS provided any necessary system maintenance. Rieger herself fielded all the e-mail, phone, mail, and in-person questions, which in the first five months totaled 82 inquiries. As with the Mann Gateway, most of these questions were technical in nature, such as "I can't connect" or "My connection failed."

Also like the Gateway, the plan for the USDA system was always to eventually mainstream user support even though the number of initial questions was manageable for one librarian. Again, this reflects an anticipation that this particular service would reach a large audience—in this case, one that was all over the world. "The goal was always to empower the rest of the reference staff to handle questions," says Rieger about the project she got off the ground in Mann's public services. "We [the original USDA project team members] never felt we were the sole authority responsible for the system."

By 1995, the increasing number of questions coming in pressed Rieger to start mainstreaming support. In the first six months, the same sorts of questions were asked frequently. so she categorized these and put them in a Gateway binder at the reference desk. Several training sessions were also held for reference staff to familiarize them with the system. Rieger created decision trees that were handouts that took reference staff through various types of questions and gave clear guidelines on what to do for each type of question.

The goal of all of these was to help empower the staff to handle questions about numeric files. which often elicit fear in librarians not trained in them. "We wanted to help them (the reference staff) overcome the mental barrier to numeric files questions. and also to help them figure out when to stop." That is. just as with the Gateway support structure, she wanted to provide the training and encouragement to help staff answer most questions but also let them know that difficult. highly technical questions could be referred to her. to Kathy Chiang (who at the time was the other numeric files specialist at Mann). or to Gregory Lawrence. the government information librarian.

As these three examples show. the process of mainstreaming in public services here at Mann is a cooperative effort that usually doesn't start that way. The lone bushwhacker. like Lewis and Clark. goes on ahead into unmapped territories trying to ferret out the dangers in the wilderness and make it safe for everyone who wants to travel that way. Should there be enough settlers—I mean. patrons—who want to venture there. then the trail-breaking librarian trains the whole staff. providing the group with the maps that will allow them to be capable guides.

As a last point. I would emphasize that even though this mainstreaming philosophy is central to much of what we do at Mann. it is not true that we only pursue services and projects that will be heavily trafficked. If GIS and census data remain more or less forever wild in the information world. we will still continue to maintain them if we think they are important to a core group of our patrons.

Notes

1. It's not the case—yet—that more reference interviews are done in cyberspace than in the library. but there is a noticeable shift taking place. From 1997–1998 to 1998–1999. the annual number of reference questions asked at the Mann reference desk dropped 8%. from 8020 to 7412: in that same time period. e-mail reference questions answered by Mann reference staff jumped 93%. from 368 per year to 711.

2. This team approach to reference service. where all members of the reference staff share support of most services. is also reflected in the composition of the staff itself. While all public services librarians work the reference desk, a number of other units in the library are represented on the desk. This includes the information technology section (ITS). access services (circulation). technical services. and collection development. In the case of collection development. all bibliographers—including Mary Ochs. the head—work reference.

3. In 1996–1997, Mann spent nearly $6000 on printing supplies for the reference room: $3600 on Apple Stylewriter cartridges, $1325 on dot-matrix printer ribbons, and $925 on computer paper. And the introduction of major networked full-text databases like Proquest and Dow Jones came after this period.

4. CONCLUSION

Electronic collections are growing significantly and are still in a period of remarkable expansion. The large publisher- and subject-based collections of e-books and e-journals that are now available are only the beginning of what could be available in a few short years. Statistical resources and geographic information systems with no print equivalents are changing the nature of research. Many users already prefer to access the latest journal issues from their offices, and technology for more user-friendly and transportable access to electronic publications is being developed. Certainly, such developments will have a significant impact on the services of any library, and the challenge can be more effectively met with the efforts and knowledge of many rather than a select few.

In recent issues of *American Libraries*, it has been clear that even though some positions were advertised with job titles identifying the "electronic" component of the positions' responsibilities, most positions—regardless of the job title—had responsibilities for the collections and services that involved all formats, including electronic publications. There are still specialist positions in many libraries; for example, GIS and statistics specialist, data services librarian, digital projects librarian, metadata analyst, and so on. Electronic resources and services are vastly changing the face of libraries, and the role of specialists, particularly in larger research libraries, is still important. It is clear, however, that without mainstreaming the routine activities for electronic resources, specialists would be overwhelmed with processing and service demands. Specialists must be assisted by their colleagues.

Integrating the processing and services for electronic resources into the library's mainstream activities is an evolutionary process. Its success very much depends on each library's staffing resources. It also depends on the resources available to staff for training and for the hardware and software available to them to more efficiently handle their responsibilities. Since this is still an evolutionary period, it is essential to be flexible. The best-laid plans and procedures of only a few years back will need to be adapted to developments often out of the local control of libraries. Regardless of whether they are due to the relatively sudden expansion of titles for the collection in electronic form or other technological and/or nontechnological changes, the library will need to accommodate these developments.

Librarians and libraries are not strangers to change. Adapting existing policies, procedures, and services to handle new challenges or streamline operations was an essential part of library management long before the current digital age. The rate of change has increased, but libraries have not been static. Rather, they have been users of new technology to process materials more quickly and provide better services to library patrons. The automation of activities, creation of online catalogs, development of MARC standards, and use of word processing and other software packages have all been part of the computerization of library operations and services for over two decades. The skills needed to utilize these resources have created a foundation on which the increasingly electronic library can build.

One critical element in Mann's efforts to handle the changes brought by technology is a belief that libraries should not be followers but leaders, especially for those technological advances involving collections and services for information resources. Librarians are information specialists and have much to contribute to this evolution. A second element, forming the framework to fully integrate electronic resources into the core library operations, was that this effort to utilize and develop technology would not be restricted to few staff, but that the entire organization would be involved in building the electronic library. Only through such involvement would the library and individual members of the staff realize their potential. The organization would be stronger for the commitment and skills of many rather than a few.

Without integrating the handling of electronic resources into each of the core functional areas of the library, the library organization misses an opportunity to truly involve staff in these dramatic changes and build and use their skills to meet the challenge to provide quality and innovative library services. Through the involvement of staff and their combined skills in a shared effort, a library can better meet the challenges and opportunities that the 21st century is bringing.

REFERENCES

1. Demas S, McDonald P, Lawrence G. The internet and collection development: mainstreaming selection of internet resources. Lib Res Tech Serv 1995; 39(3):275–290.
2. For further information on the history and development of this service, see Lawrence GW. U.S. Agricultural Statistics on the Internet: Extending the Reach of the depository library. J Govt Info 1996; 23(4):443–452.

3

Resources for the Digital Library

Mary Anderson Ochs and John M. Saylor
Cornell University, Ithaca, New York, U.S.A.

This chapter addresses definitions of digital libraries and presents Mann's approach to building its digital collection within the context of Cornell University Library.

- Definitions based on ownership, control, or challenges.
- Selection criteria must go beyond content to metadata quality, commitment to access and preservation, and services.
- Changes in scholarly publishing have brought wide variations in pricing and delivery options.
- Libraries and the scientific research community have initiated attempts to gain more control in the scholarly publishing arena.
- Cornell provides digital access through its Library Gateway, which manages user authentication and authorization behind the scenes.
- The Library Gateway grew out of the Mann Library Gateway, created in 1991 to provide user-friendly access to digital resources, and it continues to evolve.
- Licensing can be very complex, especially when licenses include large, geographically dispersed communities.
- Preservation and archiving receive high priority, not only for "born-digital" resources but also for digitized historical collections.

- Other issues of concern in building digital collections include staffing, funding, and technological infrastructure.

This chapter introduces the general concept of a "digital library" and relates it to material selection for a digital library collection. While these concepts are to some extent universal, this chapter focuses on science libraries in a large university setting. In this setting, digital library resource selection can require the cooperation of multiple selectors with multiple budget lines, making the selection process quite complex. Such is the case at Cornell, and thus, this interrelationship between libraries within a large system will be addressed. This chapter also looks at some of the advantages and disadvantages of digital collections and their impact on the scholarly research process. Local selection practices and decision making, as they have evolved in response to these changes in the scholarly communication process, are described. Preservation of digital collections has an impact on selection and is also addressed here.

1. WHAT IS A DIGITAL LIBRARY?

The exponential growth of digital information and the significant differences between digital and physical collections offer many new opportunities and difficult questions for selectors in what they try to collect and in how to permit users' access. Peter Lyman provides an exhaustive estimate of just how much information there is in all formats in his article, "How much information." He suggests, "The world produces between 1 and 2 exabytes of unique information per year, which is roughly 250 megabytes for every man, woman and child on earth" [1]. Emerging resource types such as data sets, geographic information systems, scientific data and visualization tools, digital images, and Web pages do not always fit into traditional library collection development practices. The challenges of managing materials to which a library provides virtual access are different from those of managing a collection that is owned and housed in a controlled physical space.

One definition and classification of digital libraries reflects issues of ownership and control that arise. In their paper "Digital libraries on the Internet," Sharon and Frank classify digital libraries into three categories. Definitions for their classifications are excerpted below:

1. Stand-alone digital library (SDL). This is the regular classical library implemented in a fully computerized fashion. SDL is simply a library in which the holdings are digital (scanned or digitized). The SDL is self-contained—the material is localized and centralized. In fact, it is a computerized instance of the classical library with the benefits of computerization. Examples of SDLs are the Library of

Congress (http://www.loc.gov/) and the Israeli K12 Portal Snunit (http://www.snunit.k12.il/).

2. Federated digital library (FDL). This is a federation of several independent SDLs in the network, organized around a common theme and coupled together on the network. An FDL composes several autonomous SDLs that form a networked library with a transparent user interface. The different SDLs are heterogeneous and are connected via communication networks. The major challenge in the construction and maintenance of an FDL is interoperability (since the different repositories use different metadata formats and standards). Examples of FDLs are the Networked Digital Library of Theses and Dissertations (http://www.ndltd.org/) and the National Engineering Education Delivery System (NEEDS) at http://needs.org/.

3. Harvested digital library (HDL). This is a virtual library providing summarized access to related material scattered over the network. An HDL holds only metadata with pointers to the holdings that are "one click away" in cyberspace. The material held in the libraries is harvested (converted into summaries) according to the definition of an information specialist (IS). However, an HDL has regular DL characteristics; it is finely grained and subject-focused. It has rich library services and has high-quality control preserved by the IS, who is also responsible for annotating the objects in the library. Examples of HDLs are the Internet Public Library (http://ipl.sils.umich.edu) and the WWW Virtual Library (http://www.vlib.org/) [2].

However, in order to have a comprehensive collection, there are two more digital library classifications that we have identified at Cornell as part of an NSF-funded National Science Digital Library Project (NSDL) [3,4]. These are

4. Gathered digital library (GDL). This is much the same as the HDL, with the exception that the material in the collection is automatically "gathered" by automatic programs such as Webcrawlers that are instructed to look for material on a broad subject area. In other words, material is collected without any cooperation from the data producer other than it having been posted on the Web.

The GDL is intended to broaden the comprehensiveness of the collection to allow for material to be automatically collected from sources that won't put the effort into describing their material for harvesting or federation, both of which are more expensive for the creator to do. Experimental work on building a gathered collection is part of the National Science Foundation's funded research on the NSDL. An example of a tool for automated collection building is WebQuery. J. Carriere and R. Kazman provide an excellent introduction in the *Proceedings of the Sixth International World-Wide Web Conference* [5].

5. Services for using the digital library (SUDL). SUDL are tools built to navigate, tune, channel, filter, customize, unify, and use the digital resources from distributed collections. These tools are both for the user or information seeker and for the resource creator as well. The Cornell Library Gateway at http://campusgw.library. cornell.edu is an example of a portal service that provides search and other navigational tools for users. Most university digital libraries today are a combination of SDL, HDL, and FDL collections whose access is provided to users by service portals.

Another definition of the term "digital library," from Mel Collier in the 1997 International Symposium on Research, Development, and Practice in Digital Libraries, points out even more challenges:

A managed environment of multimedia materials in digital form, designed for the benefit of its user population, structured to facilitate access to its contents, and equipped with aids to navigate the global network ... with users and holdings totally distributed, but managed as a coherent whole [6].

The challenges that this definition presents include

Defining the user population (Should university libraries provide access for alumni? What about geographically distributed learners?)

Constructing navigational aids that are much more sophisticated and powerful (and therefore more complicated to develop)

Managing holdings that are distributed (i.e., not geographically in the same place or necessarily even owned by the library)

2. SCOPE STATEMENTS FOR DIGITAL LIBRARIES

This wide range of challenges therefore forces any library to define the scope of its collecting responsibility. A scope statement is important because

It describes the types of resources that are suitable for inclusion in the library.

It is an important guide for users, resource creators, catalogers, and collection providers.

It is short and easy to understand.

It is easy to apply quickly and consistently.

The scope statement for the Digital Library for Earth Systems Education (DLESE) at http://www.dlese.org/documents/policy/collectionsScope_final.html provides a good example of a clearly written scope statement. This statement provides an overview of the library holdings and guidelines for such key issues as subject coverage, geographic coverage, types of resources available, copyright restrictions, technical requirements, metadata, and quality filters.

The Calflora database provides a well-formulated policy statement at www.calflora.org/about-database.html. Calflora is a comprehensive database of plant distribution information for California. Its policy statement briefly outlines the purpose of the database and then provides more detailed information about the contents of the database's different components.

Selectors must look at other criteria in addition to content. Some of these include metadata quality, commitment to access and preservation, and services. The Arts and Humanities Data Service of the U.K.'s Higher Education Funding Councils and the Arts and Humanities Research Board has developed an exemplary model of "managing digital collections" at http://ahds.ac.uk/managing.htm. They present a clear collection scope and have extended and modified the concept of digital collection levels originally proposed by the SunSITE Digital Library at Berkeley (http://sunsite.berkeley.edu/Admin/collection.html). "There are five AHDS collection levels, which may also include designation of commitment to long-term preservation of a resource:

> Archived—the resource is archived by the AHDS and the AHDS intends to preserve and keep the intellectual content of the resource available on a long-term basis. The resource will also normally be disseminated by the AHDS unless special arrangements have been agreed with a depositor, e.g., to restrict access for a specified period of time.
> Served—the resource is accessioned, catalogued and disseminated by the AHDS but another institution has primary responsibility for content, maintenance and long-term preservation. This collection level may include 'mirrored' resources where a copy of a digital resource residing elsewhere is hosted by the AHDS to improve access, or resources held, maintained, or preserved by collaborating and commercial agencies, which are licensed and disseminated by the AHDS.
> Brokered—the resource is physically hosted elsewhere and maintained by another institution but the AHDS has negotiated access to it with a collaborating agency and includes metadata and links for the resource in its catalogue, or AHDS users are able to locate and cross-search, and in some circumstances acquire access to it.

Linked—the resource is hosted elsewhere and the AHDS provides a Web link pointing to it at that location from its Web pages. The AHDS has not accessioned that resource or negotiated a collaboration agreement with the agency which maintains it and has no control over the information or formal agreements for access to it.

Finding aids—electronic finding aids and metadata held by the AHDS which will facilitate discovery and searching of digital resources. This metadata is associated with digital resources such as collections at the AHDS or elsewhere but may be stored, managed and maintained separately from them [7]."

Comparing the AHDS model with the digital library model proposed by Sharon and Frank shows the levels of collecting to be similar:

Collecting Level	Digital Library Classification
Archived	Stand-alone digital library (SDL)
Served	Federated digital library (FDL)
Brokered	Harvested digital library (HDL)
Linked	Gathered digital library (GDL)
Finding aids	Services for using the digital library (SUDL)

The AHDS collection levels thus reflect varying degrees of responsibility for the preservation, location, or control of digital materials in a physical or virtual collection and accurately reflect the five categories of digital libraries described above. Models such as these help selectors to define the digital material they collect in relationship to the

Quality of the metadata provided by the resource (which determines the material's interoperability)

Commitment of the resource creator to preserving the material

Commitment of the resource creator/provider to making the resource available on a long-term basis

Services provided by the digital collections to enable use (both in and out) of the collection.

Metadata quality, which determines the level of interoperability of one resource with another (or one collection with another), is important to the development of distributed digital libraries. However, better metadata brings higher cost. This issue is being addressed by a new initiative called the Open Archives Initiative (OAI, at http://www.openarchives.org/). The OAI is developing interoperability standards that aim to facilitate the efficient dissemination of content. According to Carl Lagoze and Herbert Van de Sompel,

The fundamental technological framework and standards that are developing to support this work are, however, independent of both the type of content offered and the economic mechanisms surround-

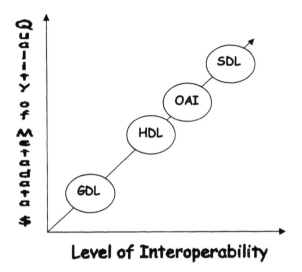

Level of Interoperability

FIGURE 1   The principle of cost versus functionality. SDL, Stand-Alone Digital Library; OAI, Open Archives Initiative; HDL, Harvested Digital Library; GDL, Gathered Digital Library.

ing that content, and promise to have much broader relevance in opening up access to a range of digital materials [8].

This principle of cost versus functionality was first modeled in a table used by William Y. Arms of Cornell University in his book *Digital Libraries* [9]. It is used again in an article by Arms et al. in *D-Lib Magazine* [10]. Figure 1 is an adaptation that Arms has used to relate the quality (and therefore cost) of metadata to the level of interoperability of digital libraries:

An initial goal of the OAI is to prove that minimal levels of coope-ration (metadata standards such as Dublin Core and a communi-cation protocol) can provide a useful level of interoperability among distributed digital resources.

For more on the OAI, see the excellent article by Clifford Lynch, Executive Director of the Coalition for Networked Information, titled "Metadata harvesting and the Open Archives Initiative [11]."

3.   DISTRIBUTED OPEN ACCESS DIGITAL COLLECTIONS

Open Access resources are those materials on the World Wide Web that their creators make available for use without access restrictions, such as cost or membership. Open Access may include metadata that points to restricted materials, but the fact that the metadata is open means that the availability of the resource is made known at a basic level of interoperability. Digital library services can be built to manage the restrictions placed on the material for both the user and the resource provider. For more on the controversial subject of Open Access Information, see papers from the Freedom of Information Conference, The Impact of Open Access on Biomedical Research [12].

4. INFLUENCES ON DIGITAL LIBRARY DEVELOPMENT

In this era of great change in libraries, daily collection development tasks and decisions require thoughtful consideration of theoretical issues. Understanding evolving new technologies and considering their impact on building digital collections is necessary for effective collection development. Two strong forces are driving the day-to-day development of the digital library: rapidly advancing technological capabilities plus the ever-increasing expectations of our users.

4.1. User Expectations

A science library in a research university serves multiple clienteles, with varying needs and expectations. First, the undergraduate: Today's 18-year-old freshman probably started using computers when he or she was in kindergarten, if not earlier. Most of them have never used a card catalog, and many think the Web holds the answer to any research question. For many, if it is not online, it is not worth pursuing. As James G. Neal of Johns Hopkins University has said, "The music television/video games revolution is cultivating a generation of new learners and consumers who demand a more graphical, integrated, and interactive multimedia presentation of information" [13]. While most users are becoming more computer-savvy, undergraduates often are the ones pushing the limits of the new technologies.

Research faculty and graduate students need access to a high-quality research collection. Timely access to key journals in their fields of research is essential. Computer-savvy researchers are aware that access to data, reports, maps, scientific drawings, and 3D models is made possible by current technology. They may not know that the barriers to providing all these resources often are not technical, but financial, legal, or logistical.

Teaching faculty deal with both of these issues. They must be able to offer their students scholarly online information that meets the expectations of this "networked generation." Without it, their students will turn to other online sources, which often lack the credibility of traditional scholarly publications. Teaching faculty are themselves also researchers, so they need access to research collections for their own work as well.

So, as construction of the digital library proceeds, librarians must ask many questions. Here are just a few of them: How do we use staff time, financial resources, and technology in the most effective way to build the digital library? What should the digital library contain, and how do we help users understand the difference between our digital library and the general World Wide Web? In building digital collections, are we simply reacting to a perceived need for convenience or is it much more than that? James G. Neal cites 25 trends that are affecting the environment in academic libraries today. His list of "revolutions" runs the gamut from the "network revolution" and the "cellular revolution" to the "intellectual property revolution" and the "global awareness revolution." We are truly experiencing a revolution in libraries.

TWENTY-FIVE REVOLUTIONS

The personal computing revolution is at the core of individualized technology and the expanding power to access, communicate, analyze, and control information.

The electronic revolution is producing vast amounts of digital information in all media and intelligent software that enables effective search and retrieval.

The network revolution is creating a vast telecommunications web and critical platforms for a renaissance in such areas as personal communication, publishing, distributed learning, and commercial development.

The cellular revolution is enabling an expanding sense of freedom from place, of being able to communicate and access information whenever and wherever.

The music television/video games revolution is cultivating a generation of new learners and consumers who demand a more graphical, integrated, and interactive multimedia presentation of information.

The robotics revolution is advancing programmed mechanical tools and intelligent agents to take on routine and repetitive processes.

The virtual reality revolution is enabling a variety of computer-generated experiences and simulations with broad applications in entertainment, education, and work settings.

The security/encryption revolution presents a pressing information access challenge, as we seek to implement authentication tools for enabling appropriate uses of information and to protect privacy and security of network communication.

The hypertext revolution is building robust and powerful links among the millions of networked files and enabling navigation among the rich intricacies of the integrated, if still chaotic, Internet.

The push revolution is shifting the nature of Web searching by narrowcasting to network users through customized packaging and delivery of information.

The privatization or outsourcing revolution is moving basic operations out of the organization to external providers.

The self-service or ATM revolution is encouraging a fundamental re-thinking of user services in an environment where user-initiated and user-controlled activities are now commonplace.

The partnership revolution is producing higher levels of cooperation and collaboration among organizations as a fundamental requirement for success and as a tool for resource sharing.

The authorship revolution is defining the facility and the creativity potential of the Web where, with a minimal investment, one can post information to numerous potential readers on a global scale.

The entrepreneurial revolution is encouraging creators and distributors of networked information to explore the commercial potential of the Internet and the new market niches being created for products and services.

The business concentration revolution is highlighting the global business linkages developing in many industries and the economic, political, and social impacts of monopolistic practices.

The new majority student revolution is bringing into the academic community waves of individuals who have not traditionally attended college and whose family, job, and personal responsibilities demand very innovative responses from higher education.

The values revolution is pointing to the growing political and social schisms under the impact of technology change and the expanding threats to intellectual freedom, privacy, and the free flow of information.

The intellectual property revolution is threatening fair-use rights for digital information and creating conflicts between the interests of information providers and information consumers.

The government information revolution is transforming the creation, distribution, and use of publication and data from the nation's and world's largest publishing sources, as they become increasingly electronic and network-based.

The digital preservation revolution is energizing us to be concerned about the integrity and archiving for the future use of the vast amount of electronic information being produced and lost.

The information as commodity revolution is increasingly viewing data and its synthesized products, knowledge, as articles of commerce and sources of profit rather than property held in common for societal good.

The global awareness revolution is supporting the internationalization of all aspects of life and encouraging a new world view of networked collections and services.

The knowledge management revolution is spawning a new relationship among researcher, librarian, and information technologist, which maximizes the usefulness of data gathering, information generation, and distribution.

The virtuality revolution is energizing all organizations to think and plan beyond the envelope of place-based capabilities and to create innovative approaches to the design and delivery of new products and services to expanding markets.

From JG Neal, in SH Lee, ed. Collection Development in a Digital Environment. New York: Haworth Press, 1999.

4.2. Changing Ways of Scholars

We know that the World Wide Web is changing the way people gather information, whether it is finding a beach house to rent or getting directions to a different city. But is the digital library changing the way scholars do their work? Of course, but we are only beginning to understand how. In addition, with change continuing to occur at an incredible rate, behavior is changing as we speak. Early on in the development of digital libraries, researchers at the Mann Library investigated user preferences in the use of online scientific journals. Richard Entlich and others evaluated user response to online chemistry journals in the Chemistry Online Retrieval Experiment (CORE). In the CORE project, researchers at the American Chemical Society, Bellcore, OCLC, and the Mann Library studied user preferences for an electronic journal system. This early system, developed at the beginning of the 1990s, allowed chemists to access the journals of the American Chemical Society in electronic form. Researchers examined user preferences as well as technical issues in bringing journals up in an online format. By analyzing user trans- actions and interviewing users, they found that portability, comfort, conve- nient access, permanence, and serendipity are key issues that needed to be addressed in order to achieve widespread acceptance of electronic journals [14]. Interestingly, the users most likely to use the system after requesting a project account in this early test of e-journals were undergraduates—an illustration of Neal's "generation of new learners."

Advances in technology have resolved many of the issues of concern to users of this early test system. Issues such as response time, image quality, and full-text searching have been dramatically improved with advances in technology in the last five years. Other concerns, such as a preference for printing out material rather than reading from the screen, are still felt by many of our users.

Linda Stewart interviewed users of the CORE system. At that time users were still pessimistic that electronic journals would ever supplant their print counterparts, but they did believe that access to electronic journals would increase productivity. More than half of the respondents said they would read more complete articles and would read them sooner after publication [15]. These comments came as a result of using a very primitive e-journal system, which predated the World Wide Web and its user-friendly browsers. Today's e-journals are far more convenient than the CORE test system.

Recent enhancements, such as links from bibliographic databases to articles and links within the articles, bring even greater potential. And with these most recent changes come more questions related to collections. How do systems that link bibliographic databases, electronic journals, and other electronic files affect the behavior of our users? And how do they affect our collections? How do libraries balance the costs of digital resources with the ongoing costs of printed materials? How can we achieve permanent archival access to the resources we buy in electronic form?

Imagine a faculty member in her research lab. She turns to her computer to look for an article she remembers reading, hoping it might address the dilemma she faces at that moment. She finds the citation and clicks on the link to the full text. The article is there. That article is linked to all the items in the bibliography, so the researcher's one recollection leads her to a wealth of related information. She also has software that allows her to automatically add the citation to her personal bibliographic database. Situations like this occur every day. Do you suppose that the same researcher would have left her lab to immediately go track down the article in print? Would she have then gone to find all the related articles in the bibliography? Probably not.

In 1997, Jan Olsen, former director of the Mann Library, wrote

> The computer revolution has introduced an anomaly into the traditional paradigm: scholarly information is now electronic in form. It is widely dispersed and not carefully organized and classified by librarians and publishers. The scholar can sit at home and access electronic information through a low-cost personal computer and national networks. The theories and practices of handling information in printed form within the traditional paradigm of the research library are being challenged by the emerging electronic library [16].

Whether information is purchased from a publisher or available for free on the Internet, it is part of the body of knowledge to which libraries must provide access.

The digital library has caused basic changes in the way our users do their research. Whether we call it a paradigm change or something else, it changes the very nature of what we do. If collection development librarians, acquisition librarians, and publishers around the world are scratching their heads ... it's no wonder. It is their job to build the collection for the digital library from the ground up. Our past practices still work in some ways, but new issues, new methods, and new partners all change the way we do our jobs.

4.3. Changes in Scholarly Publishing

Most of the major scientific publishers have e-journal packages available, but pricing and delivery options are far from standardized. Librarians are frustrated because publishers' package pricing takes away some of the flexibility libraries have traditionally had in choosing which journals to subscribe to and which to cancel. In many cases, once publishers' package contracts are in place, the option to cancel a journal from that publisher is lost or regulated by the contract. What about changes in the curriculum and changes in research programs? Collection development staff can no longer save money by monitoring these changes and adjusting their collections accordingly. On the other hand, many e-journal packages offer access to all the titles from a given publisher for the same price as a selected subset of titles. This can significantly enhance collections. Research studies from the PEAK project at the University of Michigan show that users make more use of articles from nonsubscribed journals than expected [17].

Some e-journals are free with a print subscription, but commercial e-journal packages typically cost between 5% and 15% above the print cost of the journals. Society publishers' pricing for e-journals can sometimes appear quite high as a percentage of the print price, but because their journals generally cost less than the commercial publishers' journals, the cost in real dollars is not that high. These surcharges for e-journals are having a significant impact on library budgets. Will libraries obtain new money to afford these contracts, or will something have to give? This is not clear, but what is clear is that a "state-of-the-art" academic science library must provide access to electronic journals and other digital library resources.

There have been many new developments in scientific publishing, with projects such as SPARC, CrossRef, and PubMed Central just a few of the initiatives underway. They represent an attempt on the part of libraries and the scientific research community to gain more control in a scholarly publishing arena typified by spiraling prices, increasing numbers of new specialized journals, and e-journals sold as large commercial packages. With CrossRef (http://www.crossref.org/), the world's leading scientific, technical, and medical publishers have collaborated to form a service that will link reference citations to the online content that those references cite. Participating publishers include Annual Reviews, Blackwell Science, Elsevier, and Cambridge University Press, among others.

SPARC, the Scholarly Publishing and Academic Resources Coalition (http://www.arl.org/sparc/), formed as a result of ever-increasing prices for scientific journals. SPARC is a worldwide alliance of research institutions, libraries, and organizations that encourages competition in the scholarly communications market and supports innovative uses of technology to improve scholarly communication. SPARC has helped to start several new journals as alternatives to higher-priced commercial journals. These new journals are beginning to find a secure place in the scholarly communication process.

PubMed Central (http://www.pubmedcentral.gov/) is a digital archive of peer-reviewed life science journals maintained by the National Center for Biotechnology Information at the National Library of Medicine. Access is free and unrestricted, and publishers choose whether to include their most current literature or to delay release.

These three initiatives are just a few examples of the library community's efforts to move scholarly communication in a direction that most effectively benefits the scholarly community. Mark McCabe, an economist from the Georgia Institute of Technology, presented an economist's view of the market for scholarly information at a conference, "The Economics and Usage of Digital Collections," held in Ann Arbor, Michigan, in March 2000. McCabe points out that library demand for scholarly publications is inelastic, with demand for material not significantly affected by price [18]. While libraries have cancelled journals to balance budgets, our library patrons are never pleased with this process. Now with the introduction of e-journal packages, this problem is confounded. For an excellent historical overview of the scholarly journal, scientific communication, and serial pricing crisis, see Jean-Claude Guedon's paper, "In Oldenburg's long shadow: Librarians, research scientists, publishers, and the control of scientific publishing," which Guedon presented at the 2001 Association of Research Libraries Annual Meeting [19].

Cornell's Project Euclid (http://projecteuclid.org/) represents another role for the library at a new point along the publishing continuum for a library. Project Euclid, a cooperative project between Cornell University and Duke University Press, aims to help independent journals of mathematics and statistics publish on the Web and to increase their visibility through a combined online presence. The Euclid site represents a new model of scholarly communication, as it will support the entire span of scholarly publishing from preprints to the distribution of published journals.

5.   LOCAL PRACTICES AND POLICIES FOR SELECTING
ELECTRONIC RESOURCES

5.1.   Access to the Digital Library: The Library Gateway

As a preface to this discussion of resources for the digital library, it is useful to understand how Cornell provides access to electronic resources. For more than 10 years, the Library Gateway (http://campusgw.cornell.edu) has been the primary access point to electronic resources for users of the Cornell University Library, whether they were on campus and part of the Cornell community or far from Ithaca, New York. The original Gateway was created by Mann Library in 1991 to provide user-friendly access to digital library resources and to serve as the checkpoint for ensuring that only authorized users were able to get access to the databases licensed specifically for the Cornell community [20]. The Mann Library Gateway was the product of the visionary leadership of Jan Olsen, director of Mann Library from 1982–1998, and the library staff. This vision centered on a user at a workstation who was able to easily enter the electronic library through a single gateway and obtain access to all available electronic resources without thought for passwords and special procedures. In this new age (12 years later) of multiple search engines and multiple browsers, the concept does not seem so incredible, but in 1991 it was a landmark.

Recently, the Cornell Library installed a proxy server, so that Cornell community members can reach the Library Gateway via the Internet from anywhere in the world, with any Internet service provider, and get full access to the online resources of the Cornell University Library. This has extended the idea of the "scholar's workstation" far beyond the typical office or dorm room on the Cornell campus. Cornell researchers working abroad from France to Sri Lanka can access the resources of the Cornell University Library. More information on this is presented in Chapter 5.

5.2. Selecting Free Internet Resources

Selectors in the 19 Cornell libraries choose both free resources and fee-based resources to catalog for the Gateway. Web search engines provide access to free Internet resources, so some question the need to catalog them. If one considers this question in light of the philosophy behind the Gateway, however, it makes perfect sense. Jan Olsen writes

> The research library connects scholars to society's recorded knowledge. In the paradigm for achieving this—the library based in the printed record—librarians have developed theories, practices, and standards to evaluate, organize, and provide access to the printed record of knowledge [21].

5.3. Cataloging

A comprehensive digital library needs to provide access and interoperability to all levels of information resources now available as a result of the success and wide proliferation of the World Wide Web. Many libraries have created Web sites that provide access to their electronic resources. Cornell's Library Gateway takes a different approach. The Library Gateway is not a collection of standalone pages with links to resources in specific subjects. Instead, it is created using records entered into the online catalog. Using this method, any changes made to records in the online catalog are reflected in the Gateway. Cornell participated in the CORC project, an OCLC initiative to share cataloging records for Web resources, and is considering implementing CORC as a standard operating procedure. A summary of Cornell's experience with CORC can be found at http://campusgw.library.cornell.edu/corc/. The following excerpt is taken from the executive summary of the report

"CORC at Cornell Project: Final Report," at http://campusgw.library.cornell.edu/corc/.

> CORC—the Cooperative Online Research Cataloging project—is a collaborative research initiative of the OCLC Office of Research and about 150 participating institutions, including Cornell. It provides Web-accessible shared databases and automated tools to help libraries manage and provide intellectual access to the massive amount of material becoming available on the Web. The "CORC at Cornell" project was undertaken by a small, cross-functional research team of seven people. We worked on the project from mid-May to mid-November 1999. In the approximately 400 hours we spent on the project, we
>
>> Selected and cataloged about 120 new resources for the library catalog and Gateway,
>> Experimented with a new workflow in which selectors, reference staff, and catalogers collaborated to create metadata,
>> Gained practical experience with Dublin Core,
>> Explored the features of CORC for creating subject guides (a.k.a. pathfinders),
>> Evaluated the functions and features of the CORC system,
>> Enhanced our abilities to select, manage and control electronic resources for the library....
>
> Gaining insight into new ways in which selection, description and access can work together was a highlight of the project for the Cornell team. Particularly valuable aspects of CORC are the interoperability of Dublin Core and MARC and the system's support for having selectors and reference staff participate in the resource description process [22].

The current Library Gateway, as you can see in Fig. 2, is broken down by broad subject categories as well as by genres, allowing users to select a particular type of resource, such as indexes, in a particular subject area. It is also fully searchable, so users can search for resources on a particular topic, such as "wildlife" or "ecology."

The original Gateway was constructed before our online catalog could provide direct links to electronic resources. The Gateway served then as the catalog for online resources, maintained separately from the OPAC. Cornell now has a Web-based OPAC, which includes links to Web resources, so the library is now contemplating the fate of the Gateway. Will it continue to make sense to provide a gateway to electronic resources outside the OPAC when the

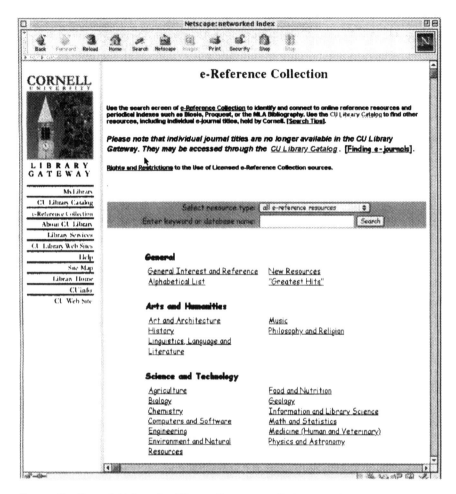

FIGURE 2   Cornell University Library Gateway e-Reference Collection.

OPAC does provide direct linking to resources? As part of this process, in August 2001 full-text journals were removed from the Gateway to streamline it as an e-reference collection. Access to electronic journals is now provided through the OPAC. Cornell will be monitoring user response to this change to see if users find it acceptable, but we have already received many requests for "single-click" access to e-journals, which the OPAC cannot provide.

Many libraries are looking at overarching software solutions to cross-database searching. This multiresource searching capability, invisible to the user, seems to be the wave of the future. Cornell must examine how the Gateway and the OPAC can and/or should evolve to provide a broader searching "umbrella" for the digital library, while still maintaining the desirable functions of the current Gateway. Cornell is also experimenting with software, such as EnCompass from Endeavor, to provide cross-collection searching of digital collections created locally.

6. COLLECTION DEVELOPMENT POLICIES FOR ELECTRONIC RESOURCES

The mid- to late 1990s found many libraries developing collection development policies for electronic resources. A search of the Web yields many hits for policies of libraries. For example, the DLF Newsletter from the Digital Library Federation provides links to collection policies at http://www.clir.org/diglib/pubs/techreps-sec2.htm. The overarching theme for digital acquisitions at the Mann Library has been mainstreaming, as outlined by Samuel Demas and others in their 1995 article, "The Internet and collection development: mainstreaming selection of Internet resources" [23], and detailed in Chapter 2.

Early on in the emergence of digital library resources, the Mann Library also identified five genres of electronic resources and developed genre statements, which stated policy on the selection of specific types of electronic resources. The five electronic information genres identified were

> Applications software
> Bibliographic files
> Full-text documents
> Numeric files
> Multimedia

Genre statements, combined with collection development policies for specific subject areas, set guidelines for Mann selectors who were trying to make sense of the new formats available. Because technology changes quickly, some aspects of the genre statements became dated in a very short period of time. However, by creating a genre statement, selectors defined the parameters under which they would select resources in certain formats and set principles that did last.

Electronic journals—a subset of the genre "full-text documents"— serve to illustrate genre statements and how they were used. First, the Mann Library applied basic selection policies to choosing all scholarly or scientific journals, regardless of format:

> They report the results of research.
> They describe the development of new methods of investigation.

They review research progress and report the state of the art.

They rigorously report and analyze scientific, technical, social, economic, political, ethical, and educational trends, policies, and developments in the core subject areas of the library.

Mann Library's "Genre Capital Statement for electronic journals" was written in July 1998 and included these additional guidelines and considerations for selecting electronic journals [23a]:

Usefulness and demand for the resource should compensate for the work required for us to catalog and support it.

Resources should preferably have a scholarly tone, but any title with perceived usefulness to the Cornell Community will be selected.

Resources should be well organized.

If two versions of a resource are to be available online, each version should present some clear advantage.

Dates of coverage should be appropriate for the subject area.

Resources are generally selected on a title level. A higher level of hierarchy may be selected for groups of resources, which are both accessible through a common front end and coherent in subject focus. In this case, individual components should be able to be searched simultaneously or be similar to each other in format.

With these two sets of guiding principles, selectors early on could make some sense of the almost infinite number of journal-like resources available for addition to the library's digital collection.

These guidelines were written before many of the commercial publishers had large package deals for their e-journals, and they came out of an environment where selectors were choosing electronic journals title by title, rather than publisher by publisher. Now libraries are working with large publishers, whose preferred sales strategy is to market a package that includes all of their journals. The debate rages on about the pros and cons of subscribing to the "Big Deal," as Ken Frazier of the University of Wisconsin has referred to it in his article, "The librarians' dilemma." Frazier points out that the "Big Deal" bundles the strongest journals with the weakest of a publisher's offerings and as a result forces libraries to subscribe to titles that they may not feel are worthwhile [24].

Cornell has signed some of these contracts through our consortium, NERL (NorthEast Research Libraries Consortium). Faculty and students rely on the library to provide state-of-the-art services in support of their research, which today includes access to electronic journals. We hope that the marketplace for e-journals will settle down and mature, as publishers gain a better understanding of how providing electronic access to their publications will affect their organizations. This maturing has the potential to include a productive exchange between librarians and publishers to allow the systems of scholarly communication to develop in ways that are mutually beneficial.

New genres are evolving within the multimedia category. In his address to the 9th ACRL National Conference, Clifford Lynch describes some of the emerging genres of scholarly communication. He encourages librarians to move forward with a lack of bias toward traditional well-understood and well-established scholarly publishing. New genres may look and act very different from those of the past [25].

Individual librarians within Mann's Collection Development Division are assigned responsibility for developing and maintaining the special expertise required to effectively select materials in the genres described above. When the genre statements were first developed, staff became genre specialists, devoting significant time and energy to develop the expertise needed to work with special formats. Today, technology has made these formats easier to acquire and use, and related tasks are rolled into the jobs of subject bibliographers. One Mann bibliographer devotes 50% to 75% of his time to the selection of electronic journals, such as investigating licensing terms, evaluating user interfaces, evaluating pricing arrangements, and working with other campus libraries on cooperative purchases. This remains a very time-consuming process, although at some point in the future, when we have signed licenses with many of the major publishers, this work should settle down. Another bibliographer devotes 25% of his time to the selection of numeric data files, developing expertise with GIS and census files and monitoring the availability of important data sets.

An important and rapidly developing area is the selection of scientific data files, particularly in the area of genetics, but also in fields such as nutrition, biochemistry, and other science disciplines. Files have been available to practitioners for some time, but the library must examine its role in making these files available to the "outsider" and its role in making sure its clientele have long-term access to these files. Who is the outsider? Is it the new graduate student, the adventurous undergraduate, or the researcher from another discipline, unaware of the existence of resources outside his or her specialty area?

So with these as the underpinnings of the selection process, let's examine the actual process of selecting electronic resources.

7. SELECTION PRACTICES

What does it mean to "select" an electronic resource? Traditionally, when a bibliographer selects a book, an order is placed, the book arrives, an amount is deducted from a specific fund, and the book is cataloged for the collection. It is not quite so simple with electronic resources. Procedures and workflow for print materials do not always work for electronic resources. But our goal has been to mainstream electronic resources to as great an extent possible. Selecting material based on its content, rather than its format, has been a guiding principle. Text that is online is comparable to that in a printed book. By "selecting" free electronic resources, they are added to the online catalog and the Library Gateway. This gives them an "added value" and brings them to the immediate attention of our community of users when they are using the online catalog. While search engines already index the Web, "selecting" a resource for the Cornell digital library gives it a level of access and credibility beyond that of a resource found only with a search engine. Clifford Lynch describes a detailed, human-expert-supplied description as "the gold standard." It is expensive, and thus selectors must evaluate carefully the resources chosen for cataloging [26].

Free electronic resources do not need to go through traditional ordering procedures. However, they still need to be evaluated carefully and then enter the cataloging stream, as directed by our policy of cataloging all selected electronic resources. As previously mentioned, selectors at Cornell have participated in the CORC project as a possible mechanism for sharing the work of selecting and cataloging free Internet resources, but as of this writing, Cornell is not a full CORC participant. At this time, catalogers create MARC records for the online catalog, and these records are modified and added to the Library Gateway.

Bibliographers at the Mann Library devote a portion of their time to "selection" of free electronic resources, although this task tends to drop down on a selector's priority list as he or she gets busy. For years selecting books has relied on "push" technology without even knowing it (i.e., publishers' catalogs arrive in the mail and approval plans deliver books and notification slips to our offices). Web selection, on the other hand, requires "surfing" for gems appropriate for adding to the collection or relying on outside sources for identifying important new resources. Mann selectors use several alerting listservs and Web sites to identify possible resources to select, but the real job of discovery resides with the selector. Without the traditional "push" technology, the process is much more labor-intensive, and noting key alerting services for "hot" sites in Mann's subject areas takes vigilance. Unlike looking through *Choice* cards or vendor slips, and very different from relying on approval plans, Web selection takes "detective" skills. Finding the gems requires an active and constant watchfulness for good resources, but the process becomes easier and more efficient as the selector gains experience.

Here are examples of sources that list new and useful resources for selectors in the Mann Library, where selection focuses heavily on the life sciences and agriculture:

The Scout Report (University of Wisconsin–Madison's Department of Computer Sciences) http://scout.cs.wisc.edu/

As described on their Web page,

The Scout Report is the flagship publication of the Internet Scout Project. Published every Friday both on the Web and by e-mail, it provides a fast, convenient way to stay informed of valuable resources on the Internet. Our team of professional librarians and subject matter experts select, research, and annotate each resource.

Published continuously since 1994, the Scout Report is one of the Internet's oldest and most respected publications. Organizations are encouraged to link to this page from their own Web pages, or to receive the HTML version of the Report each week via email for local posting at their site.

Mann selectors subscribe to the e-mail version of the Scout Report and often find useful, relevant sites that can be cataloged.

Science Magazine —NetWatch http://www.sciencemag.org/netwatch/

A regular feature in *Science* magazine, this column notes important new science Web sites. Selectors at Mann peruse this column periodically to find good science-related sites to catalog. There is a subscription fee for online access to *Science*.

7.1. Licensing Fee-Based Internet Resources

Perhaps one of the greatest challenges of purchasing electronic resources for the digital library is negotiating a satisfactory license agreement with the publisher or vendor providing access to the resource. This challenge is compounded by the complex nature of large academic institutions like Cornell. The Cornell University Library consists of 19 libraries on 3 campuses. Seventeen of the libraries are on the main Ithaca campus. Library number 18 is at the Medical College in New York City, and library number 19 is in Geneva, New York, at the New York State Agricultural Experiment Station. Adding to the complex mix are remote users who are legitimate users of Cornell library resources, such as Cornell Cooperative Extension staff scattered around New York State and staff at the Arecibo Observatory in Puerto Rico.

Other universities have even more complex licensing issues. Penn State, for example, consists of many branch campuses with libraries throughout the state. Similarly, the California Digital Library licenses resources for all of the University of California campuses. The University of Washington supports medical students over a five-state region.

At Cornell, all 19 libraries and their users obtain access to resources through the Library Gateway. As a result, licenses should include access to all resources purchased for the digital library for all members of the "Cornell community." Ideally, no users should hit "dead ends" where they are denied access because of their IP address or physical location. Publishers, however, are not so quick to agree to our definition of the "Cornell community."

7.2. Electronic Journals

Because of Cornell's complex organization, purchasing large e-journal packages requires a great deal of cooperation across campus. The individual libraries have decentralized acquisitions budgets, so selectors from multiple libraries must pool funds to make electronic purchases. The Cornell libraries have a group called the Science Team, comprised of selectors and other librarians responsible for choosing resources—both print and electronic—in the sciences. The group has collaborated in investigating a number of e-journal deals, and then decided how to cooperatively fund them, since at this time there is no central fund for the purchase of electronic journals at Cornell.

This process has worked very well. However, several issues have surfaced as we have worked our way through several "deals." For example, recently the Science Team negotiated a contract with an e-journal publisher that provided mostly science titles but a few social science titles. Should the social science selectors have veto power over a deal that will have an impact on their budgets? Another deal required title-by-title billing back to individual selectors' budgets to pay for electronic access to specific journal titles. Acquisitions and accounting staff must now pore over publishers' spreadsheets assigning billed amounts for each title. Can we afford the added investment in acquisitions staff time required to fund purchases in this way? On the other hand, do we want to create giant central funds where individual selectors lose autonomy? Large centralized funds mean that individual selectors have less control over funds they have managed in the past. Many subject bibliographers are resistant to this model.

Often in license negotiation, we talk about "deal breakers." Many publishers have clauses in their license agreements that require that an institution will not cancel any journal titles over a certain period of time. Do other industries sell products in this way and get away with it? Should this be a "deal breaker"? In some cases, the advantages of the contract may make this clause "swallowable," but not very palatable. It compounds the problem of package deals when individual selectors at a large institution are not interested in getting electronic access—or print access, for that matter—to a particular title. Another example of a "deal breaker" was the policy of *Nature* to place a three-month "embargo" on certain content, such as news features and letters to the editor, for institutional subscribers. Librarians were very outspoken in their criticism of this policy, and many refused to subscribe. As a result, *Nature* agreed to change its policy.

The packaging of electronic journals in such a way that we must subscribe to all or none of a publisher's journals reduces our ability to tailor our collections to our users' needs, yet libraries want to move forward, creating state-of-the-art electronic libraries. Large e-journal vendors may offer a very good deal, but the sheer size of the collection makes the price prohibitive. As McCabe describes, inelastic demand in a near-monopoly situation results in high prices [27]. It also results in e-journal licenses with terms not particularly favorable to libraries. "No print cancellation" clauses and pricing determined by "base year" subscriptions are examples of unfair and undesirable subscription pricing models.

Does a publisher's refusal to allow access to all of Cornell's user community constitute a "deal breaker"? In some cases "yes" and in some cases "no." However, Cornell tries very hard to negotiate deals in which our entire user community is allowed access to a resource. Some publishers charge for access based on the number of campuses the resource serves. Then the definition of "campus" seems particularly important. In the case of Cornell, some faculty members have joint appointments at the Ithaca, NY campus and the Geneva, NY, Agricultural Experiment Station 40 miles away. Yet some publishers want to charge the Experiment Station as if it were an entirely separate institution.

It is curious to observe the chaos of pricing for electronic resources. Publishers struggle to find mechanisms for charging that are often based on criteria that are no longer relevant in an electronic environment, such as physical distance between campuses. Others base pricing on student FTEs or a percentage of the current cost of print subscriptions. Clearly, publishers need to protect their investment in producing electronic versions of journals and providing the infrastructure to support access to the journals. Their policies and prices reflect their concern about institutional electronic sub-scriptions replacing many individual paper subscriptions. Unfortunately, their pricing mechanisms do not take into account that there is no way for academic libraries to quickly acquire money saved by individuals and depart-ments on personal subscriptions as the result of a library's electronic insti-tutional subscriptions. Comments from publishers' sales representatives suggesting that we just ask the departments for their share of the cost are naïve.

Another pricing mechanism, where "per use" fees are charged, is more closely tied to individual subscriptions. This pricing mechanism is difficult for libraries because there is no way of predicting costs. Individual users determine the amount of use without thought for overall costs. This model is currently being used for document delivery in place of traditional interlibrary loan in some institutions.

It is likely that pricing in the electronic journal market will settle down over the next several years. It remains to be seen how the cards will fall. Initiatives in the academic community that offer alternatives to traditional scholarly publishing, such as SPARC and PubMed Central, have the potential to cause dramatic shifts in the dissemination of scholarly information. If these initiatives are successful, we may see some overall lowering of electronic journal prices. Changes in technology that we cannot yet foresee may also play a role.

Plans among major scholarly publishers to link bibliographic databases to full-text and to link from one e-journal article to another offer potential to change the way researchers use the scholarly literature. How this impacts library collections in general remains to be seen. Recall the professor in her lab described earlier in this chapter. Can libraries cancel print, and move wholly into an environment of electronic journals? Our computer-savvy undergraduates would probably do just fine, but what of our older faculty, who are not quite ready for print to disappear? This, in addition to the archiving issue, causes us to pause before canceling many print titles. In a research library, we cannot afford to make a mistake that our clientele 100 years from now will pay for.

7.3. E-Books

Electronic books, or e-books, are perhaps the newest challenge in the digital library selection process. First to enter this market was NetLibrary (http://www.netlibrary.com), with its large collection of books for academic audiences. Librarians have criticized its approach, which mimics a traditional pattern of 1 book/1 user circulation. Here again publishers are concerned about maintaining revenue while providing electronic access. Publishers and vendors must get beyond "horseless carriage" access and pricing mechanisms and find ways of pricing their products that allow full utilization of the technology. As of this writing, the fate of NetLibrary is uncertain, as rumors of bankruptcy and purchase by OCLC float through the library community. Other e-book vendors have come and gone, while some have survived, such as O'Reilly (http://safari.oreilly.com/) and Knovel (http://knovel.com/). An article by Clifford Lynch, entitled "The battle to define the future of the book in the digital world," at http://www.firstmonday.dk/issues/issue6_6/lynch/index.html, is perhaps one of the most comprehensive discussions of "the competing visions for the future of the book in the digital environment" [28].

The Cornell University Library established a working group on e-books, which just issued its report. They characterize the e-book terrain as one of business failures, company mergers, and retraction. In making practical recommendations for everyday collection development decisions, it was necessary for the working group to examine the theoretical possibilities for e-books and make decisions for today. The group stated in its report, "If the future of the e-book appears unclear, the relationship of libraries to e-books is even more uncertain. E-book licenses and rights management systems are likely to conflict with library values and systems." The group identified collection development issues, technical services issues, public services issues, and preservation issues. They recommended cautious main-streaming of e-book selection processes and noted the need to assign a group or individual to keep abreast of e-book developments [29].

8. ELECTRONIC RESOURCES AND PRESERVATION

And what of issues of archiving? Publishers and libraries are grappling with the archiving issue. Librarians build collections not only for today's users, but also for the users 100 years from now, who—we think—will still use libraries for their research.

The digital library requires us to engage in thoughtful consideration of the preservation of the information it contains. Since the publishers of electronic journals and other electronic resources do not necessarily want to take responsibility for long-term maintenance of the resources, the library itself must ensure that its investment in these resources is secure and that users, years into the future, will still have access to the material. There are two types of materials we must consider: those born digital, and thus only available in electronic form of some kind, and those converted to digital. Each poses its own set of challenges. Within these categories fall materials that are unique and material that may be owned by many institutions, and thus cooperative preservation plans might be possible.

8.1. Born Digital

Let us begin this discussion with an example. At the Mann Library, we provide access to several important bibliographic databases, BIOSIS, CAB Abstracts, and AGRICOLA, through regular local loading of the tapes. The databases run under BRS software and have a simple text-based Telnet interface. BRS was one of the early vendors of online database searching and also licensed its software for locally loaded databases. We have cancelled the print counterparts to the databases and have relied on local efforts to maintain access to these files, with the backup of purchasing temporary online access to these files in an emergency.

Because commercial interfaces to these databases have become more sophisticated and linking between databases and electronic journals has become widespread, we now plan to switch over to providing access to these databases through a commercial vendor. Since we no longer subscribe to the print counterparts to these files, we are relying completely on the database producers and vendors to ensure long-term access. Certainly archival access to these databases is important for a multitude of institutions. Even if the publisher assures perennial access to the databases, are we comfortable with its assurances? Every academic library in the country need not duplicate the preservation efforts necessary to ensure access to these databases, but who will be the one to do it? New cooperative arrangements may be necessary, where publishers and libraries work together on preservation efforts. Cornell is just one of several institutions looking at long-term archiving issues for electronic content.

Numeric files represent another area where long-term preservation is necessary. Two methods for ensuring access are migration, where the data is moved forward into new formats as technology changes, and emulation, where software mimicking the software originally used to create the files is used to read them on new platforms. The Mann Library has undertaken a project to assess the risk involved in migration of several common file formats. Results of this study are available at the CLIR Web site, at http://www.clir.org/pubs/abstract/pub93abst.html. This document provides "a practical guide to assessing the risks associated with the migration of various formats and to making sound preservation decisions on the basis of that assessment" [30].

Mann is the host of the USDA Economics and Statistics System Web site at http://usda.mannlib.cornell.edu (see Chap. 2 for more details). As host for the site, it is the Mann Library's role to ensure that content is preserved and made available for the long term. Sometimes organizations that produce statistical information only maintain the most recent version of a report, forgetting that 50 years from now, each annual edition might hold key facts for researchers. By creating the USDA archive, the reports will be available long into the future. But as a result of our role, we must understand and solve the problems of digital preservation.

Particularly difficult is dealing with files where the physical medium has become antiquated; for example, files purchased or received 10 or more years ago on $5\frac{1}{4}$-inch floppy disks. Our stacks contain many volumes with accompanying material on diskette that may not be readable. And although CD-ROM is still a usable medium on standard computer equipment, the software needed to manipulate data may or may not be available. Staff at the Mann Library are considering these problems and looking for solutions.

8.2. Creating the Digital Library: Providing Access to Historical Material

While standards for digitizing for preservation purposes are still far from set, digitizing offers incredible possibilities for enhancing access to historical collections. Research libraries throughout the country are filled with brittle books published between 1850 and 1950 when the problems created by the use of acid paper were not well understood.

Several large projects, such as the "Making of America Project" (http://cdl.library.cornell.edu/moa/) at Cornell and the University of Michigan and Mann Library's "Core Historical Literature of Agriculture" project (http://chla.library.cornell.edu), provided valuable early experience in creating digital libraries. By digitizing and using OCR technology to create searchable full-text for these collections, users have unparalleled access to the contents of these historical materials. It is critical that we find ways to maintain the quality and accessibility of historical digital repositories created in our libraries. Awareness of the risks to these files, which include changes in file formats over time and the need for proprietary software or special equipment in order to read the files, helps libraries be on guard for problems that may occur, rather than realizing too late that their files are inaccessible. Cornell has established a Digital Preservation Policy Working Group, which is examining the issues surrounding ensuring long-term access to Cornell's in-house digital image collections. The group has recommended specific requirements for deposit in a central archival repository, including content considerations and technical requirements. Their guidelines are available at http://www.library.cornell.edu/preservation/IMLS/image_deposit_guidelines.pdf [31].

8.3. Copyright Issues

While copyright issues have been debated and settled to some extent in the print environment, copyright in the digital era is far from settled. Many Cornell projects have for the most part focused on material in the public domain, but both the Core Historical Literature of Agriculture and Project Euclid have copyright clearance aspects. It is important to realize that it is a very complex and time-consuming aspect to any digital project if materials still under copyright restriction are included.

8.4. Staffing for the Digital Library

The role of the librarian has certainly changed dramatically with the advent of the digital library. However, the same skills that made early librarians so skilled in helping researchers find the information they needed in the print environment are still valid. They are simply transformed to take full advantage of the technology we have available to us. Imagine the traditional bun and glasses librarian morphed through a machine you might see on "Star Trek." She comes out on the far side, changed, yet not changed. That is who we are. Librarians of today and yesterday have two critical skills: (1) knowledge and understanding of how metadata enables information discovery, and (2) knowledge and understanding of how people gather and use information.

All library staff must be willing to train themselves to understand information technology well enough to recognize its value and apply it in their daily work. Technical staff (who in many cases will be librarians) with an understanding of how libraries work must work along with librarians to build the digital library. Chapter 4 discusses staffing for the digital library in greater depth.

8.5. How Do We Pay for the Digital Library?

Paying for the digital library represents a large challenge for library directors and heads of collection development. With electronic access adding from 0% to 100% to the price of a print subscription, librarians must look for ways to supplement funds. At the Mann Library, gifts and endowments play a major role in allowing the library to expand its digital library. With a growing endowment to devote to monograph purchases, some of the budget can be diverted to pay for electronic resources. Some of our endowments have been used to "jump-start" our electronic resource purchases.

However, endowments alone are not adequate to fund a major digital library effort. Strong support from faculty and students must be used to lobby for budgetary support for digital library resources. While it is possible to cancel print resources to achieve savings when comparable electronic resources are purchased, this is not always desirable. As previously mentioned, we are in a transition period where many of our users are not ready to move to "electronic only," and the archival standards for electronic resources are not yet certain. This is a financially difficult transition because we must maintain a robust print collection while building our electronic collection. It is likely that this problem will be resolved over the coming years, but at this time it appears risky for the research library to dispense with print copies of important materials. Cooperative archiving of print materials may be another answer.

8.6. Technological Infrastructure for the Digital Library

Clearly, the digital library requires a different infrastructure from that of the traditional library. At the Mann Library, we still have the same number of staff that we had when the library opened in 1952. However, some of those positions have changed significantly in scope and purpose. Our Information Technology Services Unit consists of a staff of six full-time computer analyst/ programmers and computer specialists who provide technical support for staff and provide the expertise to create and support the Library Gateway, the USDA Economics and Statistics System, and other digital library projects. Without this investment in technical staff, the digital library cannot be a reality.

In addition to staff, state-of-the-art hardware and software are needed to provide fast and reliable access to digital library resources. Whether a library is creating resources for the digital library through digitizing projects or providing access to commercial information resources, systems must be easy to use and available when users want them. In 1984, the Mann Library had one microcomputer. In 2003, the library offers 110 public-access micro-computers, provides wireless access for users on three of our four floors, and lends laptops from the Circulation Desk. The university has recognized that the library represents the link to information resources for its students, staff, and faculty and has supported the installation of appropriate technology.

9. CONCLUSION

In scientific research, the disciplines are becoming blurred. More than ever before, biology overlaps with physics, and engineering overlaps with medicine. A digital library breaks down old borders, too, making the building of the digital library—at Cornell and elsewhere—very much a team effort. In multilibrary large institutions, acquisitions dollars spent in one library benefit users all around the campus in ways they never did before. Consortia of libraries, large and small, work together to provide access to digital library resources. As we continue to build digital collections, we must keep careful watch on trends in scholarly communication, digital preservation, and electronic publishing, as we work to enhance the productivity of the research community we serve.

REFERENCES

1. Lyman P. How much information. Berkeley, CA: Regents of the University of California, 2000. http://www.sims.berkeley.edu/how-much-info/summary. html.
2. Sharon T, Frank AJ. Digital libraries on the Internet. 66th IFLA Council and General Conference, Jerusalem, Israel, Aug. 13–18, 2000. http://www.ifla.org/IV/ifla66/papers/029-142e.htm.
3. Zia L. The NSF National Science, Mathematics, Engineering, and Technology

Education Digital Library NSDL Program: A Progress Report. http://www. dlib.org/dlib/october00/zia/10zia.html.

4. NSDL (National Science, Mathematics, Engineering, and Technology Education Digital Library) Communication Portal. http://comm.nsdlib.org.

5. Carrière J, Kazman R. WebQuery: Searching and visualizing the Web through connectivity. Proc. 6th Intl. World-Wide Web Conf., Santa Clara, CA, Apr. 1997. http://www.scope.gmd.de/info/www6/technical/paper096/paper96.html.

6. Collier M. International Symposium on Research, Development, and Practice in Digital Libraries. ISDL '97. Tsukuba, Ibaraki, Japan: University of Library and Information Science, 1997. http://www.dl.ulis.ac.jp/ISDL97/proceedings/collier.html.

7. Pressler C. Managing Digital Collections. AHDS Policies, Standards and Practices. Arts and Humanities Data Service, July 2001. http://ahds.ac.uk/policies.htm.

8. Lagoze C, Van de Sompel H. The Open Archives Initiative: Building a low-barrier interoperability framework. JCDL '01, June 17–23, 2001, Roanoke, VA. http://www.openarchives.org/documents/oai.pdf.

9. Arms WY. Digital Libraries. Cambridge, MA: MIT Press, 2000.

10. Arms WY, Hillmann D, Lagoze C, Krafft D, Marisa R, Saylor J, Terrizzi C, Van de Sompel H. The British Library. A Spectrum of Interoperability: The Site for Science Prototype for the NSDL. D-Lib Magazine 8(1), 2002. http:// www.dlib. org/dlib/january02/arms/01arms.html.

11. Lynch C. Metadata harvesting and the Open Archives Initiative. ARL Bimonthly Report 217, 2001. http://www.arl.org/newsltr/217/mhp.html.

12. Freedom of Information Conference. The Impact of Open Access on Biomedical Research, July 6–7, 2000. New York Academy of Medicine. http://www. biomedcentral.com/info/conference.asp.

13. Neal JG. Chaos Breeds Life: Finding Opportunities for Library Advancement During a Period of Collection Schizoprenia. In: Lee SH, ed. Collection Development in a Digital Environment. New York: Haworth Press, 1999.

14. Entlich RG. Testing a Digital Library: User Response to the Core Project. Library Hi-Tech 1996; 14(4):99–118.

15. Stewart L. User Acceptance of Electronic Journals: Interviews with Chemists at Cornell. College Res Lib 1996; 57(4):339–349.

16. Olsen J. The Gateway: Point of Entry to the Electronic Library. In: Dowler L, ed. Gateways to Knowledge. Cambridge, MA: MIT Press, 1997:123–134.

17. Thomes K. The Economics and Usage of Digital Library Collections. ARL Bimonthly Report 210. http://www.arl.org/newsltr/210/econ. html.

18. McCabe MJ. Academic journal pricing and market power: A portfolio approach. Paper Presented at The Economics and Usage of Digital Library Collections, Ann Arbor, MI, March 23–24, 2000. http://www.si.umich.edu/PEAK-2000/mccabe.pdf.

19. Guedon J-C. Oldenburg's long shadow: Librarians, research scientists, publishers, and the control of scientific publishing. Association of Research Libraries, Proc. 138th Annual Meeting, Toronto, Ontario, May 23–25, 2001. http://www. arl.org/arl/proceedings/138/guedon.html.

20. Olsen J. The Gateway: Point of Entry to the Electronic Library. In: Dowler L, ed. Gateways to Knowledge. Cambridge, MA: MIT Press, 1997:123–134.

21. Olsen J. The Gateway: Point of Entry to the Electronic Library. In: Dowler L, ed. Gateways to Knowledge. Cambridge, MA: MIT Press, 1997:123–134.

22. Calhoun K. CORC at Cornell. Feb., 2000. http://campusgw.library.cornell.edu/corc/.

23. Demas S, McDonald P, Lawrence G. The Internet and Collection Department: Mainstreaming Selection of Internet Resources. Lib Res & Tech Serv 1995; 39(3):275–290.

23a. Weintraub J, Entlich R. Genre Statement for Electronic Journals. Ithaca, NY: Mann Library, 1998.

24. Frazier K. The librarians' dilemna. D-Lib Magazine 7(3), 2001. http://www.dlib.org/dlib/march01/frazier/03frazier.html.

25. Lynch C. On the threshold of discontinuity: The new genres of scholarly communication and the role of the research library. ACRL National Conf., Detroit, MI, April 1999. http://www.ala.org/acrl/clynch.html.

26. Lynch C. On the threshold of discontinuity: The new genres of scholarly communication and the role of the research library. ACRL National Conf., Detroit, MI, April 1999. http://www.ala.org/acrl/clynch.html.

27. McCabe MJ. Academic journal pricing and market power: A portfolio approach. Paper Presented at The Economics and Usage of Digital Library Collections, Ann Arbor, MI, March 23–24, 2000. http://www.si.umich.edu/PEAK-2000/mccabe.pdf

28. Lynch C. The battle to define the future of the book in the digital world. http://www.firstmonday.dk/issues/issue6_6/lynch/index.html.

29. Working group on e-books, Cornell University Library. Report of the Working Group on E-Books, Dec. 2001. Ithaca NY:Cornell University Library, 2001.

30. Lawrence GW, et al. Risk Management of Digital Information: A File format Investigation. Washington, DC: Council on Library Resources, 2000. http://www.clir.org/pubs/abstract/pub93abst.html.

31. Kenney A, Rieger O, et al. Report of the Digital Preservation Policy Working Group on Establishing a Central Depository for Preserving Digital Image Collections. Part I: Responsibilities of Transferee. Version 1.0. Ithaca, NY: Cornell University Library, 2001. http://www.library.cornell.edu/preservation/IMLS/image_deposity_guidelines.pdf.

4

Investing in Staff: Hiring, Training, and Mentoring

Thomas P. Turner and Howard Raskin
Cornell University, Ithaca, New York, U.S.A.

A library's staff is as fundamental as its collection, equipment, and physical facility. Consideration of organizational needs and work skills are essential hiring criteria, but potential and personal qualities are equally important.

- Hiring begins with a carefully crafted, interesting job description.
- Job descriptions must be revised as the work environment changes and technology becomes more complex.
- In a library, every job is a service position.
- Recruitment and retention are improved by attention to variety, the ability to solve problems and be innovative, a balance between individual activities and teamwork, opportunities for growth, and responsibilities for supervising people or projects.
- Creativity in advertising jobs, such as use of the Internet and visiting professional schools, broadens the pool of potential applicants.
- Cultivation of a more diverse staff requires special attention and may involve working with new partners such as nonlibrary organizations.
- Search committees comprising staff from various departments contribute a variety of perspectives, demonstrating that the library works as a team.

- Broad-based search committees also provide useful experience to staff, improve collegiality, and foster a shared organizational culture.
- The hiring decision is the library director's responsibility, with careful attention paid to all input.

An excellent staff is one of the key elements that differentiate good libraries from great libraries. This is as true for libraries with digital collections as it is for libraries without them. In addition to their specific roles, staff members determine the quality of service provided to library patrons and the overall atmosphere of the library. When people think of investing in a library, they usually think of investing in its collection, equipment, and physical facility. These expenditures are fundamental, of course, but staff are at least as important an investment for the library. Staff members impact the organizational culture, provide the service, and define the operation. The best collection and latest technology are useless without outstanding, service-oriented staff.

An organization can invest in staff by taking the time to hire well, by training staff, by providing development and growth opportunities, and by mentoring staff. Choosing the right staff member involves not only defining organizational need but also finding a personality mix that works for the position, the person's unit, and the library as a whole. Staff should be prepared for the changes that are inevitable in the current environment. The burden for this preparation is the responsibility not only of staff members but also of library managers. By making the best hiring decisions possible, library managers can help library staff and the entire organization weather difficult challenges and transitions. It is also important to give staff the opportunity to grow and change in their jobs—to tailor their responsibilities to meet the organization's needs and their own personal and professional growth. This can be accomplished through effective training and mentoring.

This chapter is concerned with hiring and training staff. It includes perspectives from administrators as well as from staff themselves. It discusses qualities needed in staff as well as qualities staff members want in their jobs and work environments. It also describes the hiring process at the Mann Library, which emphasizes the need to include staff in hiring peers as well as supervisors. Training, which is as important to the library as hiring, is described by addressing the who, what, how, and why of staff training. Mentoring is also discussed.

Throughout this chapter, the opinions and perspectives of staff members will be used to reflect the Mann Library's procedures related to hiring, training, and mentoring. Fifteen staff members were asked about the qualities they most valued in a job, in a colleague, in staff who work for them (when applicable), and in a supervisor or administrator. This approach allowed us to learn about the hiring process from the perspective of the staff as well as of administrators. A special effort was made to talk with staff members who had been hired by the library within the past year. It was hoped that they would most be able to identify the qualities they were looking for when they applied to work in the library. Three other categories of staff that were chosen included staff members who had been employed by the library for more than five years, staff members who had served repeatedly on search committees, and staff members who supervised students. These interviews were conducted via e-mail or in person depending on the individual's preference. Thomas Turner, a nonsupervisor, junior librarian, conducted all interviews in January and February of 2000. Confidentiality was guaranteed to encourage honest answers. See box entitled Interview Questions for questions that were asked.

STAFF INTERVIEW QUESTIONS

The following questions were asked of staff being interviewed for this project:

1. For staff who had started working at the Mann Library within the last two years: When you first interviewed for your job, what appealed to you about it? For staff who have been employed at the Mann Library for more than two years: What aspects of your job do you find most satisfying?

2. What qualities do you hope for in a colleague? If the answer differs for exempt (including librarians and programmers) and nonexempt staff (including support staff), mention which qualities apply to which group.

3. What qualities do you hope for in a supervisor or administrator? If the answer differs for a direct supervisor and for an upper-level administrator (such as the library director), mention which qualities apply to which type of position.

4. For student supervisors: What qualities do you look for in student employees?

5. Have you been part of a search committee? Part of a "selected Mann staff" session with a candidate? How did you feel about the experience(s)?

Responses of the interviewed staff were then analyzed for themes that appeared in common. In presenting these thematic categories, we have used the actual language of the interviewed staff whenever possible. Throughout this summary of those discussions, staff have been either directly quoted or paraphrased if there was an unambiguous correlation between the statement and the theme language. In addition, staff have not been quoted by name but placed into categories intended to shed light on their perspectives. We have used the following adjectives to describe staff members:

Senior = having between 3 and 30 years of experience
Recently hired = hired within the past two years
Support staff = non-MLS staff who are eligible for overtime
Librarians = have MLS or equivalent degree
Programmer/analyst = information technology staff who may or may not have an MLS
Supervisors = oversee the work of others but not necessarily an entire department
Student supervisor = oversee the work of students but not necessarily permanent staff

Of the 15 staff interviewed, 6 were librarians, 6 were support staff, and 3 were programmer/analysts. In addition, nine were classified as senior and six as recently hired. Last, three were supervisors and eight were student supervisors. The staff involved represented different sections of the library as well. Five staff members work in Public Services, three in Collection Development, three in Technical Services, three in the Informational Technology Section, and one in Administration. Of the staff interviewed, one librarian and one programmer/analyst have since left the Mann Library for opportunities elsewhere.

Some other particular uses of language should be noted to avoid confusion. The authors use the term "candidates" for individuals not currently working for the library who are being interviewed for positions. The term "interviewed staff member" is used to describe staff members who were interviewed about their perspectives as part of the research completed for this chapter. Throughout this chapter, the term "staff" will be used for all levels of staff—support staff, librarians, and programmer/analysts. When the authors mean support staff, as opposed to another category of staff, the phrase "support staff" will be used. The authors have also avoided using the phrase "professional staff" to refer to librarians, because all staff members, regardless of their positions, are professionals.

1. HIRING STAFF

Personal qualities, work skills, and potential should be considerations when evaluating candidates for positions. Contributing to the work environment is, in many ways, more important than the current skills a candidate brings to the job. Job skills can be learned, but personality is harder to develop. An applicant is unlikely to succeed in a new position—even with an outstanding résumé—if that applicant's social skills or personality do not fit the organizational culture and the personalities, style, and energy of potential co-workers and supervisors. A candidate's potential must also be carefully evaluated. Does he resonate with the library's goals, the service philosophy, and the use of technology? If she is lacking a particular skill, is she interested in learning that skill and applying it on the job?

Certain attributes are expected in each person hired: a positive attitude and enthusiasm, friendliness and a willingness to communicate, ambition, a strong service ethic, and potential to grow and learn on the job. Many of these qualities cannot be determined simply by a résumé. The interview process must ensure that these attributes can be reasonably measured. Questions can be developed that will assist in the evaluation of these qualities; these questions can be asked of the applicant, his references, and his colleagues. An interview process that always involves many staff members in evaluating candidates helps determine the presence or absence of these qualities.

Candidates need to have a positive attitude about themselves and their working experiences as well as a genuine enthusiasm about the library environment and the job for which they are applying. This energy is vital for the library and must be present in all staff members. Candidates are also evaluated for their general friendliness and ability to communicate with others. The Mann Library's culture emphasizes a general friendliness among staff members and a desire to teach and learn from others. All candidates must be ambitious; not just personally but also for the organization. Candidates for all positions—not just those involving work with the public—must have a service-oriented work ethic.

Of course, work skills and experience are important as well. Valued skills include relevant experience and education, learning and teaching skills, and technology skills. Some of these qualities can be determined by a résumé or in the course of discussion. Since the Mann Library serves agriculturists, biologists, and applied social scientists, having a background (or at least an interest) in these areas is vital. The Mann Library hires a mix of staff who have direct experience in the position they will take and staff who have no direct experience. Learning skills are considered essential for staff since it is assumed that positions and responsibilities will change and develop over time. Staff members need to be comfortable with change and willing to take some risks. Encouraging creativity and innovation in meeting our users' needs means that sometimes a project or service does not quite meet expectations. Individuals should be comfortable learning, growing, and building upon these experiences. All staff should also be comfortable teaching or training others in one capacity or another. Since so much of the library's activities involve technology, being comfortable with technology is essential. Competencies in dealing with hardware and standard software packages are helpful.

2. STAFF PERCEPTIONS OF COLLEAGUES, SUPERVISORS, AND ADMINISTRATORS

Fifteen staff members, including supervisors, librarians, programmer/analysts, and support staff, were interviewed about the qualities they seek in colleagues, supervisors, and administrators. Certain themes emerged in their responses. Most interviewed staff members want colleagues to be cooperative and willing to work as a team as well as to be enthusiastic about the library and their jobs. Most of the interviewed staff members want supervisors and administrators to be supportive and to advocate for the library and its staff. Fulfilling this role is one way in which a supervisor or administrator can be part of the library's "team." They also want supervisors and administrators to motivate and inspire them and to have a vision of where the library is going and what goals should be achieved. Many qualities were emphasized in common for both colleagues and supervisors/administrators: friendly, honest, enthusiastic, respectful, and communicative. Throughout the interviews, staff stressed the importance of working toward common goals and appreciating the contributions of all staff toward them. One aspect of this was communication among staff members regardless of department or rank. Another was the sense of teamwork that staff members bring to their jobs. As one senior supervisor put it: "If it takes a village to raise a child, it takes an excellent staff to run an excellent library. We all have to feel that the strength of the library relies on our individual contributions."

The staff members were asked about the qualities they hope for in a colleague. Since staff members play a role in the interview process, this question provides insight into how staff members evaluate candidates as well as their ideal working companions. None of the interviewed staff members drew distinctions in qualities they hope for in support staff or in librarians. The vision of the ideal colleague that emerges from these interviews can be used to set a standard for a great employee. The most frequently cited quality emerged in interviews with seven staff members: the desire for a colleague to be a "team player" and to have a sense of the good of the organization. One senior support staff member stated, "I value a colleague who can step in willingly and help out; one who is aware of what is going on in the work environment and takes action when needed." Another support staff member, who recently began working for the library, said he valued "a cooperative attitude and a readiness to defer personal glory for the benefit and morale of the associates as a whole." Six interviewed staff members discussed the importance of tolerance and respectfulness. A recently hired librarian referred to this as being "considerate of others," while a senior librarian emphasized the need for staff to be tolerant and open-minded. A senior support staff member said, "I like people to care about each other's feelings and try to work together." A senior programmer/analyst likes colleagues to be "mindful of the results of their actions on their colleagues."

Many other qualities were cited as important, but by fewer interviewed staff members. Five staff members noted the importance of enthusiasm in colleagues. Those interviewed saw enthusiasm embodied in an excitement "about the library and librarianship" (a recently hired librarian), in an engagement with the work being done (a senior librarian supervisor), and in a positive attitude (a senior support staff member). Another senior support staff member said "It is good when your co-workers enjoy their jobs—it is amazing how much work gets done." Four interviewed staff members noted the importance of being interested in the mission of libraries and in the academic environment. This includes being "dedicated not only to their areas of work but to the educational and cultural mission of the library in general" (a recently hired librarian) as well as being someone "who understands that libraries are an integral part of society" (another recently hired librarian). Four interviewed staff members also stressed the importance of innovation and creativity. This includes a willingness to take risks to achieve an ambitious goal (a senior programmer/analyst). Other important qualities include being hardworking, dependable, and intelligent (three each), as well as being friendly, communicative, honest, flexible, responsible, and professional (two each). In addition, interviewed staff members want a colleague to have a good sense of humor and a willingness to learn new things (two each).

The 15 staff members interviewed were also asked about the qualities they seek in a supervisor or administrator. Although some themes appeared in both sets of responses, the expectations for supervisors and administrators differed in three notable ways—supervisors should be supportive and advocate for the library and its staff, should inspire and motivate, and should provide a vision or direction for the library. These were perceived as key ingredients in being a leader. Being communicative, friendly, and honest were frequently mentioned for supervisors as they had been for colleagues. Two interviewed staff members made distinctions between the traits of the supervisor (someone to whom you might directly report) and those of an administrator (someone to whom your supervisor might report or who might be in charge of the entire library or segment of the university). An example of such a distinction was a senior programmer/analyst who said that an "upper-level administrator would, in my ideal workplace, collaborate with lower-level supervisors in a design or strategy-building process for departments or workgroups." However, most of the staff interviewed did not draw these distinctions.

Eight of the interviewed staff hoped for supervisors or administrators who would serve as effective advocates for staff and for the library and who would support their staff. Advocacy and support were seen to have two aspects: emotional and financial. Although the interviewed staff members recognized these two senses of support and advocacy as being separate, they were usually discussed together. A senior support staff member said she likes supervisors and administrators who "stand up for their employees" and who "find ways to better the library." A recently hired programmer/analyst wants supervisors and administrators to be "loyal" to staff. In one senior support staff member's view, supervisors advocate for staff by recognizing a staff member's strengths and putting those strengths to work most effectively for the department. A programmer/analyst explained, "It is also nice to have a boss who will coach me. We all have ways in which we can improve. Having a boss who will work with you to make those improvements is invaluable." The interviewed staff members talked about support and advocacy in a financial or resource sense as well. A senior programmer/analyst said "the best organizations have leaders who are willing to embrace innovation and who will spend the time to find the resources to enable it."

Two other qualities were cited almost as frequently: the ability to motivate and inspire and the ability to provide a vision for the library and a direction for work. Six staff members indicated they hoped for supervisors and administrators who motivate, inspire, or move them emotionally. Many of the staff members talked about ways in which supervisors or administrators will "make me feel" about the library. This expectation was clearly different from expectations of colleagues since peers were not discussed as inspiring, motivating, or making people feel a particular way. A senior supervisor said, "I also want my supervisor to inspire me as well—to give me new ideas—and the support I may need to accomplish my goals." Three different senior support staff members discussed wanting to be moved emotionally by supervisors and administrators. One staff member hoped for a supervisor who was charismatic, another wanted "someone I can be proud to represent me or the library on campus or nationwide," and the third wanted supervisors and administrators who made her "proud that they are representing the library."

A recently hired librarian likes supervisors who make her "feel professional and not like a subordinate." Six staff members said they hoped supervisors and administrators would provide vision and direction for the library. One recently hired librarian said that "the ability to lead and make decisions is critical" in both supervisors and administrators. A recently hired programmer/analyst wanted them to be visionaries, while a recently hired support staff member hoped to have "a good leader." One recently hired librarian spoke about administrators and supervisors in a memorable but unique way. He hoped for someone who was "a 'benevolent despot'—someone with a sense of direction but who is nice about it." No other interviewed staff member discussed supervisors or administrators in these terms.

Interviewed staff members cited several other qualities as being important in supervisors and administrators. Supervisors should be approachable, friendly, honest, and communicative (four each) as well as having a "hands-off" approach to management and being equitable to all staff (four each). One recently hired librarian said that while "patience, consideration, fairness and a dedication to the ideals of the institution (i.e., promoting diversity, encouraging professional development, etc.) are all important," so too is "the philosophy that every job in the library is important, that no task is beneath the dignity of anyone." Staff also hoped for supervisors and administrators who listen and are decisive (three each). Other qualities included being trusting, knowledgeable, respectful, positive, humble, and involved in the day-to-day decisions of the department or library (two each). These views of supervisors and administrators leave the impression that staff of all levels hope for people in these positions to be colleagues plus. Supervisors and administrators should have all the qualities of the ideal colleague in addition to being an advocate, being supportive, inspirational, and motivational, and being a visionary.

3. THE HIRING PROCESS

The design of the hiring process is extremely important to the success of the search. The interview process is the first glimpse that potential employees get into the organizational culture and should be an opportunity for established employees to help shape the organization. Job descriptions need to accurately reflect the library's needs and should be developed to reflect the position's importance to the organization. Experience has shown that you can assemble a stronger applicant pool for librarians and programmer/analysts by recruiting for staff among professional schools and organizations in addition to posting the job in a publication or on an electronic mailing list. Involving other staff members in the hiring of colleagues allows them to bring their perspectives to the organization in an immediate way.

Recruiting and hiring new employees are exhilarating but time-consuming activities. Many staff members are asked to contribute their time and energy to the search process. However, the importance of finding the right person for the job overrides any sense of "we don't have the time for all this!"

On the contrary, staff members in the Mann Library consistently volunteer to be active participants in all phases of the recruitment process.

3.1. Job Descriptions

Drafting a job description is the first step in creating the organization envisioned for the library. Carefully crafted and interesting job descriptions will attract interesting and interested staff. The job description is the best way for library managers and staff to reach an understanding about their roles in the library and the library's responsibilities to them. Bessler suggests that the service mission of the library can best be served by "defining every job to be filled as a *service* position. Make certain that every position description in your library mentions your patrons, highlights the individual's service responsibilities, and allocates time for these activities" [1]. The job description should reflect what the staff member will be doing in the near term and should include a variety of tasks. This will prevent burnout of staff, may reduce repetitive stress and other workplace injuries, and will enable a staff member to develop a variety of skills. The library should carefully consider the qualities it requires in staff. Thomas and Russell describe the ideal professional staff member for the National Agricultural Library as someone with leadership qualities, an appropriate subject background, a focus on the user and good communication skills, technology skills, and a knowledge of the functional area of the library he or she will work in [2]. These qualities could form the basis for any excellent library employee.

One chief issue academic libraries face is the importance of a subject background in staff hired. Stuart and Drake argue that

> Without a knowledge of mathematical concepts, basic scientific principles, engineering applications and the communication channels used by scientists and engineers to acquire scientific and technical information, the non-science or engineering person begins with a disadvantage that is difficult to overcome [3].

Storm and Wei contradict this argument and reason that it may be less important for a professional librarian to have subject expertise considering that "most academic librarians spend a considerable number of hours working on operational and policy-related committees, participating in professional societies, doing research, and attending meetings" [4]. However, Beile and Adams point to the increasing number of subject announcements calling for subject specialists [5]. White analyzed subject specialist professional librarian job ads and found that three job responsibilities that appear in the great majority of announcements are reference desk services, bibliographic instruction, and collection development. As expected, these are the

areas in which a subject specialist in any field would presumably participate. Other important responsibilities for all three position types are faculty
liaison activities, database searching, and specialized reference service. The
effects of electronic information are also apparent in the announcements. The
trend toward more technology responsibilities found in the business position
announcements is also consistent with other studies. Computer technology is
a skill often listed as "desired" or "preferred." Internet or Web skills are also
relatively highly placed, especially when considering that these skills were not
necessary in the early part of the decade [6]. Storm and Wei also stress the
importance of reaching out to experts: " 'Networking' is as important to
science librarians as it is to scientists to keep current in their field. Science
librarians, however, should network not only with other librarians, but with
professional colleagues from other disciplines as well" [7]. Unfortunately,
little has been written about the subject expertise of support staff and student
employees. The library benefits also from staff at these levels who have a
strong subject expertise.

The staff member should understand that his or her job description
may often be revised to reflect both the library's needs and the employee's
desire for growth and change. Additionally, supervisors should be prepared
to revise job descriptions and to seek job upgrades as the work environment
becomes more complex and as technology becomes more pervasive. Beile and
Adams analyzed trends in academic library postings and found fewer postings requiring an MLS and a growing number requesting computer skills [8].
Upgrading jobs when appropriate, changing a job description to meet an
already-hired and established employee's particular strengths, and encouraging staff to apply for higher-level positions within the library will help the
organization in the long run. Similarly, when lines are vacated, they should
be scrutinized in terms of where the unit and library are headed, what skill
sets are needed, and what new services should be developed. In most cases,
this will result in a change to the job description before it is advertised.

Building opportunities for staff development and personal fulfillment
into a job is essential to maintain long-term employees at all levels and to build
effective organizations. For instance, one support staff member at the Mann
Library has a weekly allotment of time written into her job description to
develop new technology skills. This has resulted in improvements for all the
staff she serves. Obviously, considerations such as union or other organizational limitations and requirements must be taken into account as appropriate. At the Mann Library, although staff is not unionized, the university
and the state have strict requirements related to job classification, expectations, and alterations. All of these policies are adhered to whenever job
changes are proposed or carried through. However, finding a way to build
opportunities for staff development and personal fulfillment into a job is

essential to maintain long-term employees and to build effective organizations. For a sample job description for a librarian, see box entitled Librarian Job Description.

SAMPLE LIBRARIAN JOB DESCRIPTION

Mann Library

Academic Position Description (1/21 2000)

Position Title: Metadata Librarian
Working Title, if any:
Title of immediate supervisor: Head, Technical Services Division
Unit/Department: Cataloging Unit/Mann Library
Employee in position, if any:

Main Function:

Under the general direction of the head of Technical Services is responsible for cataloging materials in a variety of formats, including preparing original bibliographic and authority records, managing innovation, developing workflows, and implementing improvements in processing routines. Works closely with staff in Technical Services and other divisions to provide access to electronic resources. Evaluates and analyzes types and models of metadata required for organizing networked information and helps devise and implement solutions. Tracks developments and advises staff on metadata standards. Participates in local and national discussions related to providing access to resources. Works closely with staff in Technical Services and other divisions to provide access to electronic resources. Plays an active role in professional organizations and the Cornell Library community. Actively participates in the library's research and development efforts, including facilitating access to digital materials, enhancing resource discovery and navigation for the user, and assisting in the development of systems for geospatial and numeric files, full-text, and other materials. Actively participates in public services and bibliographic instruction programs.

Duties and Responsibilities:

35% I. Metadata analysis
　　　A. Work with information providers and library staff to determine the appropriate form and content of metadata for electronic resources, possibly including numeric files, full-text preservation materials, geospatial data sets, etc.
　　　B. Work with staff throughout the Cornell University Library (e.g., Technical Services, Preservation, Information Technology, etc.) to implement metadata recommendations.

C. Analyze and integrate different metadata requirements (e.g., MARC, FGDC content standard for geospatial metadata, various XML and SGML DTDs, etc.) to eliminate duplication of effort within Technical Services.

30% II. Cataloging services
   A. Perform original and descriptive cataloging for materials in various formats, subject areas, and languages.
   B. Enhance member-contributed cataloging copy that requires upgrading to meet national and/or local standards.
   C. Handle associated authority and database maintenance work.
   D. Keep abreast of, and contribute as appropriate to, the development of national and international standards and policies.

20% II. Administrative activities
   A. Coordinate assigned projects within Technical Services, including grant administration, budget preparation, workflow, etc., including preservation projects.
   B. Help plan and coordinate workflow for print and electronic resources.
   C. Analyze current policies and actively respond to trends in cataloging.
   D. Maintain strong working relationship and communicate regularly with staff in Acquisitions, Public Services, Information Technology, Collection Development, and other departments and divisions.
   E. Plan, coordinate, and participate in staff training activities related to new technologies and the workstation environment.

15% III. Professional Activities
   A. Actively participate in national and international committees.
   B. Conduct research and contribute to professional publications and forums in areas related to metadata, access to information, and the electronic library.
   C. Participate in instruction, special projects, grants, committee work, and activities within Mann Library, the Cornell University Library, and the larger Cornell community.

Supervision of Others

Although no direct supervisory responsibilities, employee may be assigned functional supervision of staff in a specific project or procedure. May be assigned student employees as projects demand.

Knowledge/Experience Requirements

Required: ALA-accredited MLS or equivalent degree. Demonstrated interest in the issues and standards related to metadata, cataloging, and full-text retrieval. Excellent communication and analytic skills including the ability to work within a team setting. Solid facility with personal computers, information retrieval software, and network navigation tools. Interest in innovation and professional development. Desired: Previous cataloging experience. Prior professional experience in an academic or special library. Working knowledge of one or more foreign languages. Background or interest in agriculture, the life sciences, or related social sciences.

Contacts

Staff at all levels throughout the Cornell University Library. Some contact with faculty and representatives of organizations involved in cooperative projects.

Physical Demands

Extensive work with computers. Requires visual concentration and attention to detail.

Job satisfaction is an important consideration in the design of a job description. Looking at the factors that cause people to remain in or leave the field of librarianship, Lanier et al. found that those individuals "most likely to leave the field of librarianship were those who reported lower levels of job satisfaction, with a pronounced dislike for the pay and actual job tasks" [9]. Although an employee's life satisfaction has been shown to have an impact on job satisfaction, other factors have an impact as well. Landry's study found that "the job facets causing the greatest dissatisfaction were pay, promotional opportunities, contingent rewards [nonmonetary rewards given for good performance], operating conditions, and communication within the library" [10]. These factors were also cited in the authors' interviews with staff and apply to all positions, not just those of librarians.

Fifteen staff members were interviewed about their job descriptions to gain insight into the features that appealed to people in a workplace and in a job description. Nine senior staff members were asked about the aspects of their jobs that they found most satisfying. Of these nine staff members, four were support staff, three were librarians, and two were programmer/analysts. Six recently hired staff members were asked about what appealed to them about the job and what led them to apply for the position. Three of these staff members were librarians, two were support staff, and one was a programmer/analyst. The responses to these questions led to answers that extended beyond the responsibilities of the position and touched on the collegial work environment within the library. For example, one recently hired librarian commented,

It was a collaborative environment with everyone involved on committees. I also liked the size of the library and how involved people are with each other and how much they understand one another's work. There's a lot of friendliness, respect and recognition of others. This comes across in the interview because so many people are involved; it's not a situation where a small group has all the power.

Both sets of interviewed staff members mentioned the importance of teamwork as an appealing aspect of a job. Several of them also discussed the need for a balance of work that allows individual initiative and work that relies on a group. Both groups also discussed the appeal of having a variety of responsibilities and of having room for professional growth and development. These answers suggest that job descriptions need to talk about more than work responsibilities and requirements. They should also describe the degree of teamwork and collegial atmosphere within the library. They also suggest that the interview can play a big role in how a potential staff member perceives the job for which he or she is a candidate.

The two aspects of their jobs that senior staff members interviewed cited most were variety and the ability to solve problems and be innovative. Four interviewed staff members, all support staff, cited variety as an important aspect of their job satisfaction. This usually meant not having one repetitive set of tasks. Three senior support staff members used the word "variety" specifically. One added that she particularly enjoyed "working on special projects." Another senior support staff member explained he liked his "job to have movement and physical activity to predominate over too much time that is sitting and passive." Four interviewed staff members said they enjoyed problem solving and developing innovative solutions to problems. One senior supervisor said, "As a supervisor, I also enjoy helping staff find solutions to problems. Staff often need a sounding board, a facilitator, or a sympathetic ear." Another senior supervisor said he liked being "creative and innovative" without fear of being chastised for trying. A programmer/analyst said she liked "resolving problems" and removing "road blocks for patrons and staff."

Two other aspects were highly ranked by senior staff members: the ability to work on teams and the responsibility for supervising staff, students, or projects. One senior supervisor said she liked coordinating "the work of staff to accomplish departmental goals." A senior support staff member noted that she enjoyed working with and supervising students. Teamwork was another feature of job satisfaction for three of the senior staff members interviewed. A senior supervisor said, "Although individual initiative and innovation are nurtured, there is also the recognition that teamwork can make the idea or the innovation happen." One senior programmer/analyst said he was very satisfied by the "relatively flat organizational hierarchy at Mann, which is conducive to collaboration, enabling me and my colleagues to discuss our work and ideas rather freely. The creativity, and ultimately the productivity, of the organization is thus enhanced." Several other qualities were mentioned as contributing to satisfaction: the room for individual initiative; opportunities for taking part in planning; and the chance to take part in professional development (two interviewed staff members each). Two interviewed staff members cited a collegial work environment as important. One senior supervisor said, "Working in an environment where trust, collegiality, collaboration, humor, and creativity are all valued is wonderful." Another noted his appreciation of the "respect and camaraderie amongst my colleagues in my division and throughout the organization."

Six recently hired staff members were asked about the features of the job posting that they found most appealing. Four of the respondents noted that having opportunities for professional development and for "room to grow" were very important features for them. One recently hired librarian said she "liked the fact that the job description left some room for me to develop interests and also stressed the importance of professional development." A recently hired programmer analyst said,

> The description made the position sound very much like it would be a diverse, dynamic, project-based position allowing for much professional growth and development for the chosen candidate. This was very appealing to me. Often library positions, and job descriptions in general, can sound as though the position will be very stagnant once you've learned your job. Also, the position had a "rookies encouraged" type of clause which let me know that Mann was a library looking for the right people rather than a box of skills.

One recently hired support staff member said the job "would be a continuation and expansion of what I did previously at another campus library." Another support staff member noted that she wanted a "job where I would be learning new skills on a regular basis" and so the position she applied for was a match for her. Three interviewed staff members also cited the importance of having a variety of tasks and projects to work on.

Two other aspects frequently mentioned were having a variety of tasks in a position and having a collegial atmosphere. Three interviewed staff members mentioned wanting positions that offered the chance to work on a variety of tasks or projects. One recently hired librarian said he liked "the opportunity to work on projects that put data on the Web." A recently hired programmer/analyst said, "The diversity in the position description appealed to me. There was a wide variety of areas that would be involved in the work." A recently hired support staff member said she saw her job having "potential for diverse job duties and a busy atmosphere." Three of the recently hired staff members were also attracted to the collegial atmosphere of the library.

This often came through not in the job description but during the interview. One recently hired librarian said, "Above all other considerations, the fact that the library was made up of dedicated, friendly and professional staff was the best feature. I wanted to be part of that team." A recently hired support staff member said, "I was impressed by the friendliness and high caliber of professionalism among the prospective associates."

3.2. Job Posting and Finding Staff

Libraries have traditionally used local methods for posting jobs, such as a campus or local job announcement system and, for certain levels of employee, national advertisements in professional publications or newspapers. Recently, e-mail discussion group postings have been used to find prospective employees. Using this new technology to reach a wider audience is a good thing. It has the added advantage of enabling interested people to ask questions about positions and respond more quickly than via traditional mail. Another traditional method of recruiting professional staff is to attend professional organization conferences that have placement centers. In a study of the application practices of academic library hires, Goldberg and Womack found that the

> Sources that respondents relied on the most to identify professional vacancies are not completely unexpected. It is interesting to note that professional and scholarly journals continue to be the source that is most used, with electronic bulletin boards/listservs a close second. Because those completing the survey are new to the field, it is not totally surprising that library school or professional placement services were used by more than 50 percent. The number that used internal postings is somewhat unexpected. In addition ..., other sources given were library school newsletters, networking, word of mouth, friends/librarians, cold calling, and ALA and ACRL conferences. [11]

It is also helpful to recruit for professional positions directly at professional schools. When several professional positions are vacant at once, the Mann Library administration invests the time and travel expense to visit library and information schools in various parts of the United States. This enables library staff to gain a good sense of what the various programs were like and what they have to offer. Staff can also give public presentations to the students to discuss the library and its administration's philosophy of librarianship and hiring, and to encourage students to think about their careers. It also gives library staff the opportunity to talk with students and faculty about encouraging students to move into areas of librarianship that seem to be less popular, such as technical services or collection development. Upon hearing about the real nature of these jobs, rather than the reputation that these positions have, students are encouraged to think more broadly about their career options. During trips taken by Mann Library staff, they were able to encourage several students who had never considered applying for science library positions and who never considered technical services or collection development jobs to apply for those types of positions. Several of them came to work at the Mann Library. By getting out of the library and bringing the interview process directly to the library schools, strong candidates can be added to hiring pools, and outstanding potential staff members can be found who might have been missed through more traditional avenues.

Special attention should be paid to reaching out to minority populations to ensure a more diverse staff. In many cases, as Reese and Hawkins argue, this requires new and dynamic ways of appealing to the various populations in our communities [12]. It may also involve looking for new partners such as nonlibrary organizations, which may help match applicants to jobs. Winston asserts,

> Aggressive and informed recruitment efforts must be incorporated which reflect the institution's commitment to creating, retaining, and promoting a diverse workforce and which reflect an understanding of the factors that are important to individuals as they select a profession. [13]

He suggests that libraries look to recruitment theory, and its determination of the factors that have influenced successful recruitment policies, to help attract minority candidates. If the library staff is diverse, all segments of the user population will feel more comfortable using the library and its services. In addition, this process will "broaden the number of perspectives represented in academic library decision-making, administration, and library services" [13].

3.3. Search Committees

Forming a search committee offers an opportunity to involve staff members from various departments in the hiring of colleagues, supervisors, and co-workers. These committees are essential parts of the hiring process in the Mann Library for all levels of staff except student workers. Search committees draw on staff from every area of the library and from every level. For support staff positions, committees are composed of the position supervisor (who serves as the committee chair), at least one support staff person from the department of the position, and at least one support staff person from a department that would interact with the person in the open position. For professional positions, committees are usually composed of the position supervisor or another senior professional staff member (who serves as the committee chair), a support or professional staff person from the department of the position, and several other professional staff members representing different departments of the library, especially the departments with which the employee will interact. For managerial or administrative positions, the library director or a department head serves as the committee chair, and support and professional staff from the department of the position (including staff who the person would supervise) and representatives from other departments in the library serve as committee members. These committees are structured differently based on the needs of the particular position. When shaping the committee, consideration is given to how much interaction the staff member will have with staff outside the hiring department. Often, one person on the committee is a staff member who has been hired within the past year. This person is able to speak to candidates about his or her experience joining the staff and the development or direction that his or her job is taking.

We strongly believe the staff member who will supervise the person to be hired should chair the search committee; this applies to both professional and support staff positions. The supervisor has the most accurate and thorough knowledge of the position's responsibilities, what it entails, the potential for growth, and the skill/personality set necessary for an applicant's success.

The composition of the search committee is important for several reasons. It demonstrates to candidates that the library works as a team and that they will be expected to interact with staff members from divisions throughout the library. It also enables staff members of different levels to directly influence the hiring process and to participate on a team comprising colleagues from across the library. These staff then can have an immediate impact on the organization. The library benefits because a variety of perspectives are brought to the decision-making process. Junior members of the staff get a chance to see how search committees function, and they gain useful experience from observing the chairperson's handling of the group dynamic, delegation of tasks, etc. Bessler [14] suggests that all aspects of the search process should also be run in a way that makes the library's vision of service apparent throughout.

The search committee is involved in the process in a fundamental way. The committee talks about the open position in detail and the hiring supervisor ensures that everyone understands the position fully. Search committee members discuss the qualities desired in the position regardless of the level and compile an attributes list. This helps bring the committee to a similar understanding of the process. For example, during a recent search for the director, the search committee was composed of representatives from all areas of the library. The group discussed the qualities that were most desired in someone in this position. This list included, among other qualities, having a vision for the library, respect for staff, and the ability to challenge and to listen. In many cases, these qualities were not likely to appear on a list generated solely by the person to whom this position reports. Creating an attribute list also ensures that committee members verbalize their expectations and gives the committee chair a chance to correct any mistaken assumptions or unreasonable expectations. In addition, this list can be used as a starting point for creating a list of questions to ask candidates. It also provides a chance for the committee chair to reinforce the need to avoid questions and attitudes toward candidates that violate the law and institutional policy. See box entitled Sample Interview Questions for examples of some interview questions created in this way.

SAMPLE INTERVIEW QUESTIONS

Sample Telephone and or Campus Interview Questions

> What appeals to you about this position?
> Describe your ideal work environment.
> What computer skills do you feel would be appropriate for someone in this position to have or acquire?
> Describe a situation in which you had to work with a group of colleagues.
> What is your approach to starting a project that requires information gathering and working with a team of people? Have you ever led a group project or a team?
> The Mann Library concentrates in the life sciences and, to some degree, applied social sciences. What is your experience working with these subject areas? [For candidates without a background in science or in science libraries: What do you feel about working with these types of materials?]
> What makes a good day and what makes a bad day?
> In your opinion, what makes a "great" library?
> How do you juggle an assortment of responsibilities (numerous meetings, handle interruptions, meet the demands of training)?
> What do you feel are your special skills and qualifications for this position?
> What qualities do you look for in a colleague? A supervisor? A mentor?
> Describe a project that did not go ideally. What happened? What would you do differently?

(Additional position-specific and candidate-specific questions are also included.)

The committee also reads and discusses all applications based on the job description and the criteria established. For support staff positions, the committee conducts interviews with candidates and provides feedback to the committee chair (usually the direct supervisor for the position) and to the library director. For librarian and programmer/analyst positions, the group conducts preliminary interviews, in some cases via telephone. In conjunction with the library director, the search committee decides which candidates will be invited for on-site interviews. This process allows staff to provide feedback and to shape the process in a way that would not be possible if the library director or the staff supervisor were involved alone. The final pre-interview task of the search committee is to organize the interview schedule for the candidate. This is done as a group so that concerns from various departments can be addressed.

Eleven of the 15 staff members interviewed for this chapter had served on search committees. They were asked what they liked about the experience. The most common response among interviewed staff members was to cite an enjoyment from getting to work with staff throughout the library. Seven interviewed staff members talked about the satisfaction they get from working on search committees with staff from other departments. One senior support staff member said that she thinks serving on a search committee "involves us with other members of the staff that we might not normally have contact with." Another senior support staff member said she "liked getting to know the other people on the committees that I don't usually have much contact with." Related to this is the opportunity that being on a search committee provides for staff to learn from others. Four respondents liked having the opportunity to gain insight into library operations and into their colleagues' perspectives. A senior librarian said "you learn more about your co-workers during these exercises." A senior support staff member said he "enjoyed getting to know co-workers in a unique way by virtue of seeing how and what they considered important to ask a prospective candidate about ... and just being part of a group that cut across department lines to nurture a bit of library-wide camaraderie." Another senior support staff member said the "questions asked and the answers given sometimes give me ideas on things that maybe I would like to try." A senior programmer/analyst said,

> I like the sum of the questions and ideas that the members of the group create. In other words, I know that I have only one point of view and can generate questions and ideas from that point only. I like how each of us contributes questions that combine to make a more-inclusive whole, an environment where we learn about candidates by observing them respond to a number of different individuals.

The staff members interviewed noted several other positive aspects of serving on search committees. Three interviewed staff members indicated that it gave them pride in working in the library. A senior support staff member said serving on a search committee "impresses [her] that Mann takes such care to try and find the best employee possible." A recently hired librarian said, "I like telling people about working here and exchanging experiences. I also like the feeling of pride in where I work." Three people also indicated that they just enjoyed being part of the process. A senior supervisor said, "Participating in interviewing new staff is re-energizing. It requires you to think about issues in librarianship and values that you hold as an organization and find staff that understand the issues and hold similar values." Another senior supervisor said,

> There is a sense of adventure in the recruitment process. It's a quest to find a good colleague—the right match for the person, the library, and the position. Finding someone we would enjoy working with—someone who would enjoy working with us—one who would bring new skills and new energy to the library.

A recently hired programmer analyst said,

> I have just recently been selected [to serve on a search committee], but I think I like the fact that there are search committees at all. I think it's fantastic that representatives from across the staff have a voice in the hiring of new staff. It's great that we all get a chance to share our opinions in the hiring of new employees even if they're not in our own department.

3.4. Interview (Staff Involvement and Organizational Culture)

The interview itself broadens the candidate's exposure to the library staff and culture. Candidates are given the opportunity to meet with their potential colleagues and supervisors, evaluating the library and its staff as much as the library staff members are evaluating the candidate. It is important that the candidate leaves the interview with a realistic portrait of the library, the position, and the library's culture. There are some notable differences in how interviews are shaped for support staff and for librarians and programmer/analysts. These differences stem from differing expectations in the positions rather than in differing commitments to staff. Librarians and programmer/analysts are often expected to represent the library and its staff at local and national meetings and conferences in a manner that is not expected of support staff. As a result, the interview process for those positions often includes a public presentation. All staff members are invited to attend and are asked for feedback on the candidates. Support staff positions are often focused more on the local needs of the library, so presentations are not appropriate in most cases. As a result, it is not as easy to request feedback from all staff because fewer people have the chance to hear the candidate's ideas. In these cases, the search committee plays the crucial role of representing the staff and its concerns. Moreover, each search should be customized when possible to best reflect the needs of the position at hand. In this way, it would be possible to add to a basic interview for positions with instructional or supervisory responsibilities. Despite these differences, attention, time, and consideration are given to the interview process for all levels of staff.

Support staff positions usually involve half-day interviews in which the candidate meets with the search committee, the supervisor for the position, staff from the department he or she might be working in, benefits staff, and the library director. Depending on the nature of the position, the candidate may also meet with a group of Mann Library staff selected from throughout the library. For support staff positions, the search committee evaluates the candidates. If other staff were involved, they are solicited for feedback about the candidate, usually by the search committee chair. The search committee then meets to discuss the candidates and come to a consensus about whom they would recommend for the position.

Librarian and programmer/analyst interviews are generally an entire day. The overall goal of the interview is for the candidate to meet and interact with staff of all levels from throughout the library. The candidates for these positions are asked to give a presentation about a relevant topic to the entire staff. For instance, a reference librarian might be asked to conduct a mock instruction session. A potential collection development librarian might be asked to talk about changes in online journal options and pricing structures over the next decade. Most staff members attend these presentations, resulting in a typical audience of 40 to 50 people. Cover letters and résumés of all candidates interviewed are circulated among the staff prior to the interview. Staff are encouraged to ask candidates questions about their presentations, cover letters, résumés, and opinions about library issues relevant to the position they are seeking. Refreshments are served after the presentation, and staff are encouraged to introduce themselves to the candidate. This provides some downtime for the candidate and lets staff meet him or her in a more relaxed setting. These candidates also formally meet with the search committee, a group of Mann Library staff who represent various areas and levels of library staff, and staff from the department they might be working in. For more senior positions or positions involved with many campus initiatives, candidates meet with colleagues from other libraries on campus. The only one-on-one interviews held during the process are with the potential supervisor, the library director, a representative from library personnel, and a representative to discuss benefits. Numerous informal meetings take place as well. In addition to the refreshments after the presentation, candidates have lunch with a number of staff (usually those with whom they would be interacting if they came to work at Mann), and a dinner following the interview is common.

SAMPLE INTERVIEW SCHEDULE FOR LIBRARIAN

Evening of arrival   .

4:00–6:00 p.m.	Tour of Ithaca area
6:00–8:00 p.m.	Dinner with colleagues

Interview schedule

7:45 a.m.	Pick up candidate from hotel
8:15–8:45	Tour
9:00–10:00	Candidate presentation to staff
10:00–10:45	Search Committee
11:00–12:00	Library policies, promotion, and benefits overview— Director of Library Human Resources
12:00–1:30 p.m.	Lunch
1:45–2:30	Departmental staff
2:30–3:15	Supervisor
3:15–4:00	Selected Mann staff [Staff from throughout the library]
4:00–5:00	Director
5:00	Leave for airport or hotel

With so many staff involved in the hiring process, it is important to make available an easy-to-use electronic evaluation form. Mann Library's evaluation form was first written in the 1980s and although revisions have been made over the years, the current form is remarkably similar to the original. However, the form is customized for each job search in the library. For an example of the tool, see the box entitled Candidate Evaluation Form. The goal was to create a tool that would guide staff through the evaluation process and provide search committees with additional information to assist them in their decision making. The form provides an easy and consistent way to receive feedback from staff. It employs a rating scale of 1 (excellent) to 5 (poor) to 0 (no opinion) for a series of statements pertinent to the open position. Many departments in the library ask staff to rate a candidate's present knowledge and experience plus their future potential. Additionally, the form may contain several questions that require a short written response from staff. Signatures are optional on the form. The information gathered from the evaluation form plays a major role in the selection process; staff members are aware of this and provide thoughtful feedback on the form.

CANDIDATE EVALUATION FORM

Collection Development Bibliographer Position

Please give us your assessment of the candidate, [candidate's name], for the Collection Development Bibliographer position. Please return this form to [designated member of the search committee] (via e-mail or printout) by [date]. There are also print versions of this evaluation form available in each division. Thank you very much for your assistance.

1. Please rate the candidate's knowledge of collection development. If the candidate has limited experience in collection development, please give your opinion on the candidate's potential ability as a bibliographer. (1 = excellent; 2 = very good; 3 = good; 4 = adequate; 5 = poor; 0 = no opinion.)

   1   2   3   4   5   0   Response: _____

2. Please rate the candidate's potential to become a specialist in the selection of electronic resources and e-journals. (1 = excellent; 2 = very good; 3 = good; 4 = adequate; 5 = poor; 0 = no opinion.)

   1   2   3   4   5   0   Response: _____

3. Please rate the candidate's ability to select materials in Mann Library's subject areas. (1 = excellent; 2 = very good; 3 = good; 4 = adequate; 5 = poor; 0 = no opinion.)

   1   2   3   4   5   0   Response: _____

4. Please rate the candidate's ability to communicate with library staff. (1 = excellent; 2 = very good; 3 = good; 4 = adequate; 5 = poor; 0 = no opinion.)

   1   2   3   4   5   0   Response: _____

5. Please rate the candidate's suitability to be a member of the Mann Library. (1 = excellent; 2 = very good; 3 = good; 4 = adequate; 5 = poor; 0 = no opinion.)

   1   2   3   4   5   0   Response: _____

6. Would you recommend hiring this candidate?

   Yes   No   Maybe   Response: _____

7. Please indicate the part(s) of the interview process in which you participated. (Indicate all that apply.)

   ___ Presentation   ___ Group segment   ___ Other _____

   Additional comments:

Thank you very much!

The library literature offers additional examples of methods used to evaluate candidates. For instance, Coffey advocates the use of competency modeling to construct "a profile of abilities and attitudes that reflect the ideal worker. Such models can be used in the hiring process as another tool with which to evaluate job candidates" [15]. Arguing for the addition of objective criteria to the search process, Bednar and Stanley describe the development and use of hiring tests for technical services staff. They explain that the "objective is to develop a series of exercises that: (1) provide clear clues to individual skills and abilities; (2) are elementary enough so as not to overwhelm the candidate; and, (3) can be performed in a reasonable amount of time, one hour or less" [16]. The goal of this process is to develop "testing devices [that] may be considered fairer than the more subjective selection devices such as interviews and reference checks, which in themselves must be considered testing situations" [16]. However, Bednar and Stanley recognize that such tests should be used in conjunction with other methods:

> When all the pieces of the hiring puzzle are together, the person or persons hired may not be those with the highest test score. In fact, all issues considered, the supervisor might even decide in some circumstances to set aside the test score for perfectly valid reasons. Using valid and unbiased skill and ability tests to evaluate candidates, however, often provides one element of impartial data that help managers make better predictions about individual job success." [16]

Landry argues that since

> the level of life satisfaction is proved to influence job satisfaction, the author argues that library directors should assess the level of life satisfaction of applicants for reference positions. This could conceivably be done as part of the hiring process, in conjunction with other questionnaires and forms to complete, assuming that including assessment of life satisfaction encounters no legal obstacles. [10]

Although the authors do not have experience using these methods, they do offer alternatives some libraries might consider. The most important lesson is that careful consideration should be given to the design of a hiring process that is fair to the candidates and staff and that results in the best hire possible.

3.5. The Hiring Decision

The library director and the supervisor have the ultimate responsibility of making the decision to hire a staff member. The director meets with the search committee to hear members' feedback about the candidates. In some cases, the decision is made to repost the position because of a lack of qualified candidates, a need for more candidates before a decision can be made, or a need for candidates who are a better fit for the organization.

Issues of staff diversity are also involved in the hiring decision. The affirmative choice should be made in accordance with institutional policy and legal considerations. However, diversity concerns need to be raised well before the actual hiring decision is made. The library can make an effort to recruit diverse professional staff by reaching out via library schools, via listservs, and through other organizations. Reese and Hawkins argue that recruiting a diverse library staff must begin with making librarianship and library employment a visible choice for minorities. They assert:

> Making ethnic minorities aware of opportunities in library and information science involves more than traveling to college campuses or placing ads. The recruitment strategy must include aligning with minority-affiliated organizations. What the library profession fails to realize is that when you are looking for minority recruits, you have a special situation on your hands. In many cases, you must go down non-traditional paths to find interested or potential candidates. [17]

In addition, it can be difficult to recruit librarians and support staff from diverse backgrounds in areas without diverse populations. There are no simple solutions to these challenges.

Even with all the effort that the Mann Library places on recruiting and hiring, we have occasionally chosen the wrong person for a particular position. In these (fortunately rare) instances, care is taken to work with the employee to find a satisfactory solution. The employee's supervisor will take the extra time to mentor and assist him or her in adjusting to the new position. Other colleagues in the library may assist in this process as well. Workshop attendance and additional training may be useful. There may be another open position in the library more suitable for the employee or another project within the library that more closely matches his or her strengths. In extreme cases the employee may be encouraged to look for another position more suitable to his or her skills.

3.6. Student Employees

For academic libraries, students bring vitality to the library that helps the organization understand the community being served. This benefit is twofold. Student employees help reach other students who might not learn about library services through other means, and they help find students who would be good matches for the jobs that are available. They also provide the opportunity to reach out to other students. Kathman and Kathman comment,

> Student employees contribute significantly to the image of the library and the delivery of library services. Thus, library student em-

ployees should be considered ambassadors of the library and often ambassadors of the larger institution to guests on campus. The investment in student employee training determines the effectiveness of services offered to patrons and the image of the library projected to both patrons and campus guests. [18]

Kenney and Painter point out that "student library employees [should] be representative of the academic community and that minority, international, and disabled students are encouraged to apply for student assistant positions in the library" [19]. Kathman and Kathman argue,

Increased diversity within the library's student employee staff can contribute to the university goals related to the recruitment and retention of talented and diverse students and staff. Successful employment experiences on campus may well contribute to the retention of a diverse student population as it decreases the sense of alienation, provides for the development of useful skills, and gives the student another place in the campus community. [20]

Despite these numerous advantages, some authors caution that libraries may overuse or inappropriately use student employees. Wilder, for instance, suggests that

A confluence of factors from automation to budget cutbacks to task/skills-level evolution indicate the presence of a potential imbalance [in student employee use versus the attention given to planning for their employment by the library administration]; that our reliance on students for person-hours may now exceed the planning done to insure that libraries make the most appropriate, rather than simply the maximal use, of student help. [21]

Student employees benefit from working in libraries as well. In a 1995 survey of library literature about student employees in academic libraries, David Gregory concludes,

If there is a single dominant theme in both the descriptive and analytical writings on student workers over the past few years, it is the emergence of a win/win philosophy among practitioners, theoreticians, educators, supervisors, and administrators of such programs. It is now generally recognized that student assistants reap considerable benefits from library employment, beyond mere financial gain. Most obviously, they witness and experience firsthand a variety of practical applications of new information tools and technologies, some of which may help in their immediate academic pursuits, but all of which contribute to lifelong learning. [22]

Typically, jobs are designed to help students develop skills that will benefit them both in the workplace and after they leave the library. Like people in other positions, student employees are mentored and trained with the hope that they will develop more skills and take on more responsibilities.

Students are increasingly performing duties that used to be designated for full-time staff exclusively. More is expected from our student workers, and consequently the support system for students has improved. For example, more time is spent training student employees. Kathman and Kathman note that there are three difficulties of student employee training: "because students are part-time employees, it takes approximately four student employees (given they work an average of 10 hours per week) to equal one full-time employee. This increases the complexity and the amount of time needed for training"; "the training needs to be completed in a short period of time"; and "a large number of people need to be trained at the same time" [18]. They suggest a four-step approach to student employee training: orientation, specific training, follow-up training, and evaluation of training. Orientation can be seen as a particularly important function because one of its "primary goals for student employees is to make communication between the student employee and the supervisor and the other workers in the unit more efficient" [19]. At the Mann Library, successful student training involves a well-organized orientation to the entire library, followed by intensive training and follow-up training programs. Regularly scheduled meetings with student supervisors provide opportunities for students to have their ideas heard and their particular needs met. Kenney and Painter emphasize the importance of ongoing evaluation of student assistants, especially daily feedback because it "provides the student employee immediate, on-the-spot evaluation of how well they are performing. It also instills the importance of the student employee in the organization with this level of attention by a supervisor" [19].

As with the other topics discussed in this chapter, eight interviewed staff members who are supervisors of students were asked about the qualities they look for in student employees. These interviewed staff members all served as student supervisors in a variety of departments and all have student-hiring responsibilities. They included two senior programmer/analysts, three senior support staff members, one senior supervisor, one recently hired librarian, and one recently hired support staff member. The student supervisors most often sought dependability in student employees. Five of the interviewed staff members identified this as important and spoke about students being either "dependable" or "reliable." This quality was not as frequently cited for colleagues or supervisors and perhaps suggests a fundamental difference in the nature of employment for students. After all, the principal reason that students are at the university is to attend school, not to work at the library. Four interviewed staff members look for students who are committed to working and take their work seriously. One recently hired librarian said, "I

look for people who are not seeing this simply as a way to make money."
Other important qualities, however, show a correlation with the qualities
sought in peers and supervisors. Three interviewed staff members look for
students who are friendly; two interviewed staff members look for evidence of
collegiality. Another important quality that two interviewed staff members
cited was an interest in learning. One programmer/analyst said, "When I am
hiring students, I look for those students who see the work experience as
another form of learning. I have even had students offer to work for free
because they are eager to get some real experience." Two interviewed staff
members also hoped for students to be conscientious about the quality of their
work "even when the job is boring" (as one senior supervisor put it). In many
ways the interviewed staff members were seeing the students as true colleagues. One senior programmer/analyst said, "I expected from the students I
hired that they would someday develop the same qualities I hope for in my
colleagues. . . . I tried to direct them toward cultivating those qualities." For
student employees, working in the library can be a rewarding growth
experience and not just a source of revenue.

4. TRAINING STAFF

Investing in staff does not end with the hiring of a staff member. Training and
mentoring staff are extensions of the process begun when someone is hired
because they build a stronger staff. Having invested so much staff time, energy,
and fiscal resources in hiring staff, training and mentoring staff members stand
as other important investments. Training and mentoring can also help retain
staff and thereby cut down the amount of time spent hiring staff. Looking at
technology training, Marmion succinctly cautions that a "lack of training
invites disaster" [23]. This is true of all aspects of library work. Training helps
staff to develop new skills that are required by the library and its initiatives. It
also allows staff to increase their satisfaction with their jobs. When interviewing staff about what appealed to them in a job, the authors discovered
that the staff frequently mentioned professional development. This suggests
that many staff members regard training opportunities as a key ingredient in
an appealing position. Jones found similar results in a follow-up study about
staff perceptions of technology and training. She comments,

> The desire and need for training appears in almost every area in
> which library technology is discussed. Training is mentioned as a
> morale builder, an assurance of competence, a cure for technostress,
> and a way of creating the image of a good, carefully planned library
> whose service-oriented staff are experts in their field. [24]

Based on these findings, training appears to be a staff investment that has
multiple payoffs.

The components of a training program can range from "learning how to use tools, usually, physical or electronic ones, to accomplish" a goal, to conceptual training and the development of problem-solving skills [25]. It should begin with a thorough overview of the library, its departments, the interrelationships between departments, and the library's position in the university or community. It should include formalized training sessions with staff in the employee's department, as well as with staff in other departments where appropriate. Opportunities should be plentiful for the give and take of ideas between trainers and trainees, and follow-up training should be incorporated into the process as well. Attention should be given not only to the use of particular technologies but also to basic computer competency. In a survey of information technology training, Kirkpatrick found

> In the majority of the libraries surveyed training was available on PCs, automated systems, e-mail, and the Internet. However, the percentage of libraries that made PC training available was substantially lower than that of libraries that offered training on the other technologies. This agrees with findings in the literature that gaps exist in the area of basic computer competence. [26]

Marmion suggests that in addition to spending more time and money on staff training, library administrators should

> place more importance on the computer skills that a prospective employee will bring to the job. We need to write into job descriptions a minimum level of computer competence, and then screen out those applicants who do not meet the requirements. We might even devise a computer competency test, similar to the typing tests that employers have used for decades. [23]

One concern, however, with setting the bar too high is that libraries risk excluding candidates who have the potential to learn but have not had the opportunities to do so.

Staff members can be excellent resources for training other staff. They understand the environment, the needs of the job, and the perspective of an employee. Staff training builds trust between new employees and their colleagues and can form the basis of a strong mentoring relationship (and friendship). Training can also be done by seeking outside trainers through local high schools and community colleges. This is especially useful for training staff in more advanced computer skills. Another way to bring training costs down is to collaborate with other libraries in your area on training. This can be done through training sessions held under the auspices of local networks or professional organizations. It can also be accomplished by several libraries in an area holding a joint training session to learn a new technology or develop a skill. For instance, several institutions might share the costs of bringing in a noted trainer on how to obtain grant funding. Tennant notes,

> Staff training requires a firm commitment from library adminis-
> tration. Although a financial commitment is important, what is
> essential is allowing and encouraging staff to take the time to learn
> and utilize new methods. Staff is a library's single most expensive
> resource and should be treated that way. Any investment made in
> retooling staff skills to meet the challenges and opportunities of the
> electronic age will be repaid many times over in better service to
> clientele and a vital and engaged workforce. [27]

Nilson suggests that one of the best ways to keep training costs down is to create a workplace in which training needs can be kept to a minimum. She suggests focusing on recruiting and placement, job design and performance monitoring, skills for managing stress and change, and business planning. By focusing on these management areas, she suggests it is possible to save training for those times when it is truly needed [28].

Training occurs in a variety of ways and in many contexts. Formal training of new staff combines an introduction to the library and its staff, a series of meetings with departmental staff, and outside training activities, as needed. An orientation can be used to set a tone for a new staff member's early days in a new organization. It also gives new employees a chance to feel like part of the group and to spend time with as many of their colleagues as possible. Using staff departmental meetings is a good way to reach all staff. For instance, in Mann's reference department meetings, training sessions can be planned as part of the routine information-sharing process. Other departments may hold special staff meetings devoted entirely to training. A colleague will review a new piece of software, a new procedure, or a new policy. There is always plenty of time for questions and hands-on training in this way.

Another helpful idea is to hold a series of professional development talks led by staff working on particular projects. For instance, the Mann Library commonly holds five or six "professional roundtables" per year. These sessions help staff learn about the projects underway in the library while stretching their horizons. Recent sessions have been held about XML and its uses, plans for creating a national database of dairy science data, and a new philosophy for programming and project management. It is also important that staff training and professional development opportunities not be limited to librarians. As Purnell notes, "Libraries often invest more time and funds in development programs for professionals to carry out and present research than in programs to enhance the skills of support staff, despite the fact that support staff is the library's most stable human resource" [29].

5. MENTORING STAFF

Mentoring staff is really a special type of training. Mentoring is a type of long-term training in which a more senior member of the staff helps newer, often younger, staff members learn about the organization, deal with difficulties, and shape their careers and development. For the digital library, mentoring can play an increased role. Tennant argues,

> Mentorship can be an important and yet often overlooked form of training for virtual librarians. A mentorship arrangement, either formal or informal, can pair an experienced librarian with a new hire or someone with less experience with virtual library technologies in an arrangement that can be productive for all involved. [27]

Additionally, for established staff with less familiarity with the latest technologies, it can offer the opportunity to learn from newer staff, who might have more advanced technology skills, while contributing to the newer staff member's understanding of the library and its environment.

Mentors cannot be assigned effectively without a spark of similarity between staff members. Supervisors serve as mentors to some degree, but peers often contribute more. It is the supervisor's responsibility to ensure that mentoring by peers is actually taking place. Mentors need also to look out for for the best interests of the employee, not just the organization. In some cases, this means that employees might be encouraged to pursue new responsibilities in other libraries rather than to remain in their current positions.

Although mentoring can be a positive experience for the individuals involved, it can have unintended, negative organizational impacts. Harris argues that

> If "mentoring is a significant mechanism for enhancing the careers of only *some* individuals within an organization, the culture, practices, and procedures of that organization may pose barriers that stand in the way of participation and opportunity for all its committed employees. [30]

In a study of the mentoring relationships of women library directors, Kirkland found many respondents identified a "glass elevator" for men that made it easier for men to be promoted to senior administrative positions. She also found that the number of male mentors the respondents noted outnumbered female mentors seven to one and suggests that "librarians who have men and women mentors [may] have an advantage in advancement, possibly deriving different strengths from each, or that the more mentors she has, the better training and more confidence a woman aiming at library administration may gain" [31]. Harris proposes two key ways for organizations to make sure that opportunities are available for all committed employees: by having senior staff advocate for all entry-level staff and by ensuring that adequate support is provided for professional development and staff training throughout the library [30].

Despite Harris's important concerns, mentoring can be an important supplement to the hiring and training process of healthy organizations. Millet acknowledges that mentoring relationships can create the appearance of favoritism. However, she concludes, "We need to encourage and develop open channels of communication and shared expectations. All this requires an emphasis on mentoring, continuing education, training, and programs that allow for personal growth" [32]. Munde proposes a more radical organizational approach to mentoring that addresses negative potential consequences. Analyzing the looming crisis caused by the retirement of senior administrators, Munde argues that libraries need to rethink how mentoring is performed in their organizations to ensure that staff have the opportunity to move up quickly and to provide more opportunities for developing management skills by assigning a series of projects to less senior staff. She argues

> If libraries began to identify and groom employees for career advancement or specialization as soon as their second or third year out of library school, or even support staff members before they went to library school, would this be favoritism? It might be. Would this democratization of mentoring negate the existing career ladders? It might. Early identification and development of employees with potential for advancement to high-demand positions would be more just than the "good old boys" network, which has hampered women and minorities, or the "wait your turn" career ladder, in which librarians were rewarded for their seniority and not necessarily their competence. [33]

Moreover, without career advancement opportunities, Munde suggests new librarians will quickly leave libraries for other career options in the technology and information management sector.

A good mentor helps a new employee adjust to the idiosyncrasies of the organization. Mentors are sources of institutional history, they know the people who should be consulted for advice/answers, they know who can be trusted, fair, and so on, and they know the political landscape of the organization. In public services at Mann, for example, a new employee who has never chaired a search committee is encouraged to meet with an established employee who has had success running committees and knows the political reality of facilitating a diverse group of staff with varying interests and expectations. A good mentor is a source of wisdom about career and development. And a good mentor helps successfully complete a good hire for both the library and the employee.

6. CONCLUSION

Hiring excellent staff has always been fundamental to a library's success. In the constantly changing digital environment, the hiring, training, and mentoring of staff take on even greater importance. Staff provides an infrastructure of expertise that makes it possible to deal with the ongoing changes libraries face in the digital environment. Staff members must be creative and innovative in their approach to solving the problems associated with the creation, distribution, and access to digital information. Flexibility and the willingness to learn and grow are imperative in a time of changing technologies, infrastructures, and services. Making the investments necessary to building an excellent staff is a key ingredient in the formula that will produce an excellent library, digital or otherwise.

REFERENCES

1. Bessler JM. Putting Service into Library Staff Training: A Patron-Centered Guide. Chicago: American Library Association, 1994.
2. Thomas SE, Russell KW. The Library Perspective on Library School Education: The National Agricultural Library as Employer. J Lib Admin 1989; 11(3/4):117–128.
3. Stuart C, Drake MA. Education and Recruitment of Science and Engineering Librarians. Sci Tech Lib 1992; 12(4):79–89.
4. Storm P, Wei W. Issues Related to the Education and Recruitment of Science/Technology Librarians. Sci Tech Lib 1994; 14(3):35–42.
5. Beile PM, Adams MM. Other Duties as Assigned: Emerging Trends in the Academic Library Job Market. College Research Lib 2000; 61(4):336–347.
6. White GW. Academic Subject Specialist Positions in the United States: A Content Analysis of Announcements from 1990 through 1998. J Acad Librarianship 1999; 25(5):372–382.
7. Storm P, Wei W. Issues Related to the Education and Recruitment of Science/Technology Librarians. Sci Tech Lib 1994; 14(3):35–42.
8. Beile PM, Adams MM. Other Duties as Assigned: Emerging Trends in the Academic Library Job Market. College Research Lib 2000; 61(4):336–347.
9. Lanier P, Carson PP, Carson KD, Philips JS. What Keeps Academic Librarians in the Books? J Acad Librarianship 1997; 23(3):191–197.
10. Landry MB. The Effects of Life Satisfaction and Job Satisfaction on Reference Librarians and Their Work. Ref User Serv Q 2000; 40(2):166–177.
11. Goldberg T, Womack K. Application Practices of Recent Academic Library Appointees. College Research Lib 1999; 60(1):71–77.
12. Reese GL, Hawkins EL. Stop Talking and Start Doing!: Attracting People of Color to the Library Profession. Chicago: American Library Association, 1999.
13. Winston M. The Role of Recruitment in Achieving Goals Related to Diversity in Academic Libraries. College Research Lib 1998; 59(3):240–247.

14. Bessler JM. Putting Service into Library Staff Training: A Patron-Centered Guide. Chicago: American Library Association, 1994.

15. Coffey JR. Competency Modeling for Hiring in Technical Services: Developing a Methodology. Lib Admin Mgnt 1992; 6(4):168–172.

16. Bednar M, Stanley NM. Hiring Tests for Technical Services Support Staff Positions. Tech Serv Q 1993: 11(1):3–19.

16a. Landry MB. Ref User Serv Q 2000; 40(2):166–177.

17. Reese GL, Hawkins EL. Stop Talking and Start Doing!: Attracting People of Color to the Library Profession. Chicago: American Library Association, 1999.

18. Kathman JM, Kathman MD. Training Student Employees for Quality Service. J Acad Librarianship 2000; 26(3):176–182.

19. Kenney DJ, Painter FO. Recruiting, Hiring, and Assessing Student Workers in Academic Libraries. J Lib Admin 1995; 21(3/4):29–45.

20. Kathman JM, Kathman MD. What Difference Does Diversity Make in Managing Student Employees? College Research Lib 1998; 59(4):378–389.

21. Wilder SN. Student Assistants: Achieving the Right Balance. J Lib Admin 1995; 21(3/4):125–135.

22. Gregory D. The Evolving Role of Student Employees in Academic Libraries. Bibliographical Essay. J Lib Admin 1995; 21(3/4):3–27.

23. Marmion D. Facing the Challenge: Technology Training in Libraries. Info Tech Lib 1998; 17(4):216–218.

24. Jones DE. Ten Years Later: Support Staff Perceptions and Opinions on Technology in the Workplace. Lib Trends 1999: 47(4):711–745.

25. Brandt DS. What (How, Where, When, Why) Is Training? Computers in Lib 1999; 19(2):32–34.

26. Kirkpatrick TE. The Training of Academic Library Staff on Information Technology Within the Libraries of the Minnesota State Colleges and Universities System. College Research Lib 1998; 59:51–59.

27. Tennant R. The Virtual Library Foundation: Staff Training and Support. Info Tech Lib 1995; 14(1):46–49.

28. Nilson CD. Training for Non-Trainers. New York: American Management Association, 1990.

29. Purnell J. Glogowski MP, ed. Academic Libraries and Training. Greenwich, CT: JAI Press, Inc., 1994:109–120.

30. Harris RM. The Mentoring Trap: A Warning for Entry-Level Librarians: Mentor–Protégé Relationships May Help & Select Few, But They Haven't Catapulted Enough Women or Minorities to Leading Roles. Lib J 1993; 118(17): 37–39.

31. Kirkland JJ. The Missing Women Library Directors: Deprivation versus Mentoring. College Research Lib 1997; 58(4):376–384.

32. Millet LK. Glogowski MP, ed. Academic Libraries and Training. Greenwich, CT: JAI Press, Inc., 1994:149–158.

33. Munde G. Beyond Mentoring: Toward the Rejuvenation of Academic Libraries. J Acad Librarianship 2000; 26(3):171–175.

5

Teams and Teamwork

Philip Herold
University of Minnesota, St. Paul, Minnesota, U.S.A.

A focus on human group processes, particularly teams and teamwork, is a necessary component of successful innovation. In the ever-changing digital environment, a growing amount of library work is project-based, and its success depends on the library administration's full support of teams.

- Teams can range from project-oriented task forces to permanent leadership councils.
- Investment in effective teamwork yields intangible benefits such as trust, a sense of ownership, and improved workflows and communication.
- These lead to tangible products such as improved collections and services.
- Guiding principles: Embrace change, create an atmosphere of trust, provide necessary tools, encourage communication, practice democratic ideals, build consensus, and educate colleagues.
- At Mann, library work relies on cross-functional, self-directed groups that work together toward common goals.
- By combining diverse skills, teams enable the library to adapt to changes in the information technology landscape.

- The best outcomes are achieved when teams work toward well-defined goals, even though discussion and consensus take time.
- In the long run the group's work benefits from members' understanding how decisions were reached.

Most of us at one time or another have been part of a great "team," a group of people who functioned together in an extraordinary way— who trusted one another, who complemented each others' strengths and compensated for each others' limitations, who had common goals that were larger than individual goals, and who produced extraordinary results. [1]

In this age of explosive information growth and increasingly digital libraries, library staff are often anxious to embrace new technologies and innovations as means to improve services and collections. In a rush to keep up with change, library staff often focus on technologies or innovations, concentrating efforts on adapting and moving forward quickly. One could argue that they spend too little time considering the human group processes that must necessarily accompany that movement.

In practical terms, such an emphasis is likely to have an effect on the way that a group will work, whether it be the work of department staff in routinely held meetings or of specially assembled staff in special project groups. Perhaps foremost, it is the time-sensitive nature of many decisions and implementations that undoubtedly has the effect of influencing the focus of the individual and the group toward the product of their work and the immediacy of the need for that product. This focus is not altogether undesired. In addition, myriad other factors can also place the foci of decision makers and groups on things other than the group process. Such factors sometimes include cost (where will the funding come from?) or technological solutions (how will we make it work?) or political concerns (how will we gain support for this product?). While undue emphasis on group dynamics and process can work against "getting the work done," there must be a balance, and library leaders should not invest too little in developing an environment and set of principles that guide truly effective teamwork. Such investments yield intangible products, such as trust, staff harmony and job satisfaction, sense of ownership, sense of fair representation, efficient workflows, and better and increased communication. These intangibles ultimately make tangible products, such as services and collections, better.

This chapter describes teams and teamwork as they occur in the Mann Library. It should be obvious to anyone who works in a library that the use of teams has become increasingly important in the fast-growing digital environment. As the rate of innovation and invention affecting information management and delivery increases, so does the rate and number of digital library initiatives. Most libraries utilize teams of some kind to address these initiatives. So what is different, unique, or special about the way teams operate at Mann? The model and practice at Mann are not unique or peculiar to the institution in the sense that it does not have a novel or groundbreaking or even a fixed approach. But, the use of teams and teamwork, and the principles underlying the teamwork concept, are given special attention at the administrative level, and several important guiding principles that apply to teamwork, adopted by library management, have been accepted by the entire library staff and are evident in nearly every part of their work.

The principles of teamwork are established foremost through the organizational culture [2]. Culture—discussed in Ch. 1—sets the tone for how the members of teams will work together. While not comprehensive or exclusive, the quality of the organization culture and success of individuals and teams rely on the following principles:

> Embrace change.
> Create an atmosphere of trust.
> Provide teams with the tools necessary to succeed.
> Encourage open communication.
> Practice democratic ideals.
> Work to build consensus.
> Educate each other.

Library literature is replete with descriptions of libraries that have adopted a corporate or hybrid corporate model for teams and teamwork. Mann does not strictly adhere to any of the approaches that have popular names, choosing instead to use its own approach based on some fundamental ideas that have proven to be successful. Mann does, however, indirectly borrow ideas from a number of different team approaches, particularly from the cross-functional and self-directed team approaches. The ideas that have been fostered in teams and their leaders, the institutional culture in which individuals and teams operate, and the structures and decision-making pathways that have been put in place allowing teams to succeed do just that—they allow teams to succeed. Similarly, the practice of teamwork at Mann is not attributable to any secret formula and probably looks much like teamwork in other libraries. But Mann's approach to the management of library work requires a high degree of cross-functional, self-directed teamwork, and that is achieved by means enumerated here—means that work well. The results, in concrete terms of services and collections, some of which are described in other parts of this book, are the best evidence in support of Mann's approach.

1. DEFINING TEAMS AND TEAMWORK

Several key terms require clarification for the context in which they are used here, terms such as "teams," "teamwork," and "succeed." One can find many different definitions for "team," but a team, as defined here, is any group that works together toward a common goal or objective. The library literature addresses the differences between teams and committees (and other types of working groups). Quinn's article [3] contrasts many differences between committees and teams. It describes the nature of committees as more ephemeral, passive, and advisory than teams, and less independent, authoritative, and comprehensive. Butcher writes, "The fundamental difference between teams, committees, or task forces is the difference between implementation and recommendation" [4]. This depiction of the elements of teams versus the elements of committees does not manifest itself in practice at Mann and, in fact, has little apparent basis elsewhere. Teams may share common methods and achieve results similar to those of a committee's work, but here the use of "team" connotes the less tangible elements that accompany the group with shared purpose and democratic process, among other things. These articles put forth a prescriptive and circumstantial definition of both terms.

In practice, teams can at times be called "committees," "working groups," "task forces," or "department staffs," or they can be called "teams." What these groups are called is far less important than how they function. They are teams if they consist of more than one person working together with a high degree of cooperation and collaboration toward a common goal or vision. Furthermore, although the term "team" is applied throughout this chapter when describing the critical elements of a "successful group," the elements should remain the focus, and they apply to any group regardless of name. For example, task forces, committees, and teams alike require diversity of thought, critically applied thought, and wholesale participation of all members to achieve the best result. It is the elements of successful teams and teamwork that are the focus of this chapter.

Teams at the Mann Library include project-oriented teams, teams of a task force nature, and permanent teams with the nature of committees, but teams do not provide the primary organizational structure of the library's functional work areas (at Mann these are the technical services, public services, collection development, and administration divisions—the latter includes an information technology section). "Team" is used in a particularly generic sense that is meant to connote a harmonious constituency working in an atmosphere of trust and following self-directed, nonprescriptive work, and decision-making processes. The way in which a team operates to reach its goal is largely a byproduct of a common experience, an environment described throughout this book.

"Teamwork," as the primary product of teams, is a term used to describe the way in which people work together toward a common end, whether that be a team project, goal, specific task, or another objective. Teamwork is present when the parts of the team are working in harmony; when they are not, it is said that a team lacks teamwork.

And what is "success"? Successful outcomes are desired outcomes—those that meet or exceed expectations. The successful product of a team is achieved when the team's goals and objectives are met—particularly when they are met expediently and efficiently and to the satisfaction of the entire team. Successful outcomes often include the mainstreaming of some new product or service into the library's everyday procedures (see Ch. 2).

2. TEAMS AND THE DIGITAL ENVIRONMENT

Why is teamwork more important in an increasingly digital environment? The answer may not be immediately obvious, but there are several reasons. For one, it is important that libraries move quickly to keep pace with changing technologies and with new digital initiatives, to meet the increasingly sophisticated needs of their communities. The library that hesitates too long, or cannot move quickly because it is too encumbered with divisions, antiquated ideas of process, or any number of other problems, will be left behind. On the other hand, the library that moves quickly and can readily adapt to changes in the information technology landscape will be in a position to lead. The private business sector models these lessons in ways that libraries should heed—those best positioned for quick mobility and adaptability are most often market leaders.

One way to increase the speed at which a library can react to, or adapt to, changes in the information technology landscape is to alter the library's organizational structures. Some libraries have adopted team structures in place of traditional functional divisions [4–7]. Some organizations are based on cross-functional, self-directed teams that accomplish project-based work [8].

However, it is not always necessary to undergo the turmoil that such reorganization can bring. At Mann, where divisions are structured hierarchically, project-based teams of a cross-functional, self-directed nature are often used to manage projects from conception to completion, and often do so with great efficiency and expedience.

The academic library that leads its campus with digital initiatives will not outlive its usefulness, will likely suffer less when budgets tighten, and will be looked to as a leader for successful adoption of information technologies, not as a follower. The following sidebar illustrates a recent situation where the library might easily have been left behind, excluded from a project were it not for the formation of a cross-functional interdepartmental team. This is also an example of a team that followed many of the suggestions in Ch. 7, Project Management and Implementation.

THE LIBRARY PROXY SERVER TEAM

Thomas D. Gale
McGraw-Hill Ryerson, Whitby, Ontario, Canada

1 Background

The Cornell University Library (CUL) system supplies a large number of networked resources to its users and provides access to those resources via the Web. Each resource offered has its own set of restrictions ranging from free availability to licenses that limit use. Use is limited by authentication and authorization mechanisms such as user ID and password, proprietary scripting, or IP authentication—one of the more challenging for CUL.

Every machine connected to the Internet needs to have a unique Internet Protocol (IP) address (or must at least appear to have a unique address for the duration of its connection to the Internet) so that it may accurately communicate with other systems. Because unique addresses are required, and because IP addresses are traceable to particular individuals and organizations, the vendors of online products often use the IP address to verify that people trying to use their system are coming from a legitimate location. Vendors will check the IP address of an incoming user, verify the address on a list of IP addresses that they know to be legitimate, and either allow or reject the user based on his or her presence or absence from the list. IP checking as a means of authentication is generally quite popular among libraries and vendors because it does not require patrons to remember their own user ID and password for every vendor, and vendors are free from the troubles caused by forgotten passwords.

2 The Problem

While IP authentication frees library patrons from the burden of remembering passwords and login IDs, it can also confine them to the campus. Libraries cannot provide vendors with the individual IPs of each user who will be connecting from home or off-campus because those IPs may change as users switch Internet service providers (ISP) or as they receive different temporary IPs each time they connect to the same ISP. Thus, patrons who are off-campus cannot access resources. CUL was wrestling with this problem for some time before arriving at the solution of a proxy server.

3 Proxy Solution

A proxy server is a piece of server software that essentially allows an authorized user to assume the identity of a different machine; that is, take on a different IP that it can present to a vendor for authentication. The proxy server resides on a machine on campus. That machine has an IP that is acceptable to vendors. When a library patron wants to connect to an IP-authenticated resource, he configures his browser to connect to the proxy server, assume a new IP, and then connect to the vendor's service. Because the proxy server stands between the library patron and the vendor, the vendor sees the allowable address of the campus based-machine and lets the patron through.

Of course, not just anyone can access the proxy server. When the patron contacts the proxy server, it verifies her identity as an authorized library patron before she is allowed to assume the IP of the proxy server. The solution sounds simple—and conceptually it is. It is also an approach that is not uncommon now. But at the time it was new to Cornell, and it took a considerable amount of teamwork and organization to implement.

4 The Team

With the volume of IP-authenticated resources selected by CUL, and the number of patrons moving to fast connections on off-campus ISPs, a strong voice was calling for the implementation of a proxy solution. A programmer from Mann Library's information technology section (ITS) began to do some preliminary research and some testing with some of the proxy solutions available. He investigated free proxy servers as well as commercial products.

Following the preliminary work, it was determined that if the library were to move forward, the best method of implementation would most likely be to use a free proxy server software called SQUID. The next step would be to incorporate the current campus-wide user ID and password authentication structure. The current campus ID and password structure is used to verify faculty, students, and staff for various services on campus. This approach was desirable because users would only be required to remember the user ID and password that they already used to collect their Cornell e-mail and other commonly used services.

During the investigation of proxy technologies and authentication systems, it was discovered that Cornell Information Technologies (CIT), the central computing department for the university, had been considering the use of a proxy server for some of its own services, but had not yet begun to fully implement its project. Because CIT was already responsible for the mainte-nance of the authentication services that the library had hoped to employ in its project, management from both CIT and CUL decided that the library proxy project would be a good place for the campus-wide proxy server initiative to begin. A team was formed.

Mann staff had already begun the proxy server investigation, so it seemed the logical place to base the CUL's efforts in the proxy project. The library team members included staff from public services and the information technology section at Mann.

Meetings between CIT and the Mann Library helped to determine the members who would be required from CIT. Mann selected a programmer librarian to lead the project for the library, and a programmer at CIT became his counterpart. The remaining team players included the original programmer at Mann who had done the preliminary research, a public services librarian at Mann, a member of the CIT HelpDesk support team, and a publications and information group staff member from CIT. The project leads reported on their progress to management and to other team members, and coordinated meetings.

Tasks were divided into stages: programming, testing, maintenance, and support. The division of labor is explained as follows:

Several programming tasks needed to be covered in order to get the proxy server up and running, but division and allocation of those tasks was fairly simple. The programming responsibilities were clearly identified because of the architecture of the system. The bulk of the proxy server components would reside on the CIT machines in order to place those systems where security and authentication expertise reside. The pieces required to integrate the library's system (i.e., the networked resources section of the Library Gateway at http://www.library.cornell.edu) would be created and maintained on the library's systems. The tasks were clearly defined, and both programmers were very quick to accommodate one another with advice and solutions during the procedure. The programming stage went slightly over the anticipated schedule, due both to project problems and to competition for programmer resources from other projects. The proxy project team was very patient, as was the CUL community.

Once the programming tasks were completed, testing was needed. In order to pick up the pace and bring things closer to schedule, members of both the library community and CIT volunteered to test. Further, when some of the volunteers were unable to test because of the change in schedule, the proxy team member who represented the CIT HelpDesk (which provides technical support to students, faculty, and staff for core technologies in use on campus, focusing on helping customers configure and connect their computers to the network) offered her corps of student testers to assist in the testing. The testing went relatively smoothly and revealed only a few problems related to vendors' changing IP addresses or maintaining multiple servers. Those problems were resolved, and the team swiftly moved onto the next phase: support.

The support of the proxy server was somewhat complicated by the existence of two help structures. CIT has a structure designed to help users with their campus computing needs, while the library system has its own structure designed to help users with the specific issues involved with library resources. While the programming tasks had evenly broken down into components based on functionality and where they would reside, the user information required for configuring and understanding the proxy server for use in the library and greater campus environment was not so easily divided. In the end, it was decided that the library and CIT would maintain separate Web-based help sections on the configuration and use of the proxy server with links to and from one another's help. The help information for the library was written by the public services member of the proxy team, and the help for the CIT section was written by the CIT publications and information group representative.

After allowing some time to pass, the help structure was to be reviewed and possibly revised based on observation from support and library staff as well as on feedback from users. The time to review has recently arrived, and certain areas of the help are going to be revised and merged to alleviate redundancy and confusion.

The proxy team was able to successfully and swiftly overcome problems and implement the designated task with only minor delays. This success came from the respectful and persistent communication across divisions, a strong support from library and CIT management and the strong sense of duty and accountability individual team members held. The university paid tribute to the success of the team with an award presentation: Team members received plaques and stainless steel coffee containers brandishing the label "Big Red Security" in recognition of the team's contributions to electronic security at Cornell.

The digital environment is sufficiently complex that when libraries utilize new information technologies, the ground is rarely even and dry and the path is not always straight. When navigating this muddy, uneven terrain, only well-managed teams will facilitate the library's ability to move quickly. Libraries adhering to a traditional staff organizational chart may not lack the combination of a traditional library and the more recently necessary technical skill sets required to address all issues that appear in the complex digital environment. But they need a way to bring the right combination of skill sets together to accomplish a goal, and this cannot always be done within the confines of departmental boundaries. A well-constructed team will contain the necessary technical and related specialized skill sets to address a complex technical question. It will carry the traditional principles and values into the digital environment and will be empowered to make decisions that help direct the future of the library's services.

In situations where financial support for libraries is decreasing, or simply not increasing to keep pace with rising library costs, it is incumbent upon libraries to find more efficient mechanisms for accomplishing projects and tasks. Many organizations believe—certainly Mann does—that their employees possess the skills and abilities to make good decisions. However, in many environments the organizational structure inhibits the ability of staff to make decisions. By focusing on the principles of teamwork and utilizing self-directed, cross-functional teams, libraries can move toward empowering individuals and teams in an environment in which the ladder of hierarchy need not be ascended with each decision. Empowered teams can make their own decisions provided they are given the training, tools, and power to do so. As one librarian writes, "The accelerating pace of change requires organizational agility. If a decision could be made at the front line but is referred up the hierarchy because no one but middle management can approve it, then time, a major resource, is lost" [4].

Besemer [9] describes the changing environment that has forced libraries to review their current work structures. Some of the changes, such as shrinking budgets and increasing costs, continue to affect libraries in much the same way as they have for decades, exacerbated by the fact that these changes still exist, unabated. Other environmental change factors continue but do so at an increasing rate of change. Automation—information technology—is chief among these. The proxy server issue is an example of an information technology problem that required the library's attention, involvement, solutions, and rapid action.

3. WHY CROSS-FUNCTIONAL, SELF-DIRECTED WORK TEAMS?

To begin addressing this question, one must first set a context and define the terms "cross-functional" and "self-directed" work teams. At Mann, the two concepts are most often combined in some fashion. Experience at Mann shows that the combination of these two team characteristics achieves the best results. The term "cross-functional" describes the constituency of a team. A team that contains membership from different functional areas within and/or outside the library can be considered cross-functional. At Mann, the functional areas include

> Technical services: performs processing functions such as acquisitions, cataloging, binding, book and serial processing to prepare items for use by the public
>
> Public services: provides circulation and other document access services as well as reference, instruction, and consulting services to the public
>
> Collection development: selects resources for the library's collections
>
> Information technology staff: support the computing needs of all the library divisions and build computer systems to enable library projects and other work

When a team's membership includes several of these different functional components, it can be described as being cross-functional in content.

The term "self-directed" perhaps requires less explanation. Interpretations will necessarily vary as to the level to which a team is able to, or should be allowed to, direct its own actions, structure, decisions, schedule, and so forth. It is sufficient to say that a self-directed team at Mann is empowered to use its own discretion when making decisions. The team may use its discretion to ask for help in making a decision, or seek approval for a decision from an outside authority such as the director or the administrative council, but the salient point is that the decision to ask for approval belongs to the team and is not imposed upon it. In most cases a team's internal structure, modus operandi, training method, schedule, and other methods and means are not prescribed for it by management, but are determined by the team itself.

"Cross-functional teams help overcome isolationism, insulation, and parochialism" [10]. In most cases, regardless of the type of team being formed, adding elements from different functional areas adds a variety of professional perspectives to the group. Input from multiple perspectives will provide a built-in system of checks and balances as the group discusses issues and makes decisions. It also helps avoid the kind of parochialism that can occur in a team built of parts from the same department. "Groupthink," a pitfall in which groups lack the ability to critique their own ideas or decisions, and where conflicting ideas are not expressed, occurs in teams that lack diversity of thought. A cross-functional team is more likely to avoid groupthink than one consisting of similar elements (a team consisting entirely of public services staff, for example, or a team consisting only of managers). Including team members from different functional areas allows the team to move in concert with other areas of the library, rather than in asynchronous motion by itself. A cross-functional team containing representatives from different functional areas, departments, or divisions within a library will often help deconstruct some of the barriers that can come to be built between them. One must assume certain levels of trust and communication within a department, for example, before one can expect barriers to begin to fall; and once they are in place, such organizational divisions are difficult to remove. Building teams where each department has a representative voice (at the very minimum) is a beginning in the right direction. The team and the organization as a whole will maximize their benefits if team decisions result from the work of cross-functional teams.

4. BEYOND BASIC TEAM STRUCTURE: BEST TEAM AND TEAMWORK PRACTICES

Without becoming formulaic, there are a number of practices that Mann Library teams attempt to use and have found successful. Already, the ideas of team composition and a philosophy about the nature of team management have been introduced. Once you have a cross-functional, self-directed team in place, what works best? The best outcomes occur when team members collaborate to work toward a well-defined and concrete goal or product. This can be a great challenge, for teams often are not provided with an initial charge that sets forth clearly defined goals or objectives. It is critical that library management team leaders strive to set a clear and concrete goal(s) or milestone(s) before a team begins its work. It can be difficult for permanent teams to achieve this practice. With teams of a permanent nature, such as standing committees or departmental groups, it is important to keep a target goal in place; and when one goal is achieved, another should be set. It is also important to keep goals concrete and clearly attainable rather than vaguely stated.

For example, a reference services team may set a goal of "providing better service." This is much too ambiguous a goal to work toward in any systematic way. The team needs to take time to define what "better service" means, to break it down into concrete pieces. What is the service goal? And how can it be achieved? Specific, measurable objectives will help a team to know when it has reached its goal. What areas need improvement? The team might decide that increasing the emphasis on reference services geared specifically to remote users is an area that should be addressed. Team members can then move to set measurable objectives toward this end. Examples might include increasing the number of questions received from remote users in support of online collections, marketing new or existing services to help increase awareness within the target audience, conducting a study to understand the needs of remote users, establishing new services for remote users based on needs identified in the study, and advertising e-mail reference service to those who don't currently use it.

What is the process by which objectives and goals are set, and who makes decisions about the team goals? There are several answers. Occasionally, teams will be formed for a specific task or set of tasks and given a charge that identifies its goals. The charge may come from the library director, a division head, or the management team. Often a team will form to address a specific need and proceed to set its own course. An example from Mann was a team formed to address the need for a more focused reference services/collections presence on the Internet. The need was identified in regular meetings of all reference staff, and the team—the RefWeb team—was formed from volunteers from that group. The RefWeb team then proceeded to identify its own goals and the objectives and other tasks it would undertake to achieve these goals. In many cases, the entire process of setting the course for a team involves decision making at both the administrative and team levels. For example, goals may be set by the library management with objectives, or other means of achieving those goals, largely determined by the self-directed team.

Objectives and goals are set, and other decisions made, in what is almost always a variation of the democratic group process. In fact, some Mann Library teams have been accused of being "excessively democratic," and this is probably true. Most decisions move forward by general group consensus. When consensus cannot be reached, voting is sometimes used to identify a simple majority. The best outcomes follow group-consensual decisions. With consensual decision making, the collective wisdom of the group leads the team. Each individual is given an equal voice in the outcome and understands how the decision was reached. The worst outcomes follow authoritarian-produced decisions. Team members do not always understand the rationale for such decisions. Certainly, members who disagree with the authoritarian-produced decision may not feel they were given an equal voice in the outcome. Additionally, misunderstandings or disagreements by those who have not been given a voice in an important decision can lead to increased division between groups and individuals and can constrict the flow of communication.

Trust is the key, and leaders must place trust in the decision of the team. Although administrators and team leaders sometimes avoid this adherence to a democratic process because it is too expensive in terms of time and compromise, it is critical to team success. Team members will be most dedicated to achieving and adopting the team's goals as their own if they have each been involved in determining the team's direction. To the contrary, when team members are simply directed, they respond with less enthusiasm and a lesser sense of ownership. In an effort to reach timely decisions, team leaders need to concentrate on honing their consensus-building skills. Leaders should be adept at creating an inclusive atmosphere where all team members have an opportunity for input, have their own stake in the team's success, and have a vested interest in the success of the team—the good of the whole. Team members must realize the nature of the decisions and the time constraints placed on them, and they cannot be allowed to stand in the way of the team's progress.

5. A PRODUCTION TEAM: THE REFERENCE TEAM

One of the best examples of a permanent team at Mann, one that manages itself in a largely independent manner (self-directed) and consists of staff from many different functional work areas (cross-functional), is the reference team. This team is also a good example of one in which projects, new initiatives, objectives, and goals are not set following the top-down model.

Reference services fall under the domain of public services at Mann. Supervised by the head of public services and coordinated by the information services coordinator, reference staff number between 15 and 17 people, including librarians from each of the library's divisions (information technology section, technical services, collection development, and public services) and 2 to 3 paraprofessional information assistants. This group gathers at biweekly meetings to address reference-related issues of training, technology, information resources, and short- and long-term planning. Decisions are typically shared among the entire group. It is a large team, and therefore it can be difficult to reach consensus on some issues, but all members are empowered to voice their ideas and opinions as the team progresses to a decision.

The reference team provides reference and information services, which in practice means providing personal assistance in answering questions, or instructing or guiding users in searching for and using information resources. Services are tailored to users' perceived needs and to the varying natures of the questions they ask. Questions range from the simple directional, to the complex technical, to the in-depth research question. They can be delivered in person, via e-mail, or over the telephone. The reference team undertakes an ongoing training regimen and continually explores new and different means for improving, expanding, and innovating reference services.

Team goals are set in a variety of ways. The team's overall goal is to set a high standard of service for library users and to meet that standard. This is put into practice in many ways, through what might be described as "going the extra mile" for each individual with an information need; by paying close attention to users' needs and planning services accordingly; by always interacting in an alert, attentive, friendly manner; by establishing access to reference services in a flexible and convenient way; and by making sure reference staff are well-trained and knowledgeable about library collections and services. These are just a few examples; there are many more ways. This goal might best be described as inherited—one that has long existed at the Mann Library and that has come to be recognized and expected by the library staff and, more importantly, by Mann's user community.

Additional reference team goals, objectives, or initiatives may be championed by a library administrator—typically the director, the head of public services, or the information services coordinator. These goals are often mandated by the colleges the library serves or arrive as part of a greater consortial or national initiative.

Some goals are championed by an individual member or small group within the team. Such goals might include a natural extension of reference services to a previously underserved constituency within the library's user community. An example is the service reference staff provide to Cornell Cooperative Extension employees, who are scattered across the state of New York. Reference services are being extended to better reach this remotely located community. Efforts by one of the reference staff to increase communications and services between Extension and the library rely on the reference team to adopt and follow through with new services to a new community.

However, most goals are set by the team as a whole. For example, the group began to discuss how best to expand the information service's presence on the library's Web site. In brainstorming discussions they delineated a number of areas that could be developed, then prioritized the top three areas and formed small teams to carry out the development of each new Web-based component to reference services. The entire team considered each step leading up to the actual creation of the three components. The reference team generally follows the decision-making model described by Butcher: "Defining and limiting the problem. Analyzing the problem and gathering data. Establishing the decision criteria. Discussing possible solutions. Determining the best solution. Choosing the solution. Implementation. Revisiting the decision" [4]. The team's culture and environment are open and supportive. Solutions are most often generated through discussions. Everyone participates.

It is accurate to say that the team is "greater than the sum of its parts." Many strengths derive from the fact that reference is cross-functional. Individuals bring issues from different departments. For example, librarians from collection development communicate developments regarding access to newly acquired e-journals and other current changes impacting reference services. Individuals from different departments provide valuable perspectives outside the typical public services viewpoint. This process helps remove barriers among divisions and provides individuals in all library functional areas with public service experience and firsthand knowledge of the way users interact with the library systems and collections. This benefit is beyond valuable—it is essential.

6. THE MANAGEMENT TEAM: ADMINISTRATIVE COUNCIL

The Mann Library's management is provided primarily by its director, the heads of collection development, public services, and technical services, and the head of the information technology section. These five, together with the administrative manager, together constitute the Mann Library Administrative Council. This team gathers weekly to lead each of the library's four functional areas as well as to guide the organization as a whole. The council provides much of the library's vision, making decisions that will affect the future of its services and collections. The director is the administrative leader of the council and sets the group's agenda. Individual council members often take leadership roles on issues closely related to their respective departments.

The team conducts different types of meetings, varying its approach to concerns that come before it depending on the requirements (long-term or short-term planning, education, etc.). It uses discussion meetings to address topical agenda items that require education of team members before reaching decisions. To address the library's strategic plan, the group will conduct retreats that help to enable long-term planning. Retreats offer a change of setting and a more relaxed atmosphere in which it is easier to think out of the box. Retreats are also conducive to team building, setting goals and objectives, and establishing a vision.

For example, the university's recently announced genomics initiative will have a major impact on the nature of research at Cornell. How will the library support this research? What new collections should it be acquiring? What new services should it offer? How can the library make a proactive impact in support of the genomics initiative? The administrative council wished to be creative in thinking about these questions and their potential answers. They conducted a retreat that helped to remove the reminders and distractions that are part of everyday life in the office, allowing team members to focus squarely on the genomics questions. The retreat encouraged creative thinking and innovative approaches.

The notion of roles plays an important part in the successes of the administrative council. Roles are not assigned, but the natural differences among team members, in terms of personalities, communication styles, skills, and experiences, help create a diverse group in which members tend to serve in roles (not always the same ones) that complement one another. One member will naturally assume the role of the out-of-the-box thinker, offering many creative ideas for discussion; one or more members will bring pragmatism to the mix, explaining the potential impacts of a given idea or confirming (or countering) that an idea can indeed work, with specific implementation plans. Once the group has begun to accept an idea, one group member will often challenge the prevailing notion, providing a check to the collective thinking of the group. Sometimes the group seeks a role that does not naturally occur in the group, or it will require a person with special expertise not possessed by any of the team members. In these situations, the council will invite staff or other experts outside the team to speak on relevant issues or questions. This kind of outside stimulus helps educate and enlighten the team as the members approach decisions. The group includes a synthesizer, who brings all the pieces of an issue, or a discussion, together in a clarifying, simplifying way. There is also a gifted visual artist, who has the ability to create colorful metaphors and draw clear mental pictures of ideas. This type of illustration serves to clarify, educate, and sometimes "paint" ideas in a different light. The objectifier often presents an idea from the outsider's point of view, providing yet another picture for the group to consider.

Despite the multiple roles that together make up the management team, it does not lack cohesiveness, trust, fun, and humor. Team members are drawn together by a common purpose and vision that the group defines and accepts. The team shares the same sense of goals, it is quick to respond to problems, and it encourages open and free discussions. At the same time, members offer positive feedback to one another and carry shared responsibility and a sense of accomplishment for the decisions their team makes and the successes that result.

An important aspect of the management team, and of other teams at Mann, is that competition between members is strongly discouraged. Council members are expected to rise above simply being advocates of their respective divisions. They are expected to consider the best interests of the library as a whole. Avoidance of individual and divisional competition is an important part of the organizational culture at Mann that contributes to good teamwork.

7. DEVELOPMENT TEAM: THE CUGIR PROJECT TEAM

The Cornell University Geospatial Information Repository (CUGIR) team was created to undertake a new library project that originated from a successful proposal for a grant to fund a Web-based clearinghouse of spatial data and metadata. The process of writing the grant brought together members of the library who owned some expertise in the relevant grant topics, which included geographic information systems (GIS), government information, grant writing, and computer systems. This ad-hoc team's membership comprised a public services librarian/GIS specialist (the team leader/facilitator), the head of public services, an ITS programmer/librarian, the metadata librarian (from technical services), and the spatial and numeric files selector (from collection development). As the list of members indicates, expertise in the relevant areas was scattered throughout the library's departments, as is often the case, and less care went into creating a cross-functional team that represented every department than went into gathering the human components who knew and understood the subjects and could intelligently address them in writing.

Later, with the grant secured and the project a "go," the library formed an implementation team. In assigning people to this group, management considered a number of factors. These included (1) keeping the team to a reasonable size—one that suited the size and resource commitment of the project to be undertaken, (2) gathering staff who possessed the skills sets that were needed to accomplish the project, (3) selecting staff who would represent the functional areas within the library that would continue to develop and maintain the product long after its implementation, (4) finding people who were interested in working on the project, and (5) assigning staff who would work well together. The first three factors were necessary practical considerations, the last two strong preferences, but all were critical to the team's success. Planners also considered the future implications that this team would have for the library and the long-term development and maintenance of the clearinghouse—how would it be managed once the project ceased to be a project? Where would the expertise be located in the library when members had moved on to new responsibilities, and did this matter?

The principal grant writer and resident GIS expert, a public services librarian, presented a proposal to the library's administrative council to create a group that would include a metadata librarian, a programmer, a collection development librarian, and two public services staff with experience using and consulting in the use of GIS and spatial data. The proposal also provided specific staff recommendations, a timeline for the team's implementation schedule, and a breakdown of the broad categories of work and many specific tasks within them.

In the fall of 1997, the CUGIR implementation team convened with its charge to implement the clearinghouse and develop a plan for its long-term future. In September 1998, the Cornell University Geospatial Information Repository, a Web repository containing over 3000 data files and over 1200 metadata files, debuted at http://cugir.mannlib.cornell.edu/. In the months in between, the team worked together to educate each other, to establish a common vision, and to set attainable goals and specific objectives to be met in pursuit of those goals. The goals and objectives were met in a timely fashion, and the library developed an innovative service for the Cornell community and for data users everywhere. Since CUGIR's inception in 1998, data users have downloaded an average of 3000 spatial data files from CUGIR each month. By library standards, that is a resounding success. After all, how many libraries circulate the equivalent of their entire collection each month?

CUGIR's success is attributable to the team's structure and the emphasis on teamwork and trust as much as it is to the talents of the individuals within the team. The parts of the team were carefully put into place, and the team was given the time, resources, and support necessary to carry out its charge. The team and its members determined their own internal structure and modus operandi, defined their own roles, and allowed all individuals to increase their stake in the project's success. The team embarked on its mission by outlining these objectives:

> Establish a common vision.
> Set concrete, achievable objectives.
> Set concrete, attainable goals.
> Create an atmosphere of trust that enables team members to carry out certain tasks independently from the group and encourages open and active participation and the sharing of ideas and constructive criticism without fear of reproach.

Establish a common vocabulary.

Construct timelines.

Delegate and distribute tasks fairly and with regard to members' skills and interests.

Educate the entire team in areas previously known only to individual team members or to no one on the team.

7.1. Establishing a Common Vision

How does a team create a vision that all can clearly see and agree to pursue? This question was made difficult when working on CUGIR by the fact that several team members were not fully aware of the need for our product (a spatial data repository) and had only a loose grasp on what it would require, in terms of goals and objectives, to achieve the vision. On the other hand, the team leader and others who had worked on the initial grant proposal had a vision of the end product, knew the need for it, and had a fair understanding of the tasks required to accomplish it. Part of the group was already accustomed to working in an environment of trust and collaboration, where the group was willing to approach new ideas such as this with an open mind and without great fear or skepticism. However, rather than putting forth the vision that part of the group held as the team's, the team leader began by gathering the ideas and questions of the entire group.

In the team's earliest meetings, members discussed the clearinghouse idea, expressing individual thoughts about where it belonged in the library's mission, where it fit on the university community's instruction and research agenda, where it would fit into the greater information space. The team built on the singular vision described in the grant proposal, expanding it with questions, abstract ideas of policy, philosophy, purpose, design, and means. The resulting vision encompassed a consensually chosen set of values and a clear idea of what was still only a vaguely understood product. As that product solidified in their minds, the group began to discuss more specific questions that surrounded the repository, including timelines, metadata, and standards, computer hardware and software, and technology protocols.

7.2. Setting Goals and Objectives

The overall goal for the CUGIR team was in place from the time the grant proposal was written and ultimately funded. But a number of smaller goals, as well as a host of objectives, would need to be reached to meet each of the goals. Foremost among these objectives was the need to educate each team member to a level of expertise necessary not only to fulfill their roles on the team, but also to partake in the development of what was expected to be an innovative system. In other words, not to be at a level of competence, but to become experts—leaders in the area of GIS/spatial data clearinghouses as they relate to technical services and metadata in particular, systems and Web development, public services and reference support, and so on. Section 7.4 of this chapter, Education, further explains this objective and how it was accomplished.

Beyond education, the group's goals and objectives included many more specific ideals and plans for the project. The team opened its early meetings with free-ranging discussions that involved each member's hopes and desires for the clearinghouse. Members considered the purpose of the clearinghouse, the potential audiences for it, and the mission of the library in serving the university and the state of New York. Although these issues were considered in the grant proposal problem statement, it was necessary to specify the ways in which these issues would be handled. Out of these discussions came a number of goals that led the team throughout its work. For example, the group held tightly to the ideal that data to be included in the clearinghouse should not be accompanied by access or use restrictions—it should be freely available to anyone who wishes to download and use it. The group identified objectives including the use of a standardized file-naming protocol, one that users would be able to learn easily and apply to their own spatial data file management.

These and other, similar, goals and objectives were discussed early in the project's life and were thus in place to guide the group's work through to the project's completion. Goals and objectives helped give the team and the project a concrete sense of purpose and proved invaluable to the team. They helped keep members focused and thus eased later decisions.

7.3. Creating an Atmosphere of Trust

It is easy to say that teams need to create an atmosphere of mutual trust and respect, or that an institution must foster these traits in its culture, but it is very difficult to achieve this result. Fortunately for the CUGIR team, such an atmosphere largely existed before the group was formed. Mann's administration instills trust in its staff as a matter of routine. Leaders instill trust through example: They trust their charges with great responsibility in all aspects of work. Staff members are treated with respect and are expected to be accountable for themselves and their work. Teams are empowered and trusted to carry out the work with which they are charged and to convene, plan, and implement their plans with liberal degrees of independence and freedom. In this way a large measure of trust exists between the administration (and the library as a whole) and the teams that are formed.

To establish a culture of trust within the team is the next logical step, and this step is more easily facilitated in an organizational culture built on trust.

Within the CUGIR team, it became apparent that team members needed to get to know each other. Beyond establishing goals, objectives, planning, and training in the early team meetings, individuals had the opportunity to meet and begin to better understand one another. As the group reached consensus decisions on various plans, they each became owners of those decisions. And, after training sessions were conducted that enabled everyone to reach a minimum level of understanding of project components and issues, the level of anxiety in meetings lessened at the same time that each member's confidence in his or her own potential contribution rose.

It required some time for internal team trust to develop. The efficient and energetic group dynamic that emerged did not evolve without some growing pains. There were discussions in which members struggled to be understood, and those that required emphatic debate to reach agreement. Disparate opinions and ideas were shared, and some were necessarily discarded, while others were adopted. The key to getting through the more difficult moments was the ability to keep discussions open. In these discussions, the team would hear everyone's concerns and ideas, encouraging everyone to contribute. It is especially important to allow the prevailing notion of "how it should be done" to be challenged because, after all, a prevailing notion that cannot survive criticism should not prevail!

7.4. Education

The work of a team can be greater than its parts, but first, team members must learn the issues, standards, and technologies surrounding the project goal. Individually, the CUGIR team carried little understanding or experience in the use of spatial data and geographic information systems. Only two team members had any real GIS experience. Because of this, except for one of its members, the team was unfamiliar with the issues surrounding the creation of a public Internet data repository. What protocols would be used? What technical infrastructure would be necessary? How would the team prepare and package the data and metadata? What was the FGDC (Federal Geographic Data Committee) Metadata Standard, and how should the team use it? How did copyright laws apply? A host of questions such as these needed to be asked and answered, and the answers were either unknown or known to one or two of the team's members. The CUGIR team set about to ascertain the answers through self- and team education and training.

The team leader had experience with most of the issues related to spatial data and had used data from many different repositories similar in nature to the one planned. The group met in a series of training sessions where the leader transferred basic information related to spatial data (commonly used formats, structures, features classes, display and use, and GIS software) to the other members of the group. Providing Internet demonstrations of data clearinghouses at other institutions (the University of Connecticut's MAGIC system at http://magic.lib.uconn.edu/, for example) helped team members create their own visions of what Cornell's data repository could do and should look like. Hands-on training in the use of spatial data within a geographic information system provided each member with practical experience using spatial data in ways similar to those expected from future users. The training moved abstract concepts and issues into the realm of real, tangible things. Related concepts, such as metadata, began to take on new meanings as questions about the content, history, and quality of the data arose. Team training continued and covered several more areas in which individual team members owned some level of expertise, including Web design and related technologies such as HTML, image creation, CGI scripting, image mapping, and database management. Initially, it was not necessary that team members rise to the same level of understanding as the team leader in any area, but the project would require a basic level of understanding of all technologies and issues in order for everyone to be able to make meaningful contributions to team discussions. Eventually, as individuals focused on their own contributions to the project, each team member far surpassed the understanding of the team leader in his or her respective specialized areas of expertise.

Self-training also played a critical role in the team's work. Several important tasks would require at least one team member to develop at minimum a working understanding of some technology or standard. Where such a task was identified, a team member was assigned to investigate that area and lead the team in discussions that included it. The FGDC Metadata Standard was one such dark and gloomy area of the unknown. The metadata specialist, who had experience with other standards (mostly cataloging standards, such as MARC), bravely undertook developing a working knowledge of this standard and began to bring discussion-generating questions to the team. How would the standard be applied? Where there was room for it, how did the team want to make practical interpretations of the standard? Within the repository, what forms (e.g., SGML, HTML, text) would metadata records take, and how would the team achieve them? How would the team obtain the information needed to complete metadata records adhering to the standard? How would the team establish workflows related to the creation and publishing of metadata?

Self-training by individual team members was clearly one of the more difficult tasks the team faced. It is a daunting thing to explore a new area where the vocabulary is foreign and the concepts are unfamiliar. And there was added pressure. The team placed its trust in individual members not only to investigate a critical technical area, but also to use the newly formed understanding to educate other team members and assume a leadership role in the related decision-making process. Team members took a variety of different "trailblazing" approaches. Some read through all the related literature they could locate on their topics. Others experimented with technology solutions to a system question. The team contacted experts outside the team and the university in efforts to gather information. These methods took time and energy that required self-motivation and the support of the library administration, but sharing the burden of educating the team in all aspects of the project allowed individuals to focus on their own area of responsibility and pushed the group forward. As each member developed his or her own expertise, the entire team learned and benefited. This was an example of organized trailblazing. Read more about trailblazing in Ch. 9, New Frontiers and the Scout.

One year after the formation of the CUGIR team, the Cornell University Geospatial Information Repository at http://cugir.mannlib.cornell.edu/ was unveiled. On schedule and exceeding the expectations of the team, the resource quickly became an indispensable resource for GIS and spatial data users at Cornell and across New York State. The team continued to work, on an irregular schedule, to plan and manage the further growth of CUGIR and to complete the mainstreaming process in support of the resource.

Perhaps the greatest testament to the success of the CUGIR team and its teamwork is the continued success of the team's product. CUGIR continues to expand its collections of spatial data and metadata, having more than doubled the number of spatial data files since its inception. Statistics show that use of the system continues to grow and reach new heights with each year. At the same time, system maintenance has been streamlined for maximum efficiency, and a smooth transition has taken place.

Nearly all the original team members have assumed new and different roles within or outside the library, yet CUGIR continues to thrive. Two factors have contributed to CUGIR's successful continuation: support mainstreaming and transition. The CUGIR team is very different today from a few years ago. Rather than reacting to unforeseen changes in the library's staff that would affect the CUGIR team (and other library teams), the Mann Library took proactive steps to ease the future management of CUGIR, as it evolved from "project" status to "production system" status.

First came the "mainstreaming" of CUGIR. This took place most prominently within the information technology section (ITS). Essentially, responsibility for the system's technical maintenance and growth was shared between the ITS programmer/librarian who was a member of the CUGIR team and other programmers in his division. Carefully documenting and explaining the technical infrastructure and procedures for updating, restoring, and otherwise managing the system were paramount to this step. Rather than relying on a sole technical expert to maintain the system, the library could now be assured that ITS programming staff had at least a basic understanding of how the system worked and could continue to maintain the system in the event of a major staffing change.

To varying degrees, transitions in public services, technical services, and collection development were made to allow new staff to be included in the CUGIR team. The team leader, who accepted a major change in job responsibilities, helped train a successor in public services and continues to serve a small role on the CUGIR team. Technical services hired a new metadata librarian, who was subsequently trained to become a specialist in geospatial metadata standards and has joined the team. A new collection development librarian has also joined the team. As a group, the team is planning for the next major release of the system.

Clearly, many elements contributed to make CUGIR a successful team—the same elements that made for successful teamwork in the reference team, the proxy server team, the management team, and countless other teams at the Mann Library. Each of these teams expressed openness to change and embraced diversity of thought. Each fostered a culture of trust in teammates that began in the library's everyday organizational culture. They encouraged the participation of all team members and made efforts to include every voice in the decision-making process. These cross-functional teams included representatives from multiple divisions within the library, thus ensuring communication throughout the organization and establishing shared, institutional ownership of team products. To a great extent, the teams directed their own work, relying on the expertise of individual members and the collective wisdom of the team as a whole.

A small number of common themes in this chapter contribute to successful teams and teamwork: cross-functionality, communication, participation, empowerment, trust, and cooperation. These themes, or team elements, often do not occur, or become manifest, naturally in an organization. They are, however, latent characteristics of most organizations. Like soluble ingredients at rest within a fluid organization, they do not become part of the solution until mixed thoroughly. Library administration acts as the straw that stirs this mixture.

Organizational culture is largely defined by the leaders and administration within an organization, who must instill trust, allow participation, demand cooperation, and lead by example. The beginning chapter of this book details just how Mann has achieved its current culture. It bears emphasizing that perhaps the most essential component required to achieving harmonious teamwork by teams that are focused, self-directed, and motivated is the full support of teams by library management. Library administrators should not leave self-directed teams entirely to their own devices, nor should they meddle in the details of the team's work. They must stand aside and let the team do its work. This is a hard balance for some people in positions of authority to strike. They must provide constructive and positive feedback. This ability does not come easily to some. They must facilitate the needs of the team, provide the required resources, and do everything possible to keep teams' morale high.

A growing percentage of library work is project-based; more details on project management and implementation are provided in the following chapter. As stated previously, the speed at which information technology changes requires information providers, such as libraries, to move at a rapid pace. In order to move at this rapid pace, libraries commonly adopt transient groups—committees, ad-hoc committees, working groups, task forces, councils, etc.—that have been treated for the purposes of this chapter as varying types of teams. These teams work to identify and solve problems, to help the library implement solutions, and to attack a variety of project-based tasks that are shorter-term in nature than perhaps they once were. This is the nature of library work in a digital and ever-changing information environment. It is critical to the success of teams and teamwork that library administrations openly recognize and publicly confirm that short-term, project-based work is not peripheral to what libraries do. It is core to librarianship and essential to the current and future validity of the profession. In other words, what might be considered nontraditional tasks, whether impermanent or not, that teams address are not and should not be considered outside the realm of what is considered normal for libraries or what librarians deem normal. They are at the heart of what libraries do. Library staff need to embrace this concept, and library administrators must lead the way.

REFERENCES

1. Senge PM. The Fifth Discipline: The Art and Practice of the Learning Organization. New York: Doubleday, 1994.
2. Faiks AH, McCue JA. The Culture of Engaged Institutions. In: Barnes SJ, ed. Becoming a Digital Library. New York: Marcel Dekker, 2003:1–24.
3. Quinn B. Understanding the Differences Between Committees and Teams. Library Admin. & Management 1995; 9(2):111–116.
4. Butcher KS. Decision Making in a Team Environment. Library Admin. & Management 1997; 11(4):222–230.
5. De Jager GJJ, du Toit ASA. Self-directed Work Teams in Information Services: An Exploratory Study. S. African J. Library and Info Sci. 65(4), 1997.
6. Phipps SE, Diaz JR. The Evolution of the roles of staff and team development in a changing organization. The University of Arizona Library experience. Finding Common Ground Conference Proc., March 30-31, 1996.
7. Osif H. Manager's Bookshelf: Self-directed Work Teams. Library Admin. & Management 1995; 9(2):117–121.

8. Osif H. Manager's Bookshelf; Cross-functional Teams. Library Admin. & Management 1997; 11(1):47–51.
9. Besemer SP, et al. In: von Dran GM, Cargill J, eds. Catalysts for Change: Managing Libraries in the 1990s. New York: Haworth Press, 1993:69–89.
10. Baldwin DA. Humanistic Management by Teamwork: An Organizational and Administrative Alternative for Academic Libraries. Englewood, CO: Libraries Unlimited, 1996.

6

Information Technology Services

Tim Lynch
Cornell University, Ithaca, New York, U.S.A.

An information technology (IT) services unit is a natural fit in a library.

- Academic users are accessing information and also creating it.
- Digital information does not change a library's mission, but does change how the mission is achieved.
- Fundamental activities of identification, collection, orgranization, preservation, and access all require technology skills.
- IT unit specialization allows other library units to focus and specialize on what they do best.
- IT responsibilities include operation (day-to-day management of equipment, software, network) and development (allowing library to take full advantage of digital information in fulfilling its mission).
- Development is needed when commercial applications are not available to meet the library's needs, and to install and adapt off-the-shelf products.
- Projects are small in scale but not trivial, with open-source components bringing powerful capabilities.
- Mann's IT unit has added frontline service to its back-office operations.

- A new IT unit should start small, with staff kept integrated within the library organization.

1. INTRODUCTION: A NATURAL FIT

This chapter focuses on Mann Library's information technology services (ITS) unit. In existence since the mid-1980s, this unit was originally just one person providing support for a handful of microcomputers that had appeared in the library. Over the years, the number of microcomputers in the library grew and other technologies arrived. As Mann's digital collections and services expanded, ITS grew in staff and in the support services it provided. Today, ITS comprises both an operations unit providing desktop support and a software development group that creates new applications for library staff and patrons.

In reviewing ITS, this chapter also provides justification for locating an information technology (IT) unit within a library. Now more than ever before, there are good reasons for such a move. In fact, it makes sense to begin this look at ITS with a review of how IT is a natural fit in the library environment. Our focus is the academic setting: colleges, universities, and community colleges. What these environments have in common that is important to consider here are users who are intimately involved in not only accessing information, but also in creating the greater information space in which they operate. We'll have more to say about this user community later in this chapter. For now it is sufficient to know our focus is the academic setting.

In other chapters, we have described a library's mission: to bear the responsibility for identifying, collecting, organizing, preserving, and providing access to information. Notice that this definition does not mention format. More true with every passing day, the default, and even preferred, format of information is electronic for a growing number of library users. Does the change in format change the library's mission? Fundamentally, no, not at all. But electronic information does fundamentally change the way a library achieves its mission. We continue to review the effects of the electronic format throughout this chapter, but it is worth taking a few minutes to look at some important points before venturing further.

Let's start with identification of relevant information. If all information was *worth* collecting and *could* be collected, then identification would not be an issue: We'd just collect everything. That is obviously not the case. So, librarians must first review and assess documents, Web sites, data sets, and so forth for inclusion. In days past when everything was print, the evaluation could focus on relevancy, quality, cost, and available shelf space. Electronic information now requires librarians to consider how access to that electronic thing (Web site, data set, video clip, etc.) will be provided. In fact, some level of proficiency with electronic information access is needed just to perform the evaluation!

Once identified, the new item must somehow be collected. What does collecting mean in the electronic world? If the new thing is a Web site, it might just mean adding a URL link to the library's own Web page. Or it might require the library to create a new software application that can negotiate a secure login with a vendor's Web site. If the item is yet another new type of media (streaming multimedia formats, for example, seem to arrive every day), then perhaps new hardware and software will be required to properly "shelve" the new item. We have only come as far as collecting, but as you can easily see, the need for IT skills is essential for any modern library to complete its mission.

Let's move on to organizing the information space. Again, it is helpful to contrast the electronic information world with the world of print. In the print world, card catalogs were the prime means of searching for information. Not that card catalogs were ideal; they simply represented the best tradeoff in effort-to-create versus utility. The success of the card catalog also depended on the fact that the objects being cataloged—books, serial publications, and so on—shared important characteristics: Users had an intimate understanding of the format of the materials ("I'm looking for a book," for example, or "I'm looking for an article in a journal"). The homogeneous nature of print led to the development of card catalogs that were intuitive for users. Card catalogs were easily mastered.

One of the truly wondrous aspects of the electronic world is that information has been released from the inert bounds of the print world: Once printed, the contents of a book or journal article might as well be cast in stone. But once crafted in a word processor, there is no telling in what form an electronic document might appear today or tomorrow. Indeed, the format of any particular information item might itself change over time: One day, what you seek is in the form of a CD-ROM; the next day, it has morphed into a Web site. But the fluidity of the electronic world has created an enormous challenge as to how we might organize the information space in an intuitive and predictable way.

Until very recently, the importance of the library's role in preserving information has not been at all obvious to the casual user: After all, the books that are here today will be here tomorrow, won't they? The electronic world, however, has brought home the importance of preserving information. Who has not had the unpleasant experience of learning that their box of 5 1/4-in. floppy diskettes are no fit for their new 3 1/2-in. floppy drive? Or that the documents created with their old word processing application are no longer viewable with their newest one?

Obsolescence is bad enough when it impacts our personal collection of information. The scale and scope of the impact of obsolescence at the institutional level, however, are truly daunting. Who better than librarians to weigh in on this issue given the mission of the library? The answer is not a central IT department, for no central IT department has as its mission to identify, collect, organize, preserve, and provide access to information. IT departments exist to develop technical solutions to problems presented to them.

The last aspect of the library's mission we want to visit is providing access to information. Here, we consider what the user needs to access information. If it's print material, the answer is obvious: The user needs the material object itself. But in the electronic world, the user typically needs (1) the electronic object: PDF document, data set, video clip and so on, (2) a computer with appropriate peripheral equipment: high-resolution color screen, color plotter, speakers, CD drive, or DVD drive,-(3) an appropriate application: PDF viewer, raster image viewer, vector image viewer, streaming audio/video viewer, and so forth; and, certainly not the least, (4) the skills to use all the above!

In this electronic age, is there any aspect of a library's mission that does not require a high degree of skill with technology? Consider that all we have touched on so far are those aspects of librarianship that one might consider traditional: identifying, collecting, organizing, preserving, and providing access to information. If we were to consider nothing else, there is already sufficient justification for locating an IT unit with the library. To stop here, however, would ignore the most important change the electronic revolution has wrought in how users interact with information. The manifestation of this change is the World Wide Web.

No one need bother with the full name any more; it's enough for anyone to simply say "the Web" to make his or her idea clear. Who hasn't seen the Web? We buy books on the Web; we buy cars on the Web; we look for jobs, and job candidates, on the Web. Indeed, how many of us have a personal Web page? We display our résumés, pictures of our children and pets, and latest backyard projects on the Web. All of which, by the way, is why using a search engine can be so frustrating these days: There is a lot of detritus on the Web. (You need a librarian!)

What is most significant about the Web is that we do not simply use it to seek information; we use it to create new islands of information. While some might argue that personal pages don't qualify as "information," it certainly is true that scholars, research groups, departments, colleges, and universities are all now in the business of making significant collections of valuable information available through the Web. We don't just *access* the Web; we *are building* the World Wide Web. Today, librarians find they are responsible not just for providing access to licensed, commercially supported information repositories. Increasingly, they support navigating through and searching across the entire Web, including individual research groups' Web sites along with those of commercial entities. Users don't make or understand the distinction.

Finding, utilizing, and now creating information are all required skills for today's students and scholars. Assisting with the first two skills has traditionally been the library's responsibility. Shouldn't the last be as well? Evolving technology has brought rich opportunities for libraries to create new information spaces. An information technology unit in a library supports this creation not only by helping to strengthen staff skills but also by building and maintaining the technical infrastructure that allows a digital library to focus on its users and the collections and services they require. In other words, having a specialized IT unit allows the library's other units to do what they do best.

Up to this point we have looked at the library's mission and how that mission includes the responsibility for electronic information. We have also looked at how the electronic revolution has fundamentally changed everyone's behavior, bringing everyone into the circle of creating information and making it available to others. We have argued that the tight integration of the traditional and new activities supports the idea that strong IT skills are needed within the institution of the library.

2.   SOFTWARE ENGINEERING IN A LIBRARY

We are now going to switch gears and look at software engineering, how it has evolved over the past decade or so and, as a consequence, how now, more than ever, it makes sense to consider placing an IT shop within the library. Why should a library be involved in software engineering? There is no alternative in the digital arena, where libraries' needs often outpace commercial products. The Cornell Library Gateway (described in Ch. 3) was a software engineering project in which the Mann Library built the first entrance to its digital library. In the early 1990s, faculty and students required seamless connections to databases, but no existing product met this need. Since then, projects such as the USDA Economics and Statistics System and CUGIR (see Chs. 2 and 5) have required software development. Even when a library can purchase technology for fundamental applications, technical expertise is needed to install products and adapt them to local requirements. For example, implementing a library management package in a complex environment can require high levels of systems knowledge, skill, and creativity.

First, it needs to be noted that no single chapter can do justice to the history of software design. Entire books have been written that focus on much narrower topics than what is about to be covered here in a few pages. Nonetheless, it is worth a few minutes to look at the history of software engineering with an eye as to how today's software development environment is a good match for the library.

It was only about 20 years ago that mainframe computers dominated the computing landscape. These monsters were incredibly expensive to own and operate. In fact, when factoring all the costs of software development, the most expensive component was the computer itself; the cost of programming staff was relatively insignificant. Compounding this cost model was the fact that the programming tools were very primitive: Resulting software was prone to errors and hard to maintain. Adding new features was often cost-prohibitive.

By the early 1980s, minicomputers were beginning to appear on the scene. Computing became much more affordable and hence pervasive. The spread of minicomputers created a demand for new software applications that quickly outstripped the ability of the supply of available programmers. As computing hardware costs plummeted in relation to the cost of staff programming time, the recognition of the need to improve the overall efficiency of programmers became paramount. New software tools began to appear. The new tools allowed for more efficient development of more complex programs. As the hardware improved, graphical user interfaces (GUIs), became the expected way to interact with computers. The GUIs, in turn, placed much greater demands on the hardware as well as on the programmers who designed the GUIs. Even more powerful programming tools appeared.

This phase of rapid hardware and software tool evolution also saw the emergence of many ideas for managing the software development process: managing everything from how programmers should interact with clients in drafting project requirements to writing user documentation. Programmers' tools matured to where the tools were writing some portion of the code automatically as well as emitting documentation to manage requirements drafting! Up to this point, the process of software creation was, even with these new tools, an ever-increasingly complex process. This is exactly what one would expect: If application B is more complex than application A, then the development of B will be more complex than A. But then came the microcomputer and, even more importantly, the Internet.

Microcomputers and the Internet have introduced *component-driven* software development, which is marked by two features: (1) ready-to-use, off-the-shelf software components and (2) widely accepted open standards for how these components interact with each other. It seems hard to believe now, but only a dozen or so years ago no computer manufacturer embraced open standards. In fact, every company offered its own proprietary alternative to IP, the basic Internet Protocol all computers use today. Open standards, in particular the Internet, clearly demonstrated the advantages of allowing computers to interact and exchange information, which hastened the move to component-driven development.

Before the Internet, there was little incentive to make one computer application interact with other applications. In fact, there were often competitive advantages to keep them from interacting. But the Internet changed everything. Well, that and the fact that, as an industry, software development has somewhat "caught up" with demand. That is to say, programming tools are now very mature and while money is still to be made in creating new tools, by and large, what was perhaps a juvenile industry has settled into contented adulthood. The same can be said of the database industry and many other areas of the software industry that were hot spots for investors just a few years ago. So what's hot today? Components.

What I need today to build my new Web site is a search engine *component* that will extract and collate information from all the database *components* that now store information on my many departmental Web sites. And, while I'm at it, it would be nice to offer a calendar *component* that could automatically feed updates to my e-mail-based current awareness *component*. If that last sentence didn't make too much sense, try replacing the word "component" with the word "application." The significant difference is that an application, on the one hand, is a complete standalone package that provides all the features and functionality needed to, well, stand alone—to operate in complete autonomy. A component, on the other hand, will rely on other components to provide complementary features and functions: A database component might provide the core database functions of storing and retrieving information and not provide any user interface to speak of, instead relying on an external search engine component, a Web server component, and a Web browser to complete the interface.

What is important is that that same database component can be joined with any number of search engines, Web servers, and browsers to provide very different interface options. It's like designing a house: Look at a catalog of windows, doors, kitchen cupboards; choose those components that suit your tastes and needs; and collaborate with an architect to integrate all the pieces into something that works for you. Well, that's the idea. We aren't all the way there with designing systems, but the art of software engineering is getting mighty close.

We should consider some other interesting aspects to component-driven software development that are relevant to locating an IT shop in a library. First, there is the pace of development: It's fast. In fact, a new lightweight methodology called agile programming has arisen to support this speedy development process. Agile programming holds that the development cycle should consist of small, incremental changes by programmers with immediate feedback from the clients. Here is the popular analogy: Agile programming compared to more traditional methodologies is like driving a car fast compared to driving a car slowly. When you drive slowly, you have plenty of time to react to changes in the road and coarse corrections don't get you into trouble—you're going slowly, you have time to correct your mistakes. When driving fast, however, you must react quickly to every change and you must make small, precise adjustments. Agile programming is like driving fast: The programmer must get frequent feedback from the client with only incremental changes in between. Not surprisingly, the closer the relationship between programmer and client, the better agile development works—the feedback loop between programmer and client allows for immediate response to change, which results in quick, immediate corrections. (This approach is also called extreme programming, and you'll find more details about it in Ch. 8.)

Though at first blush it might seem counter intuitive, given what was just said about fast driving and all, dealing with changes to software specifications is actually easier with component-driven development than more traditional methods. This is true for two reasons. First, as we've just seen, the feedback loop is optimized for quick, small changes. And second, the very nature of component technology makes alterations relatively easy (or at least a lot easier than more traditional software development methodologies). First, because we are plugging together well-understood, mature components, there are few surprises; it is easier to draft accurate requirements documents that lay functionality out ahead of time. Second, we have well-understood interfaces for each component; tweaking a particular component to effect small changes (again, in a very predictable manner) is easy. And finally, if significant change is needed, we have the option of replacing entire components with others that might offer the needed functionality.

With all that review of software development behind us, we are now at a point where we can appreciate today's software developer. He or she is someone who has been freed from the technical concerns of low-level details: No programmer today worries about how best to implement a store-and-retrieve data archive; we simply pick and choose from the many efficient, robust database offerings. Programmers today do not fret about implementing a proprietary network technology so two computers can talk to each other; either our existing database/search engine/whatever already has networking built-in or we can find an add-on component to provide that functionality.

What today's programmers *do* concern themselves with is how to glue together all the components to build a system that meets the user's requirements. The collective focus has shifted from "How do I create the basic technology?" to "How do I leverage these components to meet your needs?"

All this is not to say that today's programmers are any less skilled or competent than yesterday's. What it does say is that their perspective has shifted to be much more closely aligned with their users.

3. OPERATIONS AND DEVELOPMENT

Mann's staff and users view the information technology services unit as highly successful. While it's nice to think it is because we are a smart bunch and know what we are doing, no doubt a lot of credit goes to the fact that it just makes sense, for all we've said above, to locate an IT unit in a library. To be sure, our timing did fit the historical timeline of software development we have reviewed: In the late 1980s and early 1990s, the focus of ITS was on desktop support of the rapidly increasing numbers of microcomputers the library acquired. Looking back, the failures we suffered (yes, we have had a few failures) were early in our lifecycle and did involve traditional programming methodologies. And, our most successful projects have involved component-driven development. So, what is it ITS does, and how do we do it?

The information technology services unit is a staff of nine persons. While we think of ourselves as one, we are really comprised of two subunits: operations and development. The operations group is responsible for the day-to-day running of all desktop machines and our production servers. The Mann Library has approximately 100 public access microcomputers, machines that are out and available for the public. The exact number is in flux as we are now living in temporary quarters while our main building is under renovation. We also have approximately the same number of staff computers, machines that are located in private offices or are behind a service desk. ITS operations has one person dedicated to servicing the public access machines and another person dedicated to servicing staff computers.

There is obviously considerable overlap in functionality across the public access and staff microcomputers. Thus, it is easy for the two people responsible for these two collections to back each other up. They do, however, have areas of specialization. This is particularly true of the staff support person, who is responsible for training staff on the use of their desktop machine and installed applications. Our staff person has also shown an aptitude for software development, so we have provided for him or her to dedicate a portion of his or her time to that. Several in-house applications, including a time/leave management program, are the result of this effort (and another success for component-driven development!).

Operations is also charged with administering our production servers. ITS operates several campus and national Web-based services (the USDA system and CUGIR, for example) that run on Linux, as opposed to Windows, servers. Linux is our preferred development platform for building these Web services, and, again, because our focus is component-driven, these applications easily interact with all non-Linux (e.g., Windows and Macintosh) systems. Operations has a third person who is responsible for administering our servers. This person also assists with administering our software development servers, managing a total of approximately 40 servers.

At different times, operations has employed what we refer to as a maintenance programmer, someone who does not develop new applications but is responsible for making those day-to-day tweaks and updates necessary to keeping everything running smoothly.

And finally, overseeing all this effort is our operations manager. While that is the job title, in fact, this person does much more than just manage operations staff. This person is also a key liaison with other campus units and national organizations that interact with our Web-based services.

ITS began life in the mid-1980s entirely focused on the maintenance of a small number of desktop machines. It was only in the early 1990s with the Mann Library Gateway (now the Cornell Library Gateway) that ITS took on actual full-blown software development initiatives and began to build what is now our development group. Today, the ITS development group consists of four full-time programmer/analysts. Typically, at any given time, the development group also employs one person on grant-funded development. And, at different times during the academic year, the group might also employ one or more student programmers.

With this number of developers, you are no doubt wondering what scale of development we undertake. In fact, we tend to stick to smaller projects. First, most proposals that come to us are, indeed, of a small scale. Second, larger projects that do come our way typically break down into one large piece that can be accomplished with an appropriate component (typically, an off-the-shelf database) and one or more smaller pieces that we can tackle. Though we do not have any hard and fast guidelines as to what we will pass up or take on, as rule of thumb we try to stay inside a 3×3 box: We do what can be done by no more than three programmers working for three months.

Why 3×3? Again, agile rapid development is key. If something takes significantly longer than three months, by the time you get the product out the door, it is in danger of being obsolete. If the project requires more than three programmers, the overhead of project management scales too steeply for an organization our size. Keeping projects to one or two programmers allows project management to remain much more informal yet effective. We do stretch the box in different directions. For example, we frequently take on 1×6 projects: one programmer for six months. We also find 2×6 manageable. But 5×2? No way.

Keep in mind that the 3×3 paradigm does not limit you to trivial projects when you employ component-driven development. The paradigm does, however, keep your development team keenly focused on deploying appropriate components. For example, we have used MySQL, an Open Source relational database toolkit, in a number of projects. MySQL is a very flexible database system that we have found fits well in many projects we have undertaken. That the software is Open Source means we have access to the source code, which in turn means that customization of the toolkit is entirely within our control. MySQL works well with other technologies we employ such as the Web scripting language PHP, another product of the Open Source community. PHP is an easy-to-use scripting language that simplifies the use of MySQL through the Web: Adding new records and searching for and extracting data from an MySQL database via a Web browser are easy with PHP. Over time, we have developed a level of competence with a suite of tools such as MySQL and PHP that work well together, match our development style, and are consistent with the requirements of our projects.

Finally, we are careful to anticipate the need for new programming skills to match ever-evolving software. For example, many of our projects require some sort of ability to search for content within a Web site. Whether we continue to employ a familiar search engine or tackle the integration of some new search technology is a decision that must be made not only based on expediency but also based on long-term viability of our skill set. The decision to go with known technology for expediency's sake versus spending extra time learning a new technology is not the sort of decision that lends itself to quick rules of thumb. Each such decision is on a case-by-case basis. Deciding when to migrate typically comes down to weighing the urgency of the project at hand against the gains of a new technology. About all we can offer by way of advice for making these decisions is to carefully consider the risks associated with both options and to remember that, with experience, your IT shop will get better at making the right choice.

We now need to look at how our project teams are staffed and administered. As you will see, this naturally leads into a discussion of the scope of involvement of ITS and how over the years ITS has shifted from what might be called a *back-office* operation to where today ITS is seen as a library *service*. We should cover project staffing before we jump into the scope of involvement, but to begin that conversation, we will first look at those early years of ITS and its back-office configuration.

4. BEHIND THE SCENES

In years past, most of the projects that ITS undertook could be described as back-office, which is to say ITS clientele were the librarians, not the patrons of the library. For example, in the mid-1990s ITS developed a software package that managed the recordkeeping for interlibrary loans of books and other materials. Clearly, this system ultimately benefited patrons who requested the material, but it was the librarians who used the system day to day. Until very recently, in fact, the S in ITS stood for Section rather than Services, stressing the fact that we did not have a public face; we were not a services unit. Even when an ITS project did directly touch end users, the project itself was still viewed as a *library* project, not an *ITS* project. The upshot of this is that library project teams, regardless of the IT requirements, are led by librarians from one of the services units in the library rather than someone from ITS. This style of project management is a good thing.

Why is it good? Because from project initiation through completion, the focus is solidly on the needs of the client. Think about this for a minute. Have you ever been involved in a project where you or others on your staff felt the IT staff did not understand or appreciate your concerns? It would not be a surprise if you answered "yes," as this is one of the top complaints with IT projects: "We tried to tell them that wouldn't work." "We've been asking for this from the beginning, but they keep telling us we don't need it." "They just don't listen to us." Sound familiar?

Two issues are at the root of those complaints: distance between the IT staff and the rest of the project team, and language. Let's look at the distance issue first. Distance here refers not only to the physical distance between an IT unit and the rest of the project team, but to the authoritative distance as well. A separate IT unit, distinct from the library, that reports to a different administrative unit will naturally have a perspective unique from the library: What is considered important, what constitutes sufficient and necessary, indeed, what ultimately constitutes success can be very different from what the library project team sees for each of these facets.

The autonomy of IT units seems to bestow on IT staff, if only implicitly, a perspective of *we know best*: "We are the IT unit; we know IT; this is an IT problem; we have seen problems like this in the past; we know how to solve it; we know best." Not that they ever claim to have actually *solved* the same problem. That is a critical point, because had they actually solved the same exact problem there would be no need to develop new software. What the IT staff *believes* it sees is a familiar problem and what they conclude is that they know the solution: They have a hammer and everything looks like a nail.

Our experience at Mann is that locating the IT unit within the library and involving IT staff in the daily life of the library—some of our IT staff have regularly scheduled hours at the reference desk—provides the IT unit with a perspective much more in line with library priorities. Reducing the physical distance seems to be critical, but making IT staff a part of library life is also essential. You might say we've bonded.

Another important, though subtle, aspect to locating the IT unit within the library is that ITS staff now have a *perspective*. We do not view ourselves simply as generic information technologists; we are, in some sense, librarians. Our projects have a particular focus; our skill sets have a particular focus; we have a focus. Not everything looks like a nail for us to hammer. We report to an administration that does not measure success in terms of the technology (such as in lines of code written), but rather in terms of customer satisfaction. We are able to more easily differentiate things we know something about from things we don't know about, and thus are better prepared to ask appropriate questions during the early design phase of projects. We don't hear, "You aren't listening to us" very often.

Many of the projects ITS undertakes to this day can still be considered back-office. We continue to configure our project teams with a mix of appropriate nontechnical and ITS staff and to designate a nontechnical lead for the projects. As we have described here, this approach has worked well over the years, and it continues to work to this day. But recently, the S in ITS has changed from an abbreviation for Section to Services. ITS has grown a public face. We now find ourselves taking on more projects that involve working directly with faculty and researchers of the colleges our library serves.

5. A FRONTLINE SERVICE

We began this chapter with a review of the mission of the library in terms of the involvement of technology and how technology has changed or, perhaps more accurately, has evolved the way that the mission is accomplished. In particular, we looked at how the Web has become not just the place where we look for information, but is increasingly the place where we manage our own collections of information. It is this revolution in online information management that has brought new customers knocking on the door of ITS.

From the perspective of faculty and researchers, the projects in which we collaborate do not look like library projects; from our perspective, however, they are almost one and the same with what we have always done. As an example, we have been working recently with a faculty member to build an online database of diseased-plant images. The images highlight the causative disease agents. Database users will be able to search on either the scientific or common name of the plants or causative agents in the database as well as other information associated with the images such as location on plant of infection, date of photograph, and so on.

One problem that confronted us in building this database was that the textual information was to be drawn from 3 × 5 cards boxed with each photographic negative. In most cases, the cards were as old as the negatives, with many dating back to the mid-1900s. The plan was to hire students to key in the card data, as scanning and OCR proved to be too problematic. Keying wasn't the main issue, however. The more significant problem was that obsolete terminology was contained on the majority of the cards. Scientific nomenclature has changed significantly in the past 40 or 50 years, particularly in the field of fungi. Translating from old to current terminology was seen as beyond the technical skills of students. Our solution was not to translate, but to simply incorporate the obsolete terminology in the database and use a separate thesaurus that matched old terms to new as an external translation service. This has the advantage of allowing us to leverage the thesaurus for other databases and projects that require a similar translation service.

As you can see, we have applied a very library-centric solution to a project that at least initially from the perspective of the researcher was not so library-like. Just to finish this example, we are now working to expand the descriptive nature of the thesaurus, making it into something like an ontology for plant diseases that will also specify common insect vectors of the diseases. We will then be able to link users to disparate resources in ways unanticipated by the creators of those resources. For example, a searcher working with the diseased-plant database can be prompted for relevant images of insect vectors drawn from a completely separate database. The linking of the two databases will happen through the thesaurus/ontology without any effort on the part of either the creator of the diseased-plant database or the insect images database.

In building and expanding the database of diseased-plant images, we have built channels of communication between content areas. In this new role of providing IT services to the greater community, our biggest challenge is to establish such channels between what are now isolated islands of information—the legion of Web sites created by individual researchers, research groups, and departments within the colleges we serve. Our perspective as part of the library that serves these colleges provides a substantial advantage over any outside or centralized IT unit.

As we have seen so far, locating the IT unit in a library certainly has many advantages. Up to this point our discussion has focused on project team composition and scope of activity and the effects these facets have had on ITS. We will now take a look at the reverse: the effects an in-house IT unit has on nontechnical library staff. This reverse look also brings us to that second issue, along with distance, we wanted to review: language.

6. TALKING TO EACH OTHER

Consider for a moment the process of building a new home. First, you will want to consult with an architect who will talk to you about your lifestyle and how you expect the new home to meet your needs. After learning a bit about you, the architect will begin to sketch some ideas on paper, or perhaps share a portfolio of homes and interiors with you to get you thinking about some options. You will talk about foundation siting, room placement, window and door styles, utilities, kitchen layout, and so forth. In all this discussion, the architect will no doubt introduce you to innovations in home design of which you are not aware. But what is essential to realize is that even though some innovations might be completely new, the concepts will probably be familiar. Being able to control the settings of all lights from a single point so as to enable one of a multiple set of "moods" might be new to you, but the idea of dimming lights is certainly not new. Instant, on demand hot water might be new, but hot water itself isn't. What we are getting at here is that you and the architect share the language of home design, or enough of that language, to make communication work.

In the case of home design, language works because the rate of innovation in home design—and, hence, the language that describes it—is slow enough that we can keep up. And our everyday experience with doors, windows, lights, and hot water makes this language relevant.

Contrast this interaction between you and your building architect to the experience of working with a software designer. Things begin much the same: You have an initial conversation about what your needs are, but once the process shifts to sketches on paper of what an interface might look like, or to reviewing similar applications, the comparison with the building architect begins to differ significantly. Terms like "three-tier client server" replace "full basement," and "fast, wide SCSI" replaces "wall-to-wall carpeting." Clearly, there is a disconnect.

This breakdown in communication results in frustration, mistrust, and a sense of loss of empowerment for nontechnical staff, which in turn results in frustration and mistrust for IT staff. Frustration on both sides makes for less conversation, not more, which in turn leads to more frustration.

Over the years, many software development methodologies have come into and gone out of favor—most have been designed in response to this problem with communication. What has usually been seen as the cure or fix is an elaborate, formal set of documents to be drafted and signed by all parties around the table. The differences among the methodologies have mostly to do with the details of how the documents are drafted and how, throughout the project cycle, you continually get people to review those documents and renew their faith in the objectives. While a certain amount of formality is good, it remains true that we build our homes with a lot less overhead than we build software applications with.

The reason language is not a problem when designing a new home is that we live in houses—or apartments, or whatever—that have windows, doors, light switches, and hot water. Older windows are no doubt less energy-efficient than the newest models, but nonetheless, a window is a window.

Our contact and interaction with technology are not quite the same. To be sure, we certainly interact with technology to a much greater extent that we did just a few years ago, and to that extent, our comfort with the language of technology has improved. Even so, talking about the pros and cons of USB v2 versus IEEE 1394 isn't the same as comparing casement versus double-hung sash windows.

Resolving the language problem takes time, and lots of it. You cannot resolve this problem by stretching project team meetings from one to two hours. What you must do is rethink how IT staff and nontechnical staff interact when they are not sitting in team meetings. Again, the solution is to locate the IT staff within the library and to integrate IT staff into the life of the library. Once you do this, conversation will flow. It will be casual, nonthreatening conversation over coffee or at the desk of a staff person. It will be conversation about collection priorities, undergraduate instruction, Internet searching strategies, and anything but USB v2 versus IEEE 1394. But at some point in time when the conversation does turn to USBv2 versus IEEE 1394 and why the new desktop machines came with one or the other, it will be a friendly, nonconfrontational conversation. And afterward, and this is most important, library staff will possess a confidence about technology they did not have before the IT unit came to the library.

7. GROW YOUR OWN

All right, you are convinced. You are going to grow an IT unit in your library. How do you go about it?

You would probably prefer to first hire the person who will eventually become the head of your new IT unit and let him or her worry about growing the rest of the group. The reality is, however, you will not convince whoever oversees your budget of the need to hire a manager before there is anyone who needs to be managed. But you could begin by identifying the need to review your operation with an eye toward lowering overall costs by bringing in-house certain technical operations. You need to identify someone locally whom you can talk to, who understands the big picture of where you are headed, and whom you trust. You should try to establish a formal relationship with this person by hiring him or her to do a review of your organization and make a recommendation as to the benefits of moving, for a starter, desktop services in-house.

So now you can hire your first technician. Look for someone who can work with staff one-on-one for training in the use of office packages, desktop publishing, and any other special library-centric applications. If this person can create simple Web sites for internal use (tracking staff desk hours, regulations for the public on computer use, etc.), all the better. Repair of hardware is not what you are after. The ability to swap components such as mice, keyboards, monitors, and even CD drives and hard disks is what you need.

Take your time in finding this first person. Don't hire someone just because he or she is a whiz with computers. You are after interpersonal skills as much as technical skills. Involve as many staff as possible in selecting this first person to ensure a compatibility of personalities.

Did you get someone who has a modicum of programming skills? If so, spend time talking to him about what he knows and what he can do. No doubt out of this conversation will come an idea for how to improve some aspect of your organization's daily life. Resist, however, the impulse to turn this idea into a project unless you are completely, and we mean completely, comfortable with the total failure of that project. In other words, what you want to attempt for a first project cannot be critical to the operation of your organization and should not cost any significant amount of money or time. Build a database of staff and emergency phone numbers. Build a database of local policy documents. These projects should be completely doable in 40 hours of your technician's time (that is, time spent on the project itself, which might actually translate to more than one week's worth of calendar time).

What you want to get under your belt with these first projects is some experience with designing a project, running a project, overseeing technical staff, and, not least of all, what it feels like to succeed. To help you do all this, you are going to rely on that consultant we talked about in the beginning of this section. Hiring someone on a consultancy basis has the advantage of allowing her to maintain an objective perspective on what you are doing: You are paying that consultant to give you unvarnished advice—that is what you need to insist on getting.

Once you have been around the block with a few small projects, you will be ready to tackle something more substantial. No doubt you will have come up with some ideas for bigger projects during the course of identifying the small projects you did undertake. You still have your consultant, right? You need objective advice now as to the sensibility of tackling a larger project. For this larger project, something that will perhaps take 160 to 320 hours, you will want to contract with a programmer. Do not contract with your consultant to do the work, but retain your consultant to provide you with objective advice on the progress of this other programmer.

Essentially, what we are trying to do here is hire trusted outside help on a consulting basis until the level of sustained activity necessitates hiring full-time staff. Working with outside contractors also reduces your risk, as you can replace contracted help much more easily and frequently than full-time staff. You want to hire one person to do the work while retaining your now long-time consultant to assist with project management while your own skills and confidence to manage projects grow. You might contract with a software engineer or programmer to work full-time for the duration of the project, but you will probably need your consultant's time at the rate of a few hours per week to attend project meetings and advise you one-on-one.

Again, you should be prepared to fail, as you almost certainly will with at least one project. Don't let this deter you; just make sure you are prepared for it. Contingency planning should be an integral part of your planning for any project. One indicator of the worth of your consultant will be how seriously she approaches the need for contingency planning.

All right, it has now been a few years since you began building your in-house IT expertise. Your original technician has moved on, you've rehired, perhaps more than once, for this position, and you now have someone who regularly maintains several small Web sites you operate and who oversees all aspects of training your staff. Your consultant is now overseeing two projects you have underway simultaneously, each of a duration of about 200 hours. Your nontechnical staff now eagerly come to you on a regular basis with ideas for new projects. The word of success and the utility of projects you have completed spread, and you find yourself consulting with people outside your immediate organization on projects they hope to undertake. You might consider at this point hiring a full-time programmer. Perhaps one of the contract programmers you have worked with on previous projects seems like a good fit and is interested in your organization. As a first hire, that would be ideal. You want to be extremely careful with your first hire, as you need to establish the right culture within your fledgling IT shop. Hopefully, once you have gone through the steps suggested above, you will know the right person when you meet him or her. You are better off not hiring unless you are absolutely sure. Take your time.

Once you bring someone in full-time, remember to integrate that person into the full life of your organization even if it means he is spending 4 to 6 hours a week on nontechnical work. Interest in dividing one's time between technical and nontechnical work should be one metric you use in identifying the right person.

At this phase of growth of your IT shop, you can probably still get away with you, a nontechnical administrator, overseeing the IT shop operations, given you still have an outside consultant upon whom you can rely. But once you add a second programmer, you should consider elevating one or the other to supervisory status. The overall size of your operations is such that no doubt this supervisor can split her time between supervising the one or two other IT staff members and developing software. Once you add a third or fourth person, however, your supervisor will need to switch to full-time supervision. Unless your IT shop grows to 20 or more programmers, this point of moving someone to full-time supervision should be the only "knee" you will ever hit in your productivity chart. A knee is that point where the addition of staff does not translate into an equivalent increase in productivity; your first programmer gave you 100% in programming time; your second gave you perhaps 80%, with 20% devoted to supervision; the third person added 100% programming, but the second person shifted from 20% supervision to 100%, a net gain of only 20%. Adding a fourth person, however, adds another 100% in programming effort—you are past the knee.

Our programming staff at the Mann Library now totals five full-time programmer/analysts—staff who can take on any role in a software project from leading a project team as analyst to providing software coding expertise. On occasion, we hire a sixth or seventh programmer to staff particular projects, but these hires are essentially contract hires. Given the size of our institution and the nature of the projects we undertake, we have no doubt reached the limits of our growth. Our quick how-to guide here stopped a bit short of the size of Mann's ITS, but we hope you see that the only difference between where we stopped with the guide and ITS is a few full-time hires.

You may doubt that adequate financial resources could be found for growing your own ITS. Remember, though, that the Mann Library's ITS began two decades ago with one person. Since then, the library's overall staff size has not grown. Instead, we have made decisions to reallocate our budget and personnel—decisions that have sometimes been difficult. We have also taken advantage of our staff's strengths and sought external funding. It's important to note, though, that any external funding has been for projects that further the library's mission with results that can be mainstreamed.

We have covered a lot of ground in this chapter. We began with the mission of the library, expressed in terms that conceivably could have been used at the time of Alexandria, yet that fit today's electronic milieu. From there, we looked at how the revolution in electronic information, particularly the virtual landscape that houses the new information, has extended the role of the library in academic life. We considered the role of IT staff not just as an adjunct to the library, but also as a worthy addition to be integrated into the life of a modern library. And we concluded with a brief how-to on taking those first steps in building an in-house IT unit comparable to the Mann Library's ITS unit. The next chapters provide details about managing software engineering projects, evaluating the results, and exploring new directions.

7

Project Management and Implementation

Holly L. Mistlebauer
Cornell University, Ithaca, New York, U.S.A.

Projects begin with bright people and good intentions and often end with cost and schedule overruns. A troubled project can still succeed if management recognizes problems and takes action.

- Common project pitfalls:
    - "Big-bang" implementation
    - IT staff selling a library on a project (rather than the other way around)
    - Lack of commitment from senior management
    - Communicating and documenting inadequately
    - Lacking necessary skills or proper teamwork
    - Underestimating technical difficulty
    - Using inappropriate technology
    - Rushing into programming too soon
    - Testing inadequately
    - Allowing scope to "creep"
    - Omitting careful methodology and standards to "save time"

- Strategies for success:
  - Treat library staff and patrons as customers
  - Develop written requirements
  - Conduct frequent reviews
  - Attend to morale of IT staff
  - Underpromise and overdeliver
  - Resist the lure of new technology
  - Use a project management methodology
  - Know how the project will be mainstreamed after completion

1. INTRODUCTION

Every library is engaged in multiple projects at any given time. This is the nature of our business. We identify something that needs to be and we go about doing it. The success of a project depends greatly on how the project is initiated, staffed, managed, implemented, and maintained. Chapter 5 details the composition and responsibilities of teams; this chapter provides an overview of the characteristics of projects. The goal of the chapter is to assist libraries with their projects. The focus here is on technical projects, but the basic concepts apply to nontechnical efforts as well.

2. WHAT ARE PROJECTS?

The Project Management Institute (PMI) defines a project as "a temporary endeavor undertaken to create a unique product or service" [1]. In simpler terms, a project brings about some type of change. Projects are everywhere around us, and we all do them. We are often involved in several at the same time. Some of these projects are big, while others are small. For example, an individual may be remodeling the kitchen, weeding the library's collection, shopping for a new car, cleaning out the office, and implementing a new library management system—all at the same time!

What do all projects have in common? They share the following characteristics:

1. All have a planned output [2].
2. All involve nonrepetitive tasks [2].
3. All use multiple resources, human and nonhuman [3].
4. All have a plan of attack, which is often called a "project lifecycle."
5. All appear to start with bright people and good intentions.
6. All seem to suffer from cost and schedule overruns.

There is a great deal of argument in the project management profession as to whether projects with a software development component are different from other types of projects. Some argue that they are identical, while others say almost. What are the main differences between projects with a software development component and those without? More time is spent deciding what to do when a project involves technology than when it does not [4]. It is not easy to estimate the effort needed for a project that has a large software component [5]. Another difference is that it is more difficult to know when the project is done with a software project than with other types of projects [6]. The main difference, however, is that technology is very unpredictable. It is perhaps more unpredictable than any other factor impacting a project. This difference results in software projects suffering from massive overruns and often not delivering what was promised or expected. A recent survey by The Boston Consulting Group (BCG) found that slightly more than two fifths of all software projects are either late, over budget, or both [7]. This same BCG survey found that only 33% of all software projects were viewed as having positive outcomes and that only 60% of the organizations felt that the effort was worth the end result [7]. This is not good news! It is clear that most software projects, and many other projects, suffer greatly from a variety of ailments. The point of this chapter is to explain some of the pitfalls and discuss how to avoid them.

3. PROJECT IDENTIFICATION

The first step to initiating a project is an idea. Most projects start in a very informal manner. Perhaps you had patrons complain about some aspect of library service, or perhaps you have read an article about what another organization is doing. After the initial seed is planted, the idea is usually fine-tuned as it is further discussed with individuals or groups. How does the idea blossom into a project?—when someone with the power to make it happen says, "Let's do it." The earlier a project is identified as such, the more successful the project will be. If an idea is expanded upon and turned into an objective without following proper project management procedures, you may not gather the necessary information from important sources. It is critical that the correct players, including the information technology staff, be involved as soon as possible.

4. PROJECT TEAM FORMATION

The key decision in forming a project team is who should lead it. In other words, who should be the project manager? The best person for the job is not necessarily the best programmer or the best librarian. It is important to look for specific skills that will aid in the project's success. The person selected needs to have a vision, plus the skills to implement that vision. The old joke is that great project managers are born, not made. Look for an individual with excellent organizational skills and a good sense of humor. The project manager will also need to be a people person and have a basic understanding of the underlying technology.

The next step is to identify appropriate team members. Make sure that an individual on the project team represents all impacted areas (see Ch. 5 for more about this). It is also important to ensure that those individuals who will continue after implementation are involved in some way. In a library setting, human resource management will be the biggest headache. Project team members will most likely have a full-time job in addition to being on the project team. This means that the time the project team member is willing and able to spend on the project will be limited. How can this be avoided? Perhaps have the key players reassigned to a full-time position on the project team, while filling in behind them with temporary employees or students from a nearby library school. If the project team members do not have the time to work on the project, it will not be successful. It is necessary to be highly creative in gathering the necessary resources, especially when working in a nonprofit environment. If the project is implementing a new software package and project team members do not have the skills required, hire an outside consultant who does have the skills. This will be costly, but it will definitely be worth the cost. However, do not allow this consultant to be the project manager. That would require giving away too much control. Instead, use the consultant's expertise to guide the project along the proper course. Library staff members should have the most involvement and impact on the project.

5.   WHAT IS PROJECT MANAGEMENT?

For some reason, people automatically assume that the individual in charge of a project is "managing" it. This is not necessarily true! Truly managing a project requires a unique set of skills. Some projects are successful despite the lack of good project management skills. The product may be good, but the process isn't. The organization will end up with disgruntled staff and a project that is both over budget and too late. Adequate project management will assist an organization in producing quality products in a productive manner. Just what is "project management"? "Project management is the planning, organizing, directing, and controlling of company resources for a relatively short-term objective that has been established to complete specific goals and objectives" [8]. The project manager is totally responsible for every facet of the project. Activities performed by the project manager include those described in Sections 5.1–5.9

5.1. Requirements

What is the goal of the project? What is the scope of this project? What will it do? What will it not do? The project manager does not decide the answers to these questions, but rather ensures that the requirements are documented and reviewed by all parties with a vested interest in the project. Think of generating requirements as building a house. The requirements are the foundation of the project.

5.2. Estimating and Budgeting

How long will it take to complete the project? What resources, human and nonhuman, are needed? For example, is a new piece of hardware or software necessary? It is important to document up front how much the organization will be investing in the project. This includes new hardware, software, furniture, and so forth as well as the time various employees will be investing in the project. It may be difficult to provide a precise estimate initially, so provide a figure that is "in the ballpark" instead.

5.3. Planning and Scheduling

The project manager must identify the individual tasks required to complete the project and schedule them accordingly. When scheduling, the project manager must keep in mind that some tasks are dependent on others. Timing is everything! Based on the estimate generated, it should be determined how long the project will take, given the work to be done and the staff available to do it.

5.4. Staffing

The project manager must hire or assign the right people for the right position. After the project team has been put together, the project manager must motivate the team members and resolve conflicts among them.

5.5. Coordinating

In addition to planning and scheduling the activities of the project team, the project manager must coordinate the activities with the external forces involved. This includes making sure the hardware arrives on time, the printers produce the manual in time, and so on.

5.6. Managing Change

Change in a project is unavoidable. This may be a person leaving the project team, a change in what should be delivered, or some other change. Rather than "fighting fires," establish a clear change management process. What does this mean? It means having a process for handling changes that is identified. If the scope of the project has been defined and then a new idea is presented that changes that scope, everyone with an interest in the project needs to be aware of how that change impacts the project. Will the change impact the scheduled finish date? If so, know who has the authority to say "Yes, we should do this and deliver the system later" or "No, we should wait and add this at another time."

MYLIBRARY

Holly Mistlebauer, Information Technology Section, Mann Library

1 MyLibrary Project

MyLibrary is a collection of personalized services offered to all members of the Cornell community. As of 2002, MyLibrary consists of two services: MyLinks, a collection of links used most frequently by the patron; and MyUpdates, which provides notification when items of interest are added to the Cornell University Library catalog. The future plan is to improve the two services currently offered as well as to add new services.

MyLibrary was successfully implemented during the spring semester of 2000. Although the implementation was successful, those individuals closest to the project are aware that not all aspects of the development process went as planned. The final success of the project resulted from the project team's ability to recover from problems encountered along the way and implement a quality system. As project leader for the implementation of MyLibrary, I am best qualified to share the gory details of what really happened.

The MyLibrary project was initiated when the University Librarian for Cornell formed the Personalized Electronic Services Group. This group consisted of individuals from seven different libraries on campus. Various functional areas were represented, including technical services, public services, collection development, and information technology. Each person in the group was included for a specific purpose. For example, Noni was included primarily because of her expertise in graphics and design. Tom was included because of his knowledge of MARC records. Adam had technical knowledge of our database management system, and John was our technical leader. Bob covered the patron viewpoint. You get the idea. I was chosen as project leader (or should I say "chair") because of my many years of project management experience. The team that was organized had the right skills and worked together well. We earned an A+ for project team formation.

Our charge was to implement "something" by the fall semester. Although it is never a good idea to pick a date before you know what you are doing, our plan was to make sure that "something" would be a system that could be done by the start of the fall semester. The group met every week to hash out what that something would be. It became clear to us rather quickly that we would need to keep the implementation small. We would implement MyLinks and MyUpdates without all the "bells and whistles" we had envisioned. (These "bells and whistles" included bookmark importing and exporting, look and feel customization, library announcement feature, reordering of items in a folder, plus advanced searching.) The group toyed with the idea of doing only one of the services, but decided that doing two would be more substantial. We documented what would be included in the first release and gained approval from library management. We get a B for this process, since we knew upfront that we were probably taking on too much.

     ·   I had recently completed a course in the Rational Unified Process (RUP). This is a software process developed by three project management gurus. They combined the best practices for software development into one product, RUP. Although I have used project management methodologies and software before, I was new to RUP. The programmers on this project had recently been trained in the Unified Modeling Language (UML). UML is a tool to assist project teams in clearly identifying what a system should do and then building that system. We decided that we would try using RUP and UML on this project. This decision was mostly based on enthusiasm. In hindsight, that was a terrible mistake. One should never try out an entirely new process on a large project with a tight deadline. After a month or two we scrapped that idea. We get a D for this failure, keeping in mind that I am an easy grader.

     Despite not continuing with RUP, we did benefit from the process in a big way. Let me explain. The first few steps of the Rational Unified Process (RUP) are extremely helpful in identifying what should be done, determining the risks involved, and planning the project accordingly. The very first step is to define use cases. Think of use cases as actions that will be performed by the system. For example, a patron will log in. After all the use cases have been identified, you need to determine the risks involved. The MyLibrary project team recognized that obtaining the needed data from the online catalog was critical to the project, but we were not sure how this would be done or even if it could be done. Obtaining the online catalog extract was key to the MyUpdates portion of MyLibrary. We identified several other risks, including the fact that we were using Oracle, a database management system, for the first time. We did not know how much time the learning curve would cost, how we could get Oracle to do what we wanted, and so on. After you have identified the project risks, you need to prioritize them in order of importance. Then you need to determine which of the use cases will help mitigate which of the risks. The point is to work on the portion of the project that mitigates your highest risks first. For the MyLibrary project, this meant tackling the online catalog immediately. It was critical to our project that we be able to identify records newly added to the catalog and extract all the data associated with those records. My natural inclination may not have been to start with the extract. Human nature tends to gravitate toward the easiest activities first. By starting with the online extract, we were able to come to the realization early on that it would require much more analysis than we originally thought. We also learned that we needed special processing for the online catalog extract, especially having to do with diacritics. This required developing a conversion table and coding an additional process. The use of RUP did not help us resolve this particular problem, but it did help us to recognize the problem early in the process. What if we had waited several months to start the work on the online catalog extract? We may have decided not to continue due to the online catalog extract problems. This would have resulted in two months of work thrown away. We, or should I say RUP, get an A for this aspect of the project.

As it is, the MyUpdates portion of MyLibrary did not end up being implemented the same time as MyLinks. MyUpdates just wasn't ready. The additional work required to get the online catalog extract delayed the work somewhat, but it was mostly delayed due to the programmer's being assigned to work on two projects at the same time. (That second project was ILLiad, which is also described in a sidebar for this chapter.) The MyLibrary project was taken on by the programmer while ILLiad was on an indefinite hold. Unfortunately, ILLiad became active again and was planned for implementation the same day as MyUpdates. It became necessary for one of the projects to wait, since one programmer cannot work full-time on two projects at once. MyUpdates was chosen to wait. This action was taken to ensure that both projects would be successful in the end. If we had attempted to implement both during the same timeframe, neither would have been a success. We get a D for poor staff planning and a B for quick recovery, averaging to a C.

Even though I am an experienced project leader, I still fell into the trap of biting off more than I could chew. I also failed to fully account for the Oracle learning curve. Allowing one of the programmers to be pulled in two directions at once should have been addressed sooner than it was. There is no such thing as a perfect project leader. We learn from every project we participate in. My experience assisted me in recovering from the errors made and delivering a quality project. The problem reports have only trickled in, and our statistics show that usage of MyLibrary continues to grow. As far as the patrons are concerned, we delivered an A+ product.

For more information on the MyLibrary project, please visit the MyLibrary site at http://mylibrary.cornell.edu/guest.html. Also, see our article: S. Cohen, J. Fereira, A. Horne, B. Kibbee, H. Mistlebauer, A. Smith. D-Lib Magazine 6: April 2000 (http://www.dlib.org/dlib/april00/mistlebauer.html).

5.7. Managing Risk

Most projects involve some level of risk. The risk could be the use of a new database management system, the likelihood that the environment will change during the course of the project, or something else. It is critical that all risks be identified and mitigated as soon as possible. For example, if the project will make use of a new database, it is critical that the database system is purchased, installed, and tested as the project's first step. This will assist the project team in truly understanding the impact early in the project.

5.8. Communicating

This includes preparing status reports for senior management and making sure that team members know what is expected of them. There should be no surprises! Senior management should always be aware of the current status of the project. How can they help if they do not know what is going on? By the same token, team members should know what is going on. How can they be expected to participate fully if they are not aware of the "big picture"?

5.9. Monitoring and Tracking

Having a plan is great, but it is also necessary to constantly track against it. What is tracking? It involves comparing the estimated time for a task with the time the task is actually taking. For example, if a certain activity has been estimated to take 30 hours and it is discovered that the programmer spent 40 hours on this task this week and expects to spend another 20 hours next week, the project manager needs to know. The delay in this particular activity could have a ripple effect on other activities. It may be necessary to replan the remainder of the project on occasion or to temporarily add an additional project team member.

5.10. Summary

In other words, a project manager needs to be able to walk on water. Unfortunately, perfect project managers do not exist. When project managers are unable to perform each of these skills well, projects they lead tend to suffer from a variety of problems. In other cases, the project manager refuses to delegate or doesn't have the authority needed to get the job done. It is the responsibility of the senior management to assign a qualified person to be the project manager and to give that person the support he or she needs. It is the project manager's responsibility to develop the necessary skills and to avoid the common project pitfalls. The scope of this role is highlighted in the box entitled ILLiad.

ILLIAD: IMPLEMENTING SOFTWARE OFF-THE-SHELF

Adam Smith, Cornell University Information Technologies

Many unexpected challenges were overcome to implement ILLiad, an automated system for interlibrary borrowing and lending. These challenges were unexpected because ILLiad is a commercial, off-the-shelf (COTS) software product, and our organization is accustomed to developing software in-house. As the project progressed, we learned that implementing COTS software should be approached like any other project, while paying particular attention to certain pitfalls unique to the implementation of such products.

Instead of programming, my role in the ILLiad project was to provide technical advice to the eventual end users (staff in the various interlibrary loan departments at Cornell) and act as a liaison between them and the software company. As I worked with these users, it was clear they believed that buying a COTS product meant the software would be "plug and play." Those accustomed to waiting for software to be designed and written by someone in my department saw COTS products as a way to eliminate these steps.

But as a programmer, I know very well the 80/20 rule as it describes the proportion of time devoted to a system's design and coding, respectively; the inverse proportion describes the time devoted to a system's implementation and maintenance. I quickly learned that COTS products follow much the same rules. Purchasing a COTS product does not eliminate any stages of development and implementation, but in fact adds several. The overall process, then, may be broadly defined in the following manner:

1. Gather knowledge of the problem domain, or the business rules that the system must embody. This stage includes system requirements gathering as well as a deep understanding of the domain.
2. Identify possible products, show their advantages and disadvantages, and make a recommendation.
3. Make decisions concerning tradeoffs between the costs of customization of the software versus the costs of adjusting staff workflow to the existing design of the software.
4. Request and test customizations if this option is available.
5. Plan workflow adjustments.
6. Install the product and test the software.
7. Train staff to use the product in their workflow.
8. Launch the product, troubleshoot initial use, and begin your maintenance plan.

To begin, when purchasing a COTS product, as when developing software in-house, a thorough understanding of the problem domain is the foundation of all other stages. This understanding involves not just performing requirements gathering as you would in the analysis phase of software development, but also gaining a deeper understanding of the problem domain when implementing COTS products. Unlike in-house software design, which solves problems specific to particular problem domains, the use of COTS software forces you to make difficult decisions about when to customize the software for your users and when to adjust the workflow of your users for the software. So, requirements may change or be reprioritized more significantly when implementing COTS products than when designing software in-house.

The necessity of having a deeper understanding of the problem domain becomes immediately apparent when reviewing the COTS products available and making recommendations. Your recommendations must not only account for the more or less purely technical advantages and disadvantages of the products, but they must also account for what workflow requirements each meets. The process of making your recommendations in this stage may require both you and your users to spend time installing and testing various products. This is the surest way to know to what extent each product meets your users' needs.

Once a viable product has been selected, you must decide between customizations that should be made to the software versus workflow adjustments that should be made for the software. This of course assumes that you have the option to request custom functionality from the vendor, as was the case with ILLiad.

The potential impact of these tradeoffs increases exponentially with increases in the number of end users, their varying needs, and the degree that their work is specialized. For example, if you are deciding between two very similar word processing packages for your department, your ultimate choice makes little difference as a few people learn the idiosyncrasies of the software chosen. ILLiad, however, was to be used for a very specialized purpose by many staff members and patrons in libraries and departments of varying sizes and needs. These circumstances made decisions about customization and workflow adjustment tradeoffs much more difficult.

As these decisions are made, customizations can be requested and tested, workflow can be adjusted, or both. The installation of the final product follows, then staff can be trained, the new software and workflow can be officially launched, and the job of maintaining the system can begin.

In these later stages of implementing COTS products, costs—in terms of both time and money—are more apparent. Server and possibly even workstation hardware will need to be researched, purchased, and configured. The installation and configuration of both server and workstation software will need to be tested and any problems fixed.

Be aware that as some managers believe that the decision to buy a COTS product means the system will be immediately available for use, some may also confuse the installation and configuration of the hardware and software with the official launch of the system for use by staff in their workflow. And, just as many managers forget about the time and resources needed for maintaining home-grown software, many more will assume that COTS products have no such costs.

But despite these challenges, implementing COTS products instead of designing software in-house can save significant time and money. For this reason, I believe that a deep understanding of the problem domain as well as an earnest evaluation of available COTS products should be a part of every project, even those in which it is assumed that the software will be designed in-house (and perhaps for these projects in particular). You may find a package that presents a relatively minor customization/workflow adjustment tradeoff or, at the very least, you may find the surest evidence that confirms a need to expend the resources necessary to build a custom system.

6. COMMON PROJECT PITFALLS

Projects start out for all the right reasons, but many go astray—some quickly, others slowly. Projects that are falling apart and continue on anyway are often referred to as "death march" projects. If a project suffers from one or more of the following ailments, it may be a "death march" project.

6.1. Starting a New Project with Too Many Others in the Works

A priority must be assigned to every project. Don't attempt to start another large effort if others are already in the works. The available resources will be stretched to the limit, allowing none of the projects to be successful.

6.2. Implementing with a "Big Bang"

This means that one day there isn't a system and the next day there is. Don't try to implement a large project all at once, and don't keep the project a "secret" until the last minute. As the project is developed, library staff members must be shown the system and allowed to offer input.

6.3. Trying to Do Too Much in One Release

If the project attempts to do too much at once, it probably won't succeed with any of it. It is best to provide basic functionality in the first release and add the "bells and whistles" later. The "death march" projects of the 1980s all suffered from this problem. The project bit off more than it could chew but kept going anyway. For example, one large university elected to automate all activities of the university in one large, integrated system. All activities were worked on at one time instead of focusing on one related group of activities. Project workers were designing the transcript at the same time others worked on telephone registration. Several years and $13 million later, there was very little to show for all of the effort. Project staff members recognized the error of this approach one to two years before it was officially determined to be incorrect, but the project was so visible and political that the powers that be were afraid to face the facts.

6.4. Allowing the Scope to "Creep"

Little by little the project expands and soon it has grown out of control. This is often referred to as a "runaway project"—the project keeps growing and growing until it no longer resembles the original project. The project scope needs to be clearly defined at the onset. Any changes should be evaluated and the impact to the schedule noted.

6.5. Needing to "Sell" Staff on the Idea

Too many information technology (IT) people come up with great ideas and then try to convince nontechnical employees that they need a project. This is backwards! First find out what staff need or feel the patrons need, and then make it happen. If the project manager has to work too hard to convince the staff of the worthiness of a project, perhaps it should not be done. The bottom line is that support of the staff is an absolute necessity.

6.6. Lacking Commitment from Senior Management

If the project does not have the support of someone in senior management, how will it ever get the resources needed for completion? There must be a member of senior management who is a champion for the project. If not, find out why. Perhaps the project manager has perceived the project to be more important than it is. Perhaps senior management senses that the project will not be successful, so no one wants to be associated with it. Find out!

6.7. Depending on Individuals Outside the Project Manager's Control

If the project depends on people who do not report to the project manager, the project is at outsiders' mercy. It is important to make sure that these outside individuals are committed to the project. Early on the project manager needs to find out the priority these other individuals are giving to the project. Do these individuals already have a full-time job? Is the project work going to be done with extra time the individual has? If so, the work will not get done and the project will be at risk.

6.8. Failing to Do a Cost/Benefit Analysis

Does the function in question really need to be automated? Will something be gained from this effort? Don't spend a nickel to make a dime. Instead, spend a nickel to make a dollar. Concentrate the organization's efforts on projects with the most return. No organization has the time to do everything, so projects must be selected carefully.

6.9. Ignoring the Learning Curve

This is one pitfall that organizations tend to experience again and again. If the project is using a new technology, time must be set aside for the project programmers to learn it. Learning a new technology always takes more time than anyone thinks it will or should. This is a fact of life, so plan accordingly.

6.10. Setting Unrealistic Delivery Dates

Just because senior management wants a project done by September 1 does not mean the project can be finished by then. Don't promise something that cannot be delivered. Instead, estimate the time required and present the figures to senior management. If adding people will speed up the project, it is the responsibility of senior management to do so.

6.11. Delivering the Project Late and Over Budget

If the project is already over budget and late, it won't recover on its own. Putting in 60 hours per week on a project already significantly behind is not the answer. People who are overworked not only become unhappy, but they also don't think clearly and start making mistakes. Instead, take a step back, determine what still needs to be completed, estimate the time needed, and replan the completion of the project.

6.12. Communicating Inadequately

Technical folks are often not the best communicators. There. It has been said. It is not that technical folks don't communicate; but often they don't communicate in a way that nontechnical folks can understand. If the project requirements and specifications are documented, technical and nontechnical folks are able to reach an understanding. In addition, issues and problems should be documented, as should the status of the project.

6.13. Lacking Necessary Skills

Do not just add warm bodies to a project. Instead, add warm bodies who also know what they are doing. If the project team members do not have the skills needed, either they will learn them by making many mistakes on the project or they will never learn them. Either way, the project loses.

6.14. Lacking Proper Teamwork

The days of the lone programmer are over. Software development is a job for teams. If a project has team members who "don't play well with others," there will be communication difficulties. The project manager needs to be aware of the work habits of the various team members and determine potential problem areas.

6.15. Committing Less Time Than Needed

Is this project a high priority for all of the team members? If not, one or more team members may hold up the whole show. Or, worse yet, these busy team members may do their project work but do it poorly—the result of which is not clearly seen until the project is implemented.

6.16. Providing Inadequate Training and Tools for Staff Development

Mediocre training and tools lead to mediocre systems. Part of the estimated cost of the project should include training and tool expenses. In the long run, the training and tools will cost less than the time spent trying to figure out what to do with what is available and how to correct problems after they have already occurred.

6.17. Expecting Something Other Than what was Delivered

The programmers can spend a lot of time programming and testing to produce a beautiful system that does not do what it needs to do. If the library staff do not see the system as it is developed, how can anyone know if the result will meet the needs of staff and patrons? This is the equivalent of making someone a pair of pants without having the pants fitted as the sewing progresses. The end result may be a perfect pair of pants, but they will not fit the intended wearer. Perhaps a pair of pants can be passed on to someone else, but the system is lost.

6.18. Underestimating Technical Difficulty

Don't just assume that because some other organization has already implemented a similar project, any organization will be able to do so. If an organization does not have the needed skills, it will not be able to do the work correctly or on time.

6.19. Using Inappropriate Technology

Cutting-edge technologies may not be what an organization needs. Don't fall into the trap of thinking that some technology that just came out is the answer to the organization's problems. The use of new, but inappropriate, technology has resulted in many "death march" projects. Conversely, before deciding to develop a homegrown solution, consider acquiring technology developed elsewhere. Depending on project priorities, off-the-shelf technology may be the best solution. (For an example of this, see the box entitled CUGIR.)

CUGIR: SOFTWARE DECISIONS IN PROJECT MANAGEMENT

Thomas D. Gale, McGraw-Hill Ryerson, Whitby, Ontario, Canada

As mentioned in this chapter, cost and schedule overruns are a major cause for concern in project management, and information technology is often the culprit when these overruns occur. Deciding whether to build or buy a software component can have a serious impact on project scheduling and budgeting due to the risk involved with development and purchases of software. The Cornell University Geospatial Information Repository (CUGIR) project conducted at Mann demonstrates the issue well.

1   The Project

The National Spatial Data Infrastructure (NSDA), established by the Federal Geographic Data Committee (FGDC) (http://www.fgdc.gov/nsdi/nsdi.html), is an organization dedicated to the creation, promotion, and networking of spatial data clearinghouse nodes. Each clearinghouse node hosts a repository of geospatial metadata records. The metadata records provide identification, data quality, and reference information related to particular geospatial data files as well as information on how to acquire the data files and limits on their use. The intent is to have each state have at least one clearinghouse node and to network these nodes such that users and developers of geographic information systems (GIS) can easily search for and acquire data improving knowledge and application of GIS in the United States.

Prior to 1997, New York State lacked a national spatial data infrastructure or NSDI-linked data clearinghouse node. The CUGIR project team at the Albert R. Mann Library submitted a grant proposal to fill the void by establishing a Web-based clearinghouse node and to work in close cooperation with the staff of the New York State Library (another library working to develop a GIS clearinghouse node for New York).

2   The Goals

In order to provide a system that would work well for users, we studied the existing clearinghouse nodes and the needs of our targeted users. We determined that we would need to provide three components: (1) a map-browsing interface that would allow users to click on maps of varying geographic levels to identify the metadata and data files associated with those regions; (2) a list-browsing facility that would allow users to browse for data and metadata by selecting a geographic region from a list (e.g., a list of counties) and a list of particular themes of interest to them (e.g., roads, hydrography, boundaries, etc.); and (3) a keyword and geographic search facility that would allow users to search metadata based on keywords or geographic coordinates. We wanted all three facilities to be well integrated and provide a simple, balanced interface for those relatively new to GIS as well as the advanced geospatial analyst. Further, we wanted to take advantage of the Z39.50 gateway provided by NSDI that allows users to search all NSDI clearinghouse nodes simultaneously.

3 The Problem

The primary problem was one of grant constraints. We had less than one year to complete the aforementioned interface goals as determined by our grant timeline, and we had to allocate some of our technological staff funding to hire a temporary spatial data conversion specialist to lend her expertise in the conversion and editing of GIS files that would populate our clearinghouse. Adding to the time and budget challenges was the fact that the technical lead for the project (that's me) was added to the project later and had to be brought up to speed on GIS and some of the other technologies that we would be using.

Our examination of existing clearinghouse node sites seemed to indicate that they were using one of two technologies. One option was the homegrown solution in which we would use a proprietary database software to build a Z39.50-compliant database that would house our data files and metadata files. In such a system, we could integrate custom fields with the standard required metadata fields allowing for a very flexible Web-based browsing facility when combined with common gateway interface (CGI) scripts on our Web server. We could also use the database or extracts from the database to index the metadata from our system and offer it to users and other nodes via a Z39.50 search interface. The homegrown solution would provide the utmost in flexibility and user benefit.

The alternative was to implement a software package developed specifically for NSDI clearinghouses called Isite. The software, developed by the Center for Networked Information Discovery & Retrieval (http://www.cnidr.org/), was less flexible in that it didn't provide a relational database, it was less customizable than a homegrown solution would be, and it required a login screen that was superfluous for our clearinghouse needs. However, it is a well-tested, popularly implemented indexing and searching freeware and would allow us to quickly become part of the clearinghouse node structure.

4 The Decision

In the end, we elected to go with the Isite solution rather than the homegrown solution, and we were on time and on budget. The homegrown solution did look plausible if all things went according to plan, and it looked as though we could narrowly make the timeframe and budget restrictions. However, it looked very tight, which is why we opted not to pursue it.

Given the fact that there was only one designated programmer and that he (namely, me) had just been assigned to the project, the risk of cost and time overruns seemed higher. Such overruns may have robbed the project of resources that might have better been spent on the GIS temporary programmer who would be working on resources for populating the clearinghouse node with our inaugural data.

Even using the established Isite package, we had difficulty with installation and configuration that caused the implementation process to be longer than anticipated. Further, CUGIR was not my only project, and other duties pulled me from the project more often than originally anticipated. As a result, testing was delayed and while we did make deadlines, the process wasn't as smooth and graceful as we had expected. Finally, as my understanding of (1) what was involved with the creation of a clearinghouse node and (1) what would have been involved with a custom software solution grew, it became very clear that we had made the right decision.

For more information on the CUGIR project, visit the CUGIR site at http://cugir.mannlib.cornell.edu/.

Also, see our article: P Herold, TD Gale, TP Turner. Issues in Sci and Tech Librarianship 21: Winter 1999 (*http://www.library.ucsb.edu/istl/99-winter/article2.html*).

6.20. Lacking Documentation

If the project manager does not document what needs to be done, how will he or she ever know that the project is on the right track? The project manager also needs to document what was actually done, what issues arose, what decisions were made, and so on. Project participants often think that details of a project will be etched on their brains forever, but experience shows that these details become a distant memory as soon as another project is started. Also, if a team member leaves the organization, he or she will take the information away if it is not documented.

6.21. Documenting Requirements Poorly

The number one mistake a project manager can make is having the requirements wrong. Requirements are the foundation of the project. If the requirements are not correct, the project will not be successful. The project team may eventually get it right, but the system will be very late. Document the requirements and have them reviewed by everyone who has a vested interest in the project. Better to find out the shortcomings before the project is too far along.

6.22. Rushing Into Programming Too Soon

It is a mistake to program directly from the requirements. Analysis and design must be done first. When programmers rush into programming, they end up spending more time reprogramming than doing anything else. This is expensive and frustrating.

6.23. Testing Inadequately

Software quality is critical, yet few IT professionals have been well trained in testing. The purpose of testing is not to prove that software works; it is to find errors. An "error" is a variance between actual and expected results. If no errors are found, the testing process has failed, for no value has been added.

Test for the unknown, unlikely, and invalid as well as for the expected and valid. Don't postpone testing until the end of a project. The earlier errors are found, the easier and less costly they will be to fix. Testing should include not just the software, but also manual procedures, documentation, usability, security, and so on. Testing should be performed in a well-planned and documented manner. This includes developing a test plan, designing test cases, executing the tests, and reporting a summary of test results. The end result will be a quality product that meets the needs of staff and patrons.

6.24. Failing to Bring Projects to a Close (Never-Ending Projects)

The "80/20 rule" says that last 20% of the project will take 80% of the time. Nothing could be truer! Don't overestimate the project team's ability to finish a project. A project isn't over until it has been documented and mainstreamed. Too often software is in use, but not truly finished. Don't run off to work on another project assuming that the loose ends will be tied up later. Reality has proven that this will never happen.

6.25. Outgrowing the Current System Long Before a Replacement Is Considered

If the organization waits too long, the replacement system will need to be rushed into place, resulting in mistakes caused by inadequate understanding of requirements.

6.26. Lacking Ability to Deal with Change

Projects are change, but what happens when the project itself starts changing? It's best not to resist change. Instead, manage it with minimal impact to the project. As a change is identified, discuss and document the impact. Most change will delay a project. If the change must be done, then the impact to the project schedule must be accepted as well.

6.27. Discovering Too Late That a Project has Serious Flaws

For example, performance might be bad. The project team has developed a system that does exactly what it is supposed to do, but if more than three people use it at the same time, the system operates too slowly. This should have been tested before the system was completed. The sooner problems are found, the more easily the project manager can reduce the impact to the project.

6.28. Allowing Team Members to Compete

Sometimes, it is not clear who is doing what. Two or more people may be performing some project tasks while other tasks have been ignored. Quite often a project will have team members jumping from one task to another, without actually completing anything. This is time-consuming and results in very little actually getting done.

6.29. Ditching Methodology and Development Standards Because They Take Too Much Time

This will cost the project and the organization in the long run. The project either pays now or pays later. It is always best to take the time to do it right.

6.30. Summary

Do any of these common pitfalls look familiar? Unfortunately, we are all only human and tend to repeat the same errors over and over. The good news is that a project can take some steps to limit the number of mistakes made and to ensure its success.

7. GUARANTEEING PROJECT SUCCESS

A successful project is one that comes in on time, is within budget, and meets the requirements of the staff and patrons. This may seem like a lot, but it can be done. This section details how a project manager can guarantee that a project is successful.

7.1. Treat Staff and Patrons as Customers

In some cases, IT staff and non-IT staff do not get along. Non-IT people often distrust IT staff because of past projects that were unsuccessful. Often IT staff do not respect the non-IT people because of their lack of technical skills. The best approach is for the IT staff to treat other staff as customers. This is really just common sense: The staff *are* IT customers. IT staff will need to constantly be reminded of this perspective until it sticks.

7.2. Take the Time to Do Written Requirements/Specifications

Doing specifications is very time-consuming, but in reality it saves time because project team members will not need to do a lot of rework. This includes an analysis of the workflow. There must be a clear understanding of how the work actually gets done. Doing specifications also helps ensure a surprise-free implementation. Everything that is done (design, programming, etc.) is a direct result of the requirements/specifications. The steps following requirements/specifications simply expand on what has already been done. Make sure requirements/specifications are revisited as the project progresses to ensure that the project is on the right track.

7.3. Generate Reasonable Estimates

Don't pick a date and then make the project fit into the time schedule. Don't pick an estimate so that others will agree that it should be done. The project work must be estimated at the task level. Most IT people will say that they cannot estimate the work. This is not true. At first the estimates will be bad, but over time they will improve. There are usually two types of estimators: "worst-case" and "best-case." "Worst-case" estimators assume that everything will go wrong. Their estimates tend to be grossly exaggerated. "Best-case" estimators assume that everything will go right. This is even worse! A good estimator will estimate in the middle, assuming that some tasks will go better than expected and others will go worse. Remember these words to live by: The project manager will be forgiven if the system is late, but no one will ever forget if the system is bad.

7.4. Conduct Frequent Reviews and Walkthroughs

Don't wait for feedback—seek it out! Show what is available as the project progresses. There should be no surprises. New approaches to software development recommend that systems be developed iteratively. Don't wait until the system is done before showing it to others. The project manager must also produce regular status reports. Those with a vested interest in the project must not be in the dark. Make the project as visible as possible. In addition to constantly communicating with those outside the immediate project, the project manager also needs to do so with the project team members. Project team members need to understand their role and the role of others on the project. They must also understand how their effort fits into the big picture.

7.5. Control Change Tightly

Before a change in project scope is approved, access the impact. Document and communicate change requests so that everyone is on the same page. Make sure that the involved parties understand how the change will impact the planned implementation date of the system. Nothing is free!

7.6. Assess and Manage Risk

If risk is ignored, it will not go away. Instead, risk should be embraced. Determine what parts of the project are "risky" and share this news with the senior management and other involved parties. Keeping risks to yourself will not make them go away. If the system will be using a new database management system, a new platform, and a new programming language, major risks are being taken. The work will not progress as smoothly as everyone hopes. Document the risks and mitigate them as soon as possible. Instead of first developing the software that runs on the old system and provides input data to the new system, start on the new system. Use the new database, platform, and language as soon as possible. In other words, confront the risks right away so that everyone knows what the project is dealing with. If you follow the traditional approach of working on a system in its logical order, large amounts of time may be spent before discovering a major problem that impacts the entire premise of the project.

7.7. Deal with Conflicts as They Arise

If a problem arises, don't wait for it to get worse or go away. Address the problem at the onset. For example, ignoring personnel conflicts will only allow them to fester.

7.8. Keep the IT Staff "Happy"

No, this doesn't mean giving them free pizza and cola (although that would be fine, too). Keep the IT staff happy by providing the training and tools needed in a timely fashion and by allowing for the time necessary to develop the system. Don't be afraid to get help if it is needed.

7.9. Keep Projects Small—Do a Piece at a Time

Think about the last big project the organization undertook. Starting to sweat? The project team was probably overwhelmed by the amount of work it had to do. No one knew where to start. The best approach is to identify the big project, and then break it up into smaller, more manageable projects.

7.10. Underpromise and Overdeliver

These are words to live by. Promise less than can honestly be delivered, and then actually produce more. The project team members will be beloved by all.

7.11. Resist the Lure of New Technology

The new technology may not be right for the organization or the type of project being undertaken. What works in a larger organization or a different industry may not be appropriate for the project at hand. If the organization selects a technology that is more complex than what is needed, the learning curve may be too great to bear. Just because something is the best doesn't mean it is best for every system.

7.12. Use a Project Management Methodology and Software Tool

Avoid "seat of your pants" management. For the most part, this isn't rocket science. It's been done before. Learn from others. Definitely avoid buzzword-laden approaches to system development. The latest trend may not be right for the organization or project. Instead, try a proven software process that will blend well with the work at hand. Putting these principles into practice is difficult, but practice makes perfect. Assignments and their due dates must be clearly defined, communicated, and monitored. Keep in mind that a project is late as soon as it starts slipping, not just when the system isn't implemented on the promised day. The sooner this slippage is discovered, the easier it will be to get back on track. Microsoft Project is an example of a readily available tool for managing the project. For larger organizations with more robust projects, a product like Rational Unified Process (RUP) will be useful in identifying which steps should be taken, and when to take them.

7.13. Document a Backup Plan

Assume that the project will not be completed on time. What will need to be done if that happens? This is like life insurance. Hopefully, it will not be needed, but everyone feels better that it is available.

7.14. Plan for the Mainstreaming of the Project or Service

How will this system be supported? How will this system be upgraded? The organization's investment in the system does not stop at implementation.

8. TURNING A TROUBLED PROJECT AROUND

A troubled project can still succeed. Management needs to recognize that there is a problem and take appropriate action. The problem is that managers often distance themselves from troubled projects. What is done depends on the organizational tolerance for failure. To turn around a project, the organization may want to change the scope of the project (start smaller and do another release later), improve how the project is managed (which may involve replacing the project manager or changing the project management process), add to or improve the resources, and/or get training for the staff if they don't know what they are doing. The longer the organization waits to stop and assess a troubled project, the worse the impact on the budget and morale. Unfortunately, once a project is in a downward spiral, those involved tend to lose the ability to think clearly. If an organization suspects that a project is in trouble, it is best to assign a nonproject team member to take an unbiased look.

9. CONCLUSION

If an organization is gearing up to begin a new project, or is in the midst of a troubled project, that organization should keep in mind that this road has been traveled before. Make sure the organization benefits from the successes and failures of other organizations' experiences. All projects get in trouble at some point. The end result will depend on how soon action is taken and what that action is. The size of the trouble a project gets into can be greatly reduced by keeping the project small, planning every step of the way, and communicating the plan and results with everyone impacted.

REFERENCES

1. Project Management Institute. A Guide to Project Management Body of Knowledge. Newton Square, PA: PMI, 1996:4.
2. Dinsmore PC, ed. The AMA Handbook of Project Management. New York: AMACOM, 1993:6.
3. Dinsmore PC, ed. The AMA Handbook of Project Management. New York: AMACOM, 1993:7.
4. Dinsmore PC, ed. The AMA Handbook of Project Management. New York: AMACOM, 1993:348.
5. Dinsmore PC, ed. The AMA Handbook of Project Management. New York: AMACOM, 1993:349.
6. Dinsmore PC, ed. The AMA Handbook of Project Management. New York: AMACOM, 1993:350.
7. Getting Value from Enterprise Initiatives: A Survey of Executives by The Boston Consulting Group. Boston: BCG, 2000:2.
8. Kerzner H. Project Management: A Systems Approach to Planning, Scheduling, and Controlling. New York: Wiley, 1998:4.

8

Input and Feedback from Digital Library Users

Susan J. Barnes

University of Washington, Seattle, Washington, U.S.A.

Janet A. McCue, Martin Heggestad, Nancy C. Hyland, Joy R. Paulson, and Tim Lynch

Cornell University, Ithaca, New York, U.S.A.

This chapter showcases examples of assessment and evaluation conducted by Mann's digital library practitioners.

- Digital libraries are complex and changing rapidly; we may lack adequate tools to evaluate these environments,
- We can set directions and make decisions based on studies of users' evolving needs and of whether the library is supporting those needs,
- The selections presented here include both quantitative and qualitative approaches:

  - Partnering with faculty and students
  - Using the card sort technique to organize information
  - Using "extreme programming" to make adjustments during development

- ○ Employing outcome-based evaluation to identify whether a project meets its goals
- ○ Collaborating with scholars to prioritize historical publications for digitization
- ○ Using e-mail and the Web to survey digital library users

The introduction to this book presents views of digital libraries from two communities, basic researchers and practitioners. Saracevic has contrasted the two by describing the research community as looking at a future vision of digital libraries while the practice community looks at "developmental and operational questions in real-life economic and institutional contexts, restrictions, and possibilities, concentrating on applications on the market end of the spectrum" [1]. Practitioners are building systems and services that must be effective and reliable, digital libraries that users can depend on for their information needs. Basic researchers focus more on theory and experimentation, with findings that feed into the development of working digital libraries. This book has been written by people who stand squarely within the practitioner group, conducting day-to-day management of their library's functional areas while building and expanding its digital components. These practitioners all realize that successful development does not take place in a vacuum—there is a need to remain aware of basic researchers' work and, perhaps even more importantly, a need to collect input and feedback from people for whom digital libraries are being constructed. After all, if libraries do not meet their users' needs, those users are likely to turn elsewhere, raising the question of whether libraries are necessary. Libraries that support their communities are the ones that will be supported by their communities. It is crucial for practitioners to evaluate what they do, especially amid ongoing digital library development.

However, digital libraries are very complex entities in which change is constant and rapid. Saracevic has wondered whether it is so early in digital library evolution that formal evaluation may have stifling effects and that information and anecdotal methods may have to suffice, where "the pressure of the rapid pace of evolution, the rush to do something and then to rush to something next does not leave time for evaluation." In fact, we may lack adequate tools to evaluate environments as complex as digital libraries [1]. Marchionini further delineates the problem by pointing out that digital libraries are "mutually self-adapting systems interacting in a rich environment" and that "the effects of DLs [digital libraries] will emerge over time as physical libraries, DLs, and people mutually adapt and mature; the problem of evaluation for DLs is thus one of assessing complex adaptive systems" [2].

So, how can digital library practitioners know what decisions to make and what directions to take? How can they evaluate what they do? To answer these questions, practitioners must address two other, deceptively simple, questions: What are users' present and future needs? And, is the library supporting those needs? A library is, at its core, a service organization. Instead of thinking in terms of "evaluating" digital libraries, we can instead look at our users' current and future needs and how they are changing, and keep track of how well we serve those needs. That is why this chapter is titled "Input and Feedback from Digital Library Users." It provides some strategies that the Mann Library has employed recently to keep in touch with the people whom it serves — to inform and confirm decisions made while becoming a digital library.

This chapter presents case studies, examples of applied research. Unlike basic research, which aims at producing new knowledge, these studies have addressed practical library issues. On the other hand, they have been conducted in full recognition that they benefit from basic research that has gone before. Basic researchers and practitioners need each other. After all, as Powell has pointed out, basic research often leads to practical applications, and applied research can be the foundation for subsequent work to derive new knowledge [3]. While these case studies vary in approach and structure, they all address at least one of the three types of user data that Westbrook describes: "what people do, remember, and think" [4].

We have made no effort here to provide an exhaustive overview of research techniques. Instead, we've presented selections from the abundant tapas bar of available methodologies. The point is that needs and performance assessment can provide valuable results, even if—especially if—they focus on specific digital library issues rather than "digital libraries" as whole entities. If we use tools we have at hand to examine our development efforts, those efforts will benefit. The American Council on Education recognized this in addressing research about higher education in general:

> Evidence includes both quantitative and qualitative information—sometimes data, at other times stories. It is not always a product of highly sophisticated research methodologies; while certain types of evidence may be that precise, evidence of improvement is broader and includes "softer" measures. . . .

> Stories provide important illustrations, help explain complex and ambiguous situations, and add a chronological element, connecting information in a temporal sequence. Numerical data, on the other hand, are concrete, carry legitimacy within the academy and to external groups, and lend themselves to comparison, both over time and across units. In addition, the collection of data helps avoid "proof by anecdote." Strategies that use both types of evidence will present a more complete picture of what has happened.

1. THREE CASE STUDIES OF PARTNERING*

When academic libraries form partnerships with students and faculty to assess needs and evaluate services, all groups benefit. These three cases describe opportunities for students and faculty to learn about the library while, at the same time, providing input about the library's marketing strategies and feedback about its priorities and services.

The Mann Library uses a variety of methods to evaluate its services—from formal surveys to "convenience sampling" as we talk informally with our users to learn more about their needs. In several recent surveys, we have partnered with our users. For example, a reference librarian worked with a statistical sampling class to analyze users' perceptions of digital library resources; another reference librarian partnered with a communication arts class to design a marketing strategy for the library's laptop loaner program. And, the library administration joined with a faculty committee to incorporate 10 questions related to the library in the college's academic program review. Each of these evaluative techniques provided valuable insight into our users' perceptions of the library and their behavior in using resources and services.

1.1. The Library's Role in Providing Digital Library Resources

Do users know that the library plays an essential role in delivering digital resources? One of the library's reference librarians, Angi Faiks, set out to answer this question with the help of a statistical sampling class (Industrial and Labor Relations Statistics 310). This class examines the theory and application of statistical sampling and also includes an applied project. Faiks presented the library's purpose—to determine academic library user's perceptions regarding the provision of digital library collections. The class took on the challenge for their applied project and worked with Faiks to design a national survey in the spring 2000 semester.

The class selected students, faculty, and staff at a random sampling of 26 universities to participate in the Web-based survey. Two hundred and ninety respondents answered the online survey. Most of the respondents were faculty, and half were in the sciences. The results of the survey gave us excellent insight into how users perceive the library and its resources. For example, although 67% of the faculty respondents realized that their access to electronic journals depended on the university library's subscription, 48% of the student respondents thought that electronic journals were available to everyone by virtue of being on the Web.

---

* By Janet McCue.

By working with students in this class, the library was able to do a national survey for a very small cost (the library covered the cost of cash prizes to participants—eight prizes of $50 each were awarded—as well as the snacks at the seminar reception where the results were presented). Again, the reference librarian benefited from the insight and analysis of the class members. Members of the class helped her frame specific questions that made sense to the audience as well as questions that would elicit responses that could be easily analyzed. The students, on the other hand, learned more about the economics and culture of libraries in the digital age. The good news was that more than half of all respondents believe that the role of the library in their academic work and research is the same, despite the electronic information resources now available on the Web. And, 31% think the library is even more important today. As one respondent asserted, "Just because information is moving to more of a digital form does not in any way diminish the importance of the role of the library. In fact, I believe it enhances it."

1.2. Laptop Loaners

The library initiated a laptop loaner program at the beginning of the winter term, 2001. Equipped with wireless access cards and a standard suite of software, the laptops could be taken anywhere within the building and could connect to the Internet on three of the four floors of the library. Rather than use typical library signage to market the service, the library asked a group of students in Communication 418 (Communication and Persuasion) to help us determine the best type of media to use in promoting the new laptop program. The ultimate goal was to increase both the visibility of the new services and the use of the laptops.

The students conducted a survey of current users—those who had heard about the program either through word of mouth or the library's signage—and then conducted a second survey of nonusers. Throughout the development of the survey and the marketing program, the students consulted with the head of the library's computing center. This allowed the library some input into the advertising. As a side benefit of this collaboration, we gained valuable insight into marketing strategies for students. The students created campaigns based on various theories (e.g., theory of planned behavior, stages of change model, etc.). One campaign highlighted students working on laptops in the "cushy" chairs in the informal study area. Their analysis suggested that this campaign "would influence the normative beliefs and motivation to comply, since we all like to do what our friends do." To highlight the cost/benefit component, the students suggested that the campaign should use a picture of long lines for computers, with the caption "We were tired of waiting at libraries for computers . . . then we discovered the Mann Laptop program. It's wireless, it's easy, and it's fun!"

Working with the students provided several benefits. First, the library learned more about the marketing language and images that students find appealing. Second, we learned more about how our users discovered our services as laptop usage increased 300% in the four months of the campaign. Finally, the students provided a unique opportunity for the library and the students to work together to analyze a service and come up with a better mousetrap.

1.3. Academic Program Reviews

Recently, Cornell's College of Agriculture began a multiyear program review to assess the strengths and weaknesses of the college's academic programs. As part of this review, library staff worked with the Mann Library faculty advisory committee to develop a set of questions that could be incorporated into the survey of faculty, students, and alumni. The committee acknowledged that the modern academic research library must accommodate two trends: increasing rates of expansion of knowledge; and increasing needs for electronic technology. Because these trends provide unprecedented opportunities as well as challenges, both the library staff and the faculty committee felt that assessing user needs was a priority. The committee members and the library staff developed 10 questions. These questions ranged from the adequacy of library hours to preferences for electronic formats. The results of the survey were enlightening—providing insight into services, collections, and users. The survey also helped the library prioritize its services. For example, the committee's analysis showed that the library should develop more effective outreach efforts for freshmen and transfer students. This conclusion provided excellent reinforcement for the instruction librarian, whose goal was to increase classes by 20%.

Even more valuable, though, was the engagement of the faculty in the issues facing the library. The faculty served as the advocates for the library, both in the development of the survey and in the subsequent analysis of the results. Their recommendations—from enhancing access to electronic resources to providing workshops for individuals with lower comfort levels in using technology—helped frame budget conferences and priorities within the library. Although libraries often use faculty and student advisory groups to help shape policy, there are many other sources of insight within the academy. Working with faculty and administration to incorporate questions related to the library services and collections can provide additional data and added weight for the library's program initiatives. Partnering with marketing or communication classes to help design persuasive campaigns or statistical sampling classes to design better surveys is an excellent way to learn more about our audiences. These partnerships also provide opportunities to develop and supplement the expertise of the library staff.

2. A CASE STUDY OF ORGANIZING HIERARCHICAL INFORMATION USING THE CARD SORT TECHNIQUE*

Before a committee becomes deadlocked in trying to decide on an organizational scheme for digital content, it should turn to people who will be using the materials and ask their opinions. The card sort technique is an inexpensive way to collect input from users prior to system design.

In the spring of 1999, a Cornell University library committee was charged with creating a comprehensive online help system for the Cornell University Library's Gateway at http://www.library.cornell.edu. To achieve this, the committee decided to implement a table of contents, a search mechanism, and an alphabetical index.

Gateway Help included over 100 documents on a variety of topics. The table of contents provided the main access point and served as the structure for the entire interface. A significant challenge of this project was to attain a meaningful organization in the table of contents. The committee wanted to be sure that it would be organized effectively from users' viewpoints. Despite the fact that the committee had a long collective experience in organizing information, achieving consensus was difficult. It became clear in our discussions that user input would be essential for deciding on a final structure for the table of contents. We were able to employ the card sort technique to gain user insight and organize these varying topics.

The card sort technique proved to be a highly effective and valuable method for gathering user input on organizational groupings prior to total system design. It is a useful method of capturing an individual's perception of an information space. The technique is easy to replicate, and we recommend it for any library that is wrestling with the best way to organize a set of topics in a Web interface.

The card sort technique entails providing a group of users with a set of cards. Along with an identifying number, a concept or piece of information from the set that you are attempting to organize is written on each card. Users then sort cards with similar concepts into piles. The user is then asked what title he or she would give to the different groups—which the interviewer writes down. Finally, the user is asked if any of the piles just created has any relation to any of the others.

---

* By Nancy C. Hyland.

After the user session, the cards are scored based upon their relationship to one another. The data are entered into a statistical analysis program. A statistical cluster analysis can be used to create a composite of a single user's grouping of concepts or a composite averaging all users' responses. After the cluster analysis is run, the results are presented as a tree with similar concepts grouped together in a branch. It is important to review the titles given during the session. If, for example, the user has titled one group of cards as "miscellaneous," there will be concepts grouped together in the data tree that the user might not see as related.

The technique is based on the assumption that if users group cards together, the concepts should probably be grouped together in the system. The result provides an indication of how users would organize a given set of concepts. This information can be very valuable when organizing a system or Web site. Because this input is gathered prior to total system design, it avoids design being driven by a presupposed structure or organization. Users are not in any way influenced by an existing structure, and it gives the librarian a glimpse at how users truly classify information.

By using the card sort technique, we were able to divide all of the help pages into four general categories. After reviewing items in each category, we entitled them Research Tools, Research Strategy and Process, Research

Library Research at Cornell
- Overview and clarification

Research Tools
- CU Library Catalog
- Library Gateway e-Reference Collection
- Individual CU libraries and collections
- Library catalogs worldwide
- WWW and search engines

Research Strategy and Process
- Research strategy: a tutorial
- Finding specific types of materials
- Evaluating research materials
- Citing sources

Research Services and Support
- Reference desks directory
- Ask A Librarian: email reference
- Library instruction
- Interlibrary loan
- Request purchase for library collection
- MyLibrary
- Email Notifications

Technical Support
- Computer set-up for Library Gateway
- Wireless Access in the Library
- Resolve errors and technical questions

Glossary

FIGURE 1 The card sort technique influenced the final structure of the Cornell University Library's Gateway Help Table of Contents.

Services and Support, and Technical Support. One of the help pages, a library glossary, was consistently put in its own category or into a category that the user entitled miscellaneous. The committee therefore let the item stand as its own category. Another page, giving an overview of the research process at Cornell University, was evenly distributed among different groups. In this case, we also gave the overview its own category within the help pages. The use of the card sort technique allowed the committee to create a structure for Gateway Help that accurately reflects how our patrons perceive the information (see Fig. 1).

Implementing a card sort study is actually a relatively easy task. It only requires time and a set of index cards. It is not necessary to run the statistical analysis, although it is helpful and recommended. Results can be gathered by "eyeballing" the cards if they are not too extensive or complex. Since it provides a means of end-user input, the card sort technique can positively impact system and interface decisions.

3. A CASE STUDY OF EXTREME PROGRAMMING*

After system specifications are compiled, "extreme programming" provides an approach to making adjustments during development via continuous feedback. Many small, rapid corrections can be made when users see early results in this not-so-extreme approach.

Extreme programming is the latest buzzword in software project management. The term conjures up images of programmers in baggy clothes with tattoos, green hair, and too many body piercings. Not to worry. Your programmer might have green hair, but you can relax if she says she is "into extreme programming." More a reaction to the excessively rigid formal methodologies that have preceded it than being the software coding equivalent of bungee jumping, extreme programming is all about agility: responding quickly to changes in customer specifications. In fact, the term "agile programming" is replacing "extreme programming" in some circles.

We've given extreme programming a try here in the information technology (IT) unit at the Mann Library and have found it to be a good fit for the type of projects that typically engage us. Before delving into an example, however, here's a bit more background.

Over the past two decades, the art of software project management has matured. A few might even say it has reached the point where we can call it a science, but the track record of successful on-time projects indicates "art" is

---

* By Tim Lynch.

still a more appropriate term. Not that the software management industry has failed for lack of trying. In fact, there is a plethora of solid literature on large-project management. But an interesting thing has happened with the exponential growth of the Web that, you might say, has knocked that traditional management hat into the creek.

In the wide world of the Web, what's here today is gone tomorrow. Plan to spend a year developing an application for the Web? Good luck. If it takes a year to develop something, that something will be obsolete by the time it's deployed. "Web" time is so fast, in fact, that some developers have stated "3 × 3" defines the outer limits of what's doable: If it takes more than three programmers more than three months to develop the application, forget it.

Miraculously, component-ware technologies have arrived to save the day. Sort of like Home Depot for programmers, component software provides developers with the equivalent of finished kitchen cabinets and prehung doors. Programmers can now purchase drop-in spreadsheets, streaming audio plug-ins, SQL database modules, and on and on. We can now program quickly, in Web time. Life is good. What is needed, though, is a management process that can match the deployment speed component-ware makes possible.

To gain some insight into what's needed, consider the following question: What's the difference between driving a car slowly and driving fast? Driving is a process of making continuous corrections: If your car is drifting left, steer a bit to the right; if you're slowing down, step on the gas. When you're driving slowly, the margin for error with your corrections is allowably larger than when you're driving fast. Fast driving requires you to make many small but rapid corrections. The same idea holds with rapid software development: Make a small change, gauge your customer's response, make another small change, and so on. Don't go months between software releases. Even weeks between releases is pushing the limit. Extreme programming is all about tightening the customer feedback loop.

OK, so does it really work? We recently implemented a current awareness service built around a table of contents (TOC) information feed: Users can subscribe to regular delivery of selected journal TOC or, by creating a keyword profile that we store on our server, be notified whenever a match with any TOC item is found. Using the principles of the extreme, the lead programmer met every two weeks with librarians, showed them a new working component, gauged their response, made adjustments, and repeated the cycle. To our pleasant surprise, the project finished on time and to rave reviews from its users.

Will we use this approach again? Absolutely. The extreme programming approach proved to be enjoyable by all project participants. Most notably, project expectations held to reasonable levels throughout development, which kept everyone happy.

The methodologies of yesterday, heavy on formal process, were (still are) suitable for really big projects requiring dozens of programmers working together for years on end. But that is simply not the way today's Web applications are built. The luxury of spending six months developing the technical specifications is simply not an option. In fact, what extremers would tell you is that cast-in-stone specs are a grand waste of time — the specs will change with the first customer review. Not that planning is bad, though! A favorite quote of practitioners of the extreme is from former President Eisenhower: "In preparing for battle I have always found that plans are useless, but planning is indispensable." In the extreme view, planning is something that happens throughout the development cycle; the plan is complete when the project finishes. You've got to be agile.

Intrigued? You can find more information at www.agilealliance.org and www.extremeprogramming.org.

4.   A CASE STUDY OF OUTCOME-BASED EVALUATION*

This is a description of a project that is in progress, mixing quantitative and qualitative approaches. In October 2000, the Mann Library received a grant from the Institute of Museum and Library Services (IMLS) to create the Core Historical Literature of Home Economics (CHLHE), an electronic collection of historically important home economics texts published from the mid-19th century to the mid-20th century. This grant provides two years of funding for Phase I of the project, which will digitize 2000 volumes. As a condition of funding, the Mann Library agreed to use outcome-based evaluation (OBE) to evaluate the CHLHE project.

Outcome-based evaluation is a systematic way to assess the extent to which a project has achieved its intended results. Evaluation is part of the project from its conception. OBE focuses on two key questions: How has our project made a difference? And how are the lives of the users improved as the result of our project? Often library evaluation focuses on gathering statistical information. While OBE does gather statistical information, its focus is on making a qualitative assessment.

What can outcome-based evaluation achieve? It can increase project effectiveness by providing feedback to the library on the project's impact on users. Project value can be shared with others. It provides a logical framework for program development, it generates information for decision making, and

---

* By Joy R. Paulson.

TABLE 1   Outcomes Logic Model

Influencers	Mission	Program purpose	Activities and services	Audience
Individuals and groups who influence the type and nature of services, who the project serves, desired outcomes, and what reports should say	The library's mission and its connection to the project	Program purpose is driven by assumptions about need. It relates to the library's mission statement. It defines audience, services, and outcomes.	Activities support delivery of service to project users. Services engage project participants and produce outcomes. Services and activities are driven by audience characteristics	Audience is driven by influencers, assumptions of need, and institutional mission and resources
CHLHE:	CHLHE:	CHLHE:	CHLHE:	CHLHE:
Cornell University, College of Human Ecology, CHLHE Advisory Board, Cornell University Library/ Mann Library, Users, IMLS	Collections and services support the instruction, research, and extension services of Cornell and support the faculty, staff, and students of Cornell	To provide electronic access to historically important home economics materials	Activities: Identify, select, and digitize materials, create metadata, mount materials on the web. Services: Curriculum development, bibliographic instruction, and reference services	Researchers, faculty, and students of the College of Human Ecology

it documents project successes. However, outcome-based evaluation is not formal research. OBE can identify whether a project is meeting its perform-ance goals, but the results do not necessarily demonstrate that the outcomes achieved are a direct result of the project. It can show that the project has contributed to the resulting change in attitude, behavior, or knowledge, documented in the evaluation, but it cannot demonstrate that the project is the only factor having impact.

Outcome-based evaluation defines a project as a series of activities or services directed toward intended outcomes. These outcomes are designed to change a target audience's attitudes, behaviors, or knowledge, or to increase

Outcomes	Indicators	Data source	Data intervals	Goals
Intended Impact	Observable and measurable behaviors or conditions	Sources of information about conditions being measured	When data is collected	Amount of impact desired
CHLHE:	CHLHE:	CHLHE:	CHLHE:	CHLHE:
1. Increased use of historical materials by faculty and students 2. Better skills match 3. Change in attitudes about women in 19th and 20th century America and about home economics	1 and 2: # of searches and pages viewed; # of links; # of classes using CHLHE; # of patrons taking bib. inst.classes; 3. # of students w/ changed attitudes	1 and 2: Web use statistics and Web survey Web search; Teacher assessment and student surveys Class count 3. Pre- and Post-class surveys	1 and 2: Monthly twice/year; Each Semester Each Class; 3. Each Semester	1 and 2: 25,000 searches/50,000 pages; 10 new links 2 classes with 100 students 1 class/20 students; 3. 25%

skills and abilities based on an assumed need. All projects begin with a perception of need. These perceptions are drawn from the library's experience, a project partner's experience, or formal or informal research. The project planners then assess the need and develop a plan to meet the need, including a list of assumptions, solutions, and desired results [5,6].

The project plan consists of inputs, activities, services, and outputs. Inputs are resources dedicated to a project. In the case of CHLHE, our resources are the reviewers of the bibliographies of potential titles for digitization, our advisory board, project staff, the journals and monographs to be digitized, our IT infrastructure, and funds provided by IMLS and the library. Our activities are identifying and selecting materials, digitizing materials, creating metadata, and mounting the digital images online. Our services are curriculum development with selected faculty, bibliographic instruction, and general reference support. Outputs are direct project products typically measured in numbers, such as the number of participants served or the number of materials used. CHLHE's outputs are the number of searches against the database, the number of pages actually viewed, the number of classes and students using the database, and the number of links to the CHLHE Web site. This information is then put into an outcomes logic model or evaluation plan, which is a clear, graphic representation of the links between project activities, the results these activities produce, and how the results will be measured (Table 1).

Naturally, outcomes are a central component of OBE, but what are outcomes? Outcomes describe the impact of the project, the intended results of services, and changed or improved skills, attitudes, knowledge, behaviors, status, or life condition brought about by experiencing the project. For the Core Historical Literature of Home Economics, we had several desired outcomes:

Increased use of historical materials by educators and students.
Better match of skills of students to resources available. Students who prefer online sources over print will have increased access to historical materials.
Change in attitudes about the role of women in late-19th- and early-20th-century America.
New understanding of home economics.

Evaluating these outcomes can help us prove or disprove our assumptions about the need for the project. They also provide us with a powerful narrative that can be shared with faculty, library administrators, university administrators, and grant-funding agencies about the impact of the project on faculty and students. Evaluating outcomes can help generate long-term support for the project. Instead of simply presenting statistics about the amount of use CHLHE is getting, we will also be able to provide information about how CHLHE impacted the work of faculty and researchers and assisted students in developing good research skills through the information gathered in the Web surveys, teacher assessments, and class surveys. By integrating evaluation into the activities of the project from the planning stage, it is possible to design the project to meet the desired outcomes of the project. The data gathering takes place not only during the official life of the project but can continue as long as the CHLHE database is available, allowing changes to be made to enhance its effectiveness on an ongoing basis.

5. A CASE STUDY OF SETTING PRIORITIES: THE CORE HISTORICAL LITERATURE APPROACH TO BUILDING A DIGITAL COLLECTION*

The Mann Library is conducting a multiyear digitization project to preserve historical home economics monographs and serials. This effort, the Core Historical Literature of Home Economics project, or CHLHE, uses the approach pioneered by Wallace Olsen in the Core Historical Literature of Agriculture (CHLA) project [7]. Olsen's methodology features collection of extensive evaluative information from scholars. These users of the literature provide their expert opinions regarding historical publications' relative value and importance. This results in ranked lists, addressing the fact that the quantity of materials in many subject areas that is at risk for deterioration is far greater than can be handled by available preservation resources. Olsen's approach is based on the principle that effective preservation plans should focus on a particular discipline as a whole rather than on the holdings of an individual library. This Core Historical Literature approach has brought a digitized collection of agricultural literature chosen by subject experts to the Web.

For the CHLHE project, we have been creating bibliographies for the various sub-disciplines of home economics, asking specialists to review these lists, and using their rankings to identify core texts to be preserved in a large-scale digitization effort that will, in its initial phase, cover about 2000 titles. We have relied heavily on our reviewers and have asked a great deal of them.

In seeking reviewers, we considered the needs of potential users. We anticipate that the digitized texts, which will be freely available on our Web site, will be a valuable resource for scholars in various fields, including social history, history of science, women's studies, and cultural studies. Our assumption has been that a researcher in, for example, human development would be able reliably to choose the literature that his or her colleagues have considered most influential but may overlook material that a historian might find valuable. Such concerns seem relevant for a number of the subdisciplines. In the case of the Child Care/Human Development/Family Studies list, for instance, we recruited a number of specialists in those fields, most of them approaching or beyond retirement age and thus having access to long memories, and we also invited the participation of two historians, one working in the history of science and one in social history, who have a different view of these fields.

---

* By Martin Heggestad.

Recruitment of reviewers has been a significant and sometimes time-consuming task that we have approached in various ways. We have made use of contacts such as CHLHE advisory board members, Cornell University faculty, and librarian colleagues at other institutions. We have also reviewed recent scholarly literature by home economists and by historians and have contacted the authors. Librarians with an interest in the historical literature of particular subject areas have often been willing to serve as reviewers, as have librarians and curators at museums whose missions are connected to the concerns of home economics. We have also found that specialists who have agreed to participate in the project have often been willing to recommend, and even actively recruit, their colleagues.

The CHLHE project budget does not include any funds for honoraria for reviewers, and so we have had to rely on the willingness of busy professionals to volunteer their time. Fortunately, the potential reviewers we have approached have generally been easily persuaded of the value and importance of the project. Older faculty members in home economics fields have seen CHLHE as a means of preserving the historical contributions of their fields, a goal that can seem especially significant in view of the often marginalized status of home economics within academia. Historians see the prospect of easy access to deteriorating and sometimes rare source materials as valuable for both research and teaching. In some cases, they have also been eager to have access to a comprehensive bibliography in their area of interest. Librarians and curators are well aware of preservation issues and generally need little convincing.

We have recruited as many as a dozen reviewers for each of the 11 subdisciplines. We have thus established and maintained relationships with a substantial number of people, a worthwhile but time-consuming endeavor. We will undoubtedly be relying on this large network in the next phase of the project as we begin intensively publicizing and promoting the availability of the digitized materials.

Olsen, in the CHLA project, did a citation analysis in order to identify the most frequently cited works in historical agricultural literature and used the results to create subject bibliographies. This method resulted in bibliographies that were shorter than ours and thus considerably easier for reviewers to handle. Citation analysis was not an effective tool for evaluating home economics literature, however, because much of this literature consists of practical works directed toward a general audience and thus contains relatively little scholarly apparatus.

The bibliographies have been created from a large database that has been assembled using EndNote. The sources we have looked at include home economics bibliographies, bibliographies in various subject areas such as child developments or nutrition, lists of works cited in recent scholarship (for example, social histories of etiquette and of housework), and library catalog records. Monograph titles have been identified using these sources and imported into the database from the Cornell online catalog, where possible, or from OCLC. We have applied criteria for inclusion as generously as possible, looking for any titles that may have been of importance to home economists, regardless of who the authors were, although certain categories of monographs, such as government or extension publications, were excluded because they are, or likely will be, covered under other preservation plans. Currently, the database contains about 13,000 titles. Each entry is assigned a code indicating the subdiscipline to which it belongs, making it possible to generate a comprehensive bibliography for each subject area. These lists varied greatly in length, from about 200 to about 2800 entries. (The database contains only monographs, but a number of serials will be digitized as well. These titles are selected in a more informal manner in consultation with reviewers.)

Once a bibliography for a particular subject area seems reasonably complete—always a somewhat subjective assessment—it is sent out to reviewers in print form by U.S. mail with a prepaid return envelope. Reviewers are asked to rank each title that they recognize with a number from one to three depending on their judgment of its historical significance. When ranked bibliographies are returned, the results are tabulated, and project staff begin looking for copies of highly ranked items that can be scanned and digitized. This project comes at a time of renewed interest in the historical contributions of home economics [8], and we expect that the digital collection we are building will be a valuable resource in this ongoing reassessment of an important chapter in American history.

6.   A CASE STUDY OF A DIGITAL LIBRARY USER SURVEY*

This project used the quantitative approach to collect feedback from a large, distributed user population. The USDA Economics and Statistics System, a major component of Mann's digital library, is used by people all over the nation and the world. Mann has provided access since 1984 to this collection of hundreds of numeric data sets and textual reports, produced by the Economic Research Service, the National Agricultural Statistics Service, and the World Agricultural Outlook Board of the U.S. Department of Agriculture (USDA). These publications include information about farm economics, statistics about crop production and food consumption, international agriculture reports, trade data, and much more. Some specific titles:

_____

* By Susan J. Barnes.

Acid Rain in the Northeastern U.S.; Expenditures of Food, Beverages, and Tobacco; Fruit Wildlife Damage; Farms and Land in Farms; European Agricultural Statistics; Pest Management Practices; Trout Production; and Poultry Slaughter.

The USDA Economics and Statistics System (ESS) is both a Web site (at http://usda.mannlib.cornell.edu/ess_entry.html) and an e-mail-based subscription service. During a typical week, thousands of researchers, educators, marketers, and agriculturists visit the Web site to find commodity production and pricing information and also to receive regular updates of their favorite data sets and reports. Mann receives updates from the USDA, makes them available at the ESS Web site, and, using the Majordomo automated e-mail distribution system, broadcasts them to subscribers. Each update can be sent to hundreds of different subscribers at once. These updates are similar to issues of electronic journals. Hundreds are sent out—some as often as once a week—to a subscriber population of more than 4000 people from all over the world.

Although anecdotal feedback was uniformly positive from the beginning, no formal, systematic evaluation of user satisfaction was conducted until 1998, when the library and the USDA agencies began a survey of subscribers to the e-mail update service. The goals of this survey were to

1. Collect information about system users.
2. Learn about the frequency and type of use the system receive.
3. Discover purposes of system use.
4. Investigate levels of satisfaction with the system.

The survey was administered via e-mail to all update service subscribers—approximately 4000 people. We chose e-mail as the distribution channel because e-mail addresses of all subscribers were available while surface mail addresses were not. We could be sure that all report subscribers had e-mail access because they used e-mail to subscribe to the service and received each report via e-mail. In addition, using e-mail was expected to be easier and less expensive—key considerations because the budget for this study was small.

However, the use of e-mail places severe limitations on the design of a survey. Some e-mail clients can handle text formatting and graphics but many cannot, so we used plain ASCII text and omitted any use of tabs and special spacing. E-mail surveys may be more difficult to complete than surveys in other forms, so we kept ours as simple as possible.

Respondents were asked to use their e-mail reply function and indicate their answers with an X. The e-mailed replies were received as text streams from which responses to questions could be extracted and stored with minimal human intervention. We hoped that this would make data coding and entry easier. However, although manual data entry was avoided, we still found it necessary to review a number of responses and remove extra spaces or characters—irregularities that interfered with automated processing.

Comparisons of e-mail to surface mail have found that response rate to e-mail questionnaires tends to be lower. One reason for lower response rates to e-mail surveys could be that they are not anonymous; an individual e-mail address is attached to each one. For this e-mail survey we addressed concerns about anonymity by sending an introductory message to all update service subscribers, describing the study and inviting their participation in it. We assured them that their responses would be kept confidential and that their participation was entirely voluntary. We gave them the opportunity to tell us whether or not they wished to receive and complete the survey, and we removed the addresses of any who indicated that they did not want to participate.

Those who told us that they would like to receive the survey, and those who did not respond, received the questionnaire in their e-mail. Within a week of the first e-mailing, we sent a reminder e-mail to those who had not responded. Within a week after that, we e-mailed a second reminder and an additional copy of the survey. This multiple-contact approach is recommended to increase response rate.

We provided a choice of responding via e-mail, going to a Web site to complete the survey, or printing the survey and returning it via surface mail. Since a large proportion of ESS users have World Wide Web access, the Web response option was offered in an effort to increase response rate. Respondents to Web surveys have expressed a slight preference for Web forms over printed questionnaires. Since the Web is most commonly used via graphical browsers, Web questionnaires can be more visually appealing than those sent by e-mail. However, we used uncomplicated formatting for our survey since a Web page can be displayed by different browsers in unpredictable ways. The survey on the Web contained the same questions as the e-mail survey, and data entry was performed as the respondents filled out the form. We created scripts that collected these data and stored them in a spreadsheet, where data received via e-mail were also placed. The option of using surface mail was presented in an additional effort to remove as many barriers as possible: Respondents who preferred the paper environment over e-mail and the Web could use it. Surface mail responses were entered manually. We received 1673 usable replies, for a return rate of 33%. Most responses came back via e-mail; 378 came via the Web, and 17 via fax or surface mail.

Responses provided information about subscriber location and its rural or urban characteristics; who uses the reports and why; user's type of workplace and principal occupation. More than 70% of respondents were from the United States, with California, Illinois, Texas, New York, Minnesota, and Washington, DC, being the most represented "states" (in that order). Responses came from all 50 states plus Puerto Rico and the Virgin Islands. The foreign countries most commonly heard from were Canada, Mexico, Australia, the United Kingdom, Brazil, and Argentina (in that order). Responses came from 63 different countries. Almost half the respondents were in urban areas (45%), with small city the next most frequent response (18%), and rural the next (15%).

The most frequent workplace category was School/College/University (16.5%), with Public Admin/Govt next (12%) and Farm/Ranch/Dairy next (9%). Most common principal occupation was Executive, Administrator, or Manager (22%), with Analyst next (15%) and Owner/Operator next (13%). Most frequent uses were Maintaining Current Awareness/Finding News (64%), Monitoring Trends in Prices/Production (64%), and Decision Making/Corporate Intelligence (43%).

Respondents provided feedback about preferred file formats; report display, accuracy and currency of reports, and ease of transferring data into spreadsheets or database applications. Some respondents expressed a desire to receive the reports in formats other than ASCII, with spreadsheet the first choice. Word processor and pdf essentially tied for second place. More than one third of respondents did not indicate a desire for an additional format. Many comments indicated desires to retain ASCII, even if additional formats are made available. Eighty percent of respondents find the reports easy to read as displayed by their e-mail software.

Respondents used the reports because they contain Useful Data (78%), are Up-To-Date (73%), are Timely (59%), contain Useful Analysis (51%), and are Accurate (51%). E-mail delivery is used because the reports are Delivered Quickly (79%), Delivered Automatically (78%), and Delivered to Workplace (58%); and Can Be Shared (32%) and Manipulated (22%).

Comments show a high level of satisfaction with the service. For example:

"Reports essential part of my decision making on the farm."

"The mailings are always looked forward to, and appreciated."

"This is by far the easiest way to obtain USDA reports."

"USDA material is very highly regarded by analysts, etc. for content. There is nothing that approaches this material for overall U.S. and global perspective. This is an excellent service for subscribers and obviously you can't argue with the price."

"Your reports have saved me a tremendous amount of money and heartache. Thanks a million."

"The quality of information is great. But timeliness is the major concern, especially on markets. The material is an integral part of my marketing educational efforts. The delivery system is superb.

Users have the same information at the same time that 'insiders' have it. The service is great!"

The survey, completed in 1999, has confirmed the worth of the USDA Economics and Statistics System. It provided decision-making data for the Mann Library and information useful to the USDA in describing its work and services to Congress and the American public.

Note: During the interval since we conducted our survey, a new text by Dillman was published that provides extensive, valuable details about e-mail and Web-based surveys [9]. He points out that e-mail questionnaires are easier to avoid than any other form, since the delete function can be used quickly and simply, and provides techniques to improve response rate such as use of multiple contacts, brief introductions, and alternative response modes. The principal weakness of e-mail surveys that he mentions—the fact that not everyone has e-mail—was one that we were able to avoid, since ours was a population of e-mail users by definition [9].

REFERENCES

1. Saracevic T. Digital Library Evaluation: Toward an Evolution of Concepts. Library Trends 2000; 49(2):350–369.
2. Marchionini G. Evaluating Digital Libraries: A Longitudinal and Multifaceted View. Library Trends 2000; 49(2):304–333.
3. Powell RR. Basic Research Methods for Librarians. 3d ed. Greenwich, CT: Ablex, 1997.
4. Westbrook L. Identifying and Analyzing User Needs. New York: Neal-Schuman Publishers, Inc., 2001.
5. Outcome-Based Evaluation for IMLS-Funded Projects for Libraries and Museums. Washington, DC: Institute of Museum and Library Services, 1999.
6. Perspectives on Outcome-based Evaluation for Libraries and Museums. Washington, DC: Institute of Museum and Library Services, 2001.
7. For a discussion of Olsen's methodology, see WC Olsen, ed. Agricultural Economics and Rural Sociology: The Contemporary Core Literature. Ithaca, NY: Cornell University Press, 1991, Chapters 4 and 5. For further discussion of the core literature model, see S Demas. Collection Development for the Electronic Library: A Conceptual and Organizational Model. Library Hi-Tech 12(3):81–88, 1994; D Wright, et al. Cooperative Preservation of State-Level Publications: Preserving the Literature of New York State Agriculture and Rural Life. LRTS 37:434–443, 1993.
8. See, for example, S Stage, VB Vincenti, eds. Rethinking Home Economics: Women and the History of a Profession. Ithaca, NY: Cornell University Press, 1997.
9. Dillman DA. Mail and Internet Surveys: The Tailored Design Method. 2d ed. New York: John Wiley & Sons, Inc., 2000.

9

New Frontiers and the Scout

Katherine S. Chiang
Cornell University, Ithaca, New York, U.S.A.

"No wind is favorable if you do not know which port you sail for."

Ignoranti, uem portum petat, nullus suus ventus est.
Lucius Annaeus Seneca
Epistulae ad Lucilium no. 71, sect. 3

(Translated by Robert Kibbee, Cornell University Library)

An organization that cannot change has no future. This chapter presents a principal strategy that Mann employs to set directions for change: scouting the frontier.

- "Frontier" is a metaphor for unknown information environments.
- Frontiers include technologies, behaviors, economic forces, and publication patterns.
- Scouting helps a library identify significant frontier areas.
- Scouting begins with navigational concepts: location, direction, and speed.
- Strategies involve continual monitoring of technologies and subject areas.

- Surveying—the broadest level of scouting—investigates as many trends as possible with just enough learned about each for identification of critical elements.
- Trailblazing—a more focused level—is directed to an area of interest identified through surveying.
- Good scouts have intuition, enjoy a fast pace, are comfortable with ambiguity, and can make overview assessments.
- Leaders making decisions on directions for the library take information brought back by scouts and factor in other variables.
- Scouting can lead to valuable innovations, but timing is crucial.
- At first, funding sources and administrators may find a library's ideas too new and strange.
- Soon the library's image will be enhanced by its proactive position.

1. WHY THE FRONTIER?

Stasis is not practical for a life form or an organization. Just as a life form is doomed if it cannot change in response to its environment, an organization that cannot change will be superseded or subsumed; it will have no future. For a library, it is the prospect of the future that makes our present efforts valuable. We collect and organize information for current and future users. If we do not change with our environment and are superseded or subsumed, all our efforts at collection and organization are for naught. Libraries still occupy a unique role in society. No other institution has as its core responsibility the equitable preservation and distribution of information for all audiences. If libraries are to exist in the future, the libraries of today must be able to change. In this chapter I argue that scouts can play a role in controlling that change. The primary justification for scouting—systematically surveying the library environment—is that it gives a library its best chance of continuing to carry out its mission in today's environment.

The scouting approach is applicable to many organizations: universities, corporations, as well as libraries. It is a way of leveraging the staff's natural curiosity about their future. It allows the library to be proactive in fulfilling its mission and may provide institutions a distinct competitive advantage.

This chapter defines the frontier and argues that scouting is one way for a library to respond to that frontier. It categorizes the types of scouting a library could do and explains why a library might want to employ the technique. It describes the various ways a scout might decide on the sorts of information to be gathered, how to go about it, and most importantly, how scouting should be incorporated into the decision-making processes of the library. Then the characteristics of a successful scout are enumerated. The chapter closes with a brief discussion of the risks and benefits of this approach.

2. OUR CHANGING ENVIRONMENT: THE FRONTIER

Compared to 2001, the information environment of the academic scholars (the faculty and students of a university) in 1930 was a placid place. The publication channels were few (journals, technical reports, conference proceedings) and the organization was straightforward (an abstract and index, the index-card catalog, a dictionary, a handbook). The growth of the literature was steady, but manageable [1]. The library serving the scholar was able to meet its mission of identifying, organizing, and making information available in a straightforward and predictable fashion. The scholarly process had a low information overhead. The requirements for using the library were the abilities to read; to understand the difference between a book, a journal, a journal article, and an index; and to understand the shelf classification system to locate print materials. In 1930 a student needed only to learn to use the library once, as a freshman. Faculty could memorize the path to their regular journals and read each new issue at it arrived on the shelf.

The library of 1930 paid for subscriptions to the journals, checked them in, labeled them, and placed them on the shelves. Librarians identified the resources that would be useful to the university, usually before a patron even knew they existed. The scholars of 1930 could come to the library and retrieve most of the information they needed in one location.

The information environment is radically different for the students and faculty of today. Journals are introducing electronic versions, aggregators add and subtract titles from their collections unpredictably, and scholars can access immense databases of citations, data sets, and full-text maintained in distant locations. A much higher overhead is associated with retrieving the information scholars need.

For example: The Cornell University horticulture graduate student of 1930 would retrieve 102 journals on horticulture from a search of the card catalog. The student of 1970 would have over 315 titles to look at, and the student of 2001 retrieves over 450 titles from an online catalog search. Furthermore, several of those 450 titles are available in electronic form, but only for the past few years. Today, Cornell plant geneticists routinely consult Web-based databases of gene sequences and microarray data maintained by institutions across the globe. They receive tables of contents of their favorite journals via e-mail. They search the BIOSIS, Science Citation Index, and library catalog databases from their lab workstations, where they also print recent articles from the library's digital collections. Those articles are linked to other articles and databases available via the network. The scholars e-mail requests for interlibrary loan copies of articles, and these articles are then e-mailed in return. They come into the library to photocopy older articles from the print subscriptions.

Yet a scholar's primary goals are still the understanding of information and the contribution of new knowledge to society. It is the library's mission to create the organization and delivery mechanisms to keep the information overhead as low as possible for the scholar. Since the environment is so complex, meeting that mission means the library has to organize and simplify much more in order to guarantee that the information overhead for the scholar remains low.

To fulfill our mission we must continually redesign our catalogs to incorporate digital resources, including embedded authentication (verifying individuals as licensed to use a resource) and authorization (verifying that that those individuals are who they claim to be). We must continually redesign our interfaces to convey the richness and variability of the types of information available to the scholar.

Today the library is at the center of a rapidly changing information environment. Computing technologies have accelerated the rate of information production and, consequently, the rate of change in the techniques for information distribution and delivery. One way of viewing this situation is as a physical space. Scholars have always had to "travel" through the information being produced, learning new information. Scholars read some journals cover to cover; they learn about new journals and look at them in the library. They look for a book in the stacks and find other books equally as useful sitting beside the first. They attend conferences and see new publications coming from their professional society. If that learning is viewed as a physical traversal of a space, then the acquisition of information is akin to the exploration and understanding of a frontier, an unknown landscape.

Indeed, the frontier is an apt metaphor for the unknown, rapidly changing information environment in which we operate. The information frontier for the scholar in 1930 was like an urban landscape. The changes were gradual and incremental and comprehensible—a new addition to a building in one place, a parking lot in another, the outskirts gradually expanding. Today the information frontier more closely resembles the universe in the first moments after the Big Bang. From the most physically isolated individual to the largest international corporation, almost everyone is engaged in the production, distribution, or consumption of information.

To expand the metaphor, how can the frontier be described? What are the territories to be traversed? First it is necessary to define the overall landscape being occupied. That landscape is centered in information science, which can be broadly defined as the theories and applications that further the collection, the organization, and distribution of information to humans, and the application of information technologies (hardware and software) to that collection, organization, and distribution. Information is the content, which is whatever a scholar might find useful, and the distribution of that information is, from the user's viewpoint, the retrieval of information.

Using that definition, examples of frontiers include the following:

> Technologies for the organization and distribution of information. Paper information technologies include the punch card. The punch card, invented by Hollerith and used in the 1890 Census, was the precursor to the IBM punch card. Libraries into the 1980s used types of punch cards—the McBee card was one common brand—to manage circulation records. Another familiar paper library technology was the 3 × 5 card (for the catalog) and the 5 × 3 lined card patrons signed for circulation records. Today's database and search engines are the electronic counterparts to those earlier technologies. Other computing technologies include those for transferring and communicating the content; for example, wireless and conferencing technology.
>
> Social and psychological behaviors that influence how users interact with technologies, both the software (interfaces and databases) and the hardware (screen size, peripherals, portable devices).
>
> Social and economic forces driving the developments in commercial and nonprofit information production and the subsequent changing patterns in publication.
>
> Technical developments influencing the changing patterns in publication, and how those developments drive the social and economic models, which in turn drive access to the information.

3. RESPONSES TO THE FRONTIER

An organization can respond in several ways to the changing environment, to the reality that the information "frontier" is a vast and rapidly growing space. It can attempt to stand fast against the changes and respond once a change has occurred, or it can predict changes and move to meet them. That latter scenario includes moving selectively to meet changes. In order for a library to achieve the latter response, it needs a way to look far enough ahead to see trends. A library needs to be out at the frontier. This chapter describes the possibilities and benefits of using a scouting process to deliberately navigate the frontier, treating this increasingly chaotic environment as a grand challenge for our profession.

Previous chapters have described how a library can rise to the challenge of creating new collections and services. However, no library has the infinite resources to collect everything and provide every possible service to its patrons, and certainly not in today's environment. How does a library, then, assess the information frontier and identify significant areas needing its involvement? In navigational terms: which direction, and how far? That assessment must be a considered, deliberate process in order for it to be of any benefit.

The first piece in that process is to know where you are, in which direction you are facing, and how fast you are moving. Knowing "where you are" means knowing what the library is currently engaged in with a recognition of the core and peripheral aspects of those engagements. That assessment usually requires relating aspects of the information environment to the library's mission. For example, a four-year college library will focus on assembling a general introductory suite of resources aimed primarily at the undergraduate. A library in a research institute will focus on access to the latest, most complete information in the subject areas of the institute.

Knowing "which direction you are facing" and whether it is a direction that furthers the library's mission implies a recognition of the frontier, which areas are changing and growing the fastest, and how the library's engagements relate to those areas.

Knowing "how fast you moving" (and how fast you want to move) is the final element of navigation. A library needs to assess where it wants to be in a year, or three years, or five years. The driver of a vehicle going 15 miles per hour looks halfway down the block to determine where to steer. A driver going 65 miles an hour should look considerably farther ahead.

Once you have a sense of where you are, you have a view of which general landscapes, or information environments, fall within your territory. Then the navigation becomes a three-part process: refining that view (including ongoing assessments of whether the direction and speed of change are still appropriate) and sharpening it to focus on the specific areas of interest; communicating that view to the organization; and making an organizational decision on how to proceed.

4. INVESTIGATING THE INFORMATION ENVIRONMENT

How does a library assemble information about its environment and decide what to pursue? Who in the library gathers the information? The answers to those questions vary and depend on the size and scope of an organization, but for many libraries viewing the process as one of "scouting" can be useful.

A specialized library with a limited audience may have the most straightforward time assessing its environment. The research library for a company that manufactures medium-density fiberboard will be interested in any information (via any technology) to do with its processes. This can include such diverse areas as forestry, chemicals, and health risks. This library would be gathering information for its research staff and could easily decide whether a particular resource or technology would be suitable for that audience. If the library had a small staff, it is likely most of the staff would be involved in that process and could be considered scouts.

Large libraries with broad audiences cannot use audience or subject as their narrowing parameters. Those libraries must determine other ways of selectively focusing their efforts, ways that allow for iterative overviews and detailed examinations of developments. Scouting is a way to invest a minimum of resources in the navigation process.

5. THE ICE-FISHING PROBLEM

For example, here is how scouting might help various libraries approach one current frontier. Take as the frontier the necessity for portraying the deeply nested, insanely heterogeneous information environment through a 17″ computer display screen. This is the ice-fishing problem. Users have no way of knowing whether the display screen (i.e., the hole in the ice) sits over a bucket, a deep lake, or the North Atlantic. In information terms, they could be looking at one document, an intranet with several sites, or the World Wide Web.

The following scenarios illustrate how different libraries might focus on this portrayal problem. A special library might choose to focus on interface design and develop systems that filter information and present that collection as a custom interface. A research library in a computer hardware company might focus on the possibilities of enhanced display technologies: the use of multiple screens, or digital ink, or flexible screens. A library in an academic institution with an active computer science department might focus on how virtual reality technologies could help users orient themselves in a complex environment.

As the above examples illustrate, scouting involves continual monitoring of the landscape: developments in information activities and technologies in general (such as e-publishing and national information research initiatives); developments in specific subject areas (bioinformatics, for example); or developments in specific technologies (display technologies or electronic ink). That monitoring can be quite broad, or it can be focused. The scouting can be done at different levels, from general to quite targeted.

At the broadest level scouting could be described as surveying, looking at the total landscape and as many trends as possible, and learning just enough about each area to identify the critical elements. Through surveying, the scout gets an overview of an arena. Examples of surveying include monitoring government activities in information technology (such as changing departmental responsibilities, federal initiatives, and changes in information producers) or tracking imaging technologies such as those as used in medical records or inventory systems. The goal is to gather enough information to be able to determine whether or not to worry about some development [2]. In the case of an academic library, it might be an assessment on how a development might influence scholars needing information; what the library should be doing, if anything, to implement a technology, or to provide its scholars with access to the information. Essentially, surveying is a tracking and general forecasting of the challenges facing a particular library.

An example of the outcomes of surveying was the decision to bypass Gopher server technology when the Mann Library began planning to upgrade its Telnet-based Gateway service. Upon reviewing the developments in networked access, management decided that something less hierarchical than Gopher was bound to develop, and the World Wide Web (via Mosaic) looked promising. Gopher technology was bypassed in favor of an http-based system.

A more focused version of scouting is trailblazing. It is a more directed activity in an area of interest to a library. A library's philosophies, existing collections, or mission could determine that direction. Trailblazing is an initial investigation of the "terrain" of an environment. It involves acquiring an understanding of the area and perhaps figuring out what a library could do. In most cases it is something other libraries have not done, which is why the term "trailblazing" is appropriate.

An example of trailblazing in this library has been its tracking of developments in precision agriculture. Precision agriculture is a "management strategy that uses information technologies to bring data from multiple sources to bear on decisions associated with crop production" [3]. Precision agriculture teams global positioning satellite (GPS) technologies (the ability to identify a location to pinpoint accuracy) with planting or harvesting data collected by machinery in the field. Those two streams of data are combined to create spatially referenced databases at a very large scale. Farmers can maintain databases that will tell them which square meters of their fields are giving them the best yield per pound of seed and fertilizer applied. This library collects and provides services for agricultural data in various formats and also provides consulting on data formatting and acquisition for use in geographic information systems (GIS) software. Therefore, its staff are looking at developments in precision agriculture. At this stage, trailblazing involves tracking those who are gathering the data and how they are using and disseminating it. Library staff have identified the groups involved with the application of precision agriculture data and are participating in their discussions. At some point this library may initiate projects to provide specialized archiving and dissemination services for those data sets.

Once a library has identified a promising direction of clear value to the institution, it can invest in building innovative systems. To continue the metaphor, the library has reached the production-level road building that comes after the overview surveying and more focused trailblazing. An example is this library's development of the CUGIR National Spatial Data Infrastructure (NSDI) node (see Chs. 5 and 7). Many other organizations have established NSDI nodes. This library was one of the first academic libraries to establish one, bringing library sensibilities to an existing arena of information delivery.

6. FUNCTIONS OF SCOUTING THE FRONTIERS

The focus in this chapter is on the surveying/trailblazing types of scouting, where the forecasting element is strongest. Scouting helps the library carry out its mission in today's environment. That is scouting's primary justification. Scouting also helps to keep a library moving in useful directions. This movement is part of the lifecycle of growth and renewal necessary for the survival of an organization. Scouting helps the organization's leaders translate trends into projects, which are then developed into services.

7. HOW TO WORK AT THE FRONTIER

7.1. The Scouting Process

Scouting involves lots of information gathering. The types of information a scout is looking to gather are the immutables, the trends, the inklings, the players, and the wildcards. Immutables are the underlying permanent phenomena, such as "Most commercial information providers will want to recoup their costs of collection" or "Information will be collected if someone needs it or thinks someone else will need it enough to pay for it." Trends are the variables that are changing enough to affect a library's operations. The commercialization of information, our move to an information society, and the development of Web TV are examples of trends that may affect how a library functions. Inklings are hunches about trends in an unrelated field, or seemingly minor trends (e.g., digital ink, flexible screens) that may eventually have a strong influence on a library. The players are the stakeholders who are driving the development of particular trends or who are in the library's institution or constituency. Understanding the motivations of the stakeholders is essential to being able to predict how trends will develop and affect the library. Finally, there are the wildcards, the totally unpredictable elements that may rise from nowhere to suddenly dominate a field.

7.2. Information Sources

The information can come from a number of sources. There are informal sources such as the conversation at a corporate Christmas party in 1986 with an entrepreneur who was interested in the commercial possibilities of combining proprietary data with the electronic maps underlying the Census of Population and Housing data collection and delivery. That conversation was the trigger for the Mann Library's early involvement with geographic information systems. Another time, a news story about electronic ink was stored as a possible influencing technology. Over weeks and months, trends in conversations on specialized e-mail discussion lists, articles in airline in-flight magazines, and conversations with patrons can all feed into the scouting activity.

Formal information gathering is more systematic. In any given era, research from various fields influences developments in information technologies that in turn affect libraries. In recent years those fields have included computer science (data storage, database design, search algorithms, graphic displays), cognitive psychology (user behavior, human interaction with computers), education (learning styles), and communication (organizational adoption of innovations, the effects of computer mediation on interpersonal communication, etc.). A scout who is the only librarian at a conference has escaped preconceived notions of where a library is supposed to be. Course-work, including workshops, short courses, and even full courses, helps a scout to develop the expertise to assess the various trends.

Scouts can also consult futures studies literature using the LC subject heading Forecasting. The World Future Society publishes *The Futurist*, sponsors an annual meeting, and has an online Futurist Bookstore stocked with titles such as *Encyclopedia of the Future*, and *Futures, Concepts and Powerful Ideas*. It publishes the *Futures Research Directory* in two parts: Individuals ("nearly 1000 people professionally involved in the study of the future"), and Organizations and Periodicals ("180 international organiza-tions and over 120 journals devoted to the field of futurism and futures research"). The Futurist Bookstore is at http://www.wfs.org/bookstar.htm.

Field trips and interviews are also useful. Scouts can visit other environ-ments that are involved in some aspect of information science: laboratories, offices, corporations, research organizations, or societies. Interviews—with patrons, information producers, commercial information service providers, and other players in related fields—provide an additional way of gathering information about trends.

The goal is to find information relevant to different aspects of the frontier. A scout looks deliberately and systematically at the trends (obvious and subtle), the technological developments, the research developments (from fields such as human computer interaction studies, cognitive psychology, and perception), and the status and behavior of organizations involved in information collection and distribution. The key message is that the scout needs to look beyond the library literature to see what other people are doing.

8. WHICH FRONTIERS

How does a scout or an organization decide which of the many frontiers to investigate? Where does one start? Does one start small or big? Organizational culture plays a role in this determination. A scout in an organization that prides itself on risk-taking can reach quite far ahead. A scout in a library with a large staff and significant resources can look at large-scale projects. A library with a small staff and limited resources may take a boutique approach and identify specialized projects. The organization's leaders set the overall directions, and thus they determine the overall directions for the surveying. Scouting directions should be in line with the general goals of the library, based on the role the library plays (or feels it should play) in the institution. An academic library is different from a library in a corporation, which in turn is different from a rural public library.

Another guideline: go to where the information universe is expanding most rapidly. In the late 1990s, there was an explosion in the amount of genomics data due to developments in sequencing technology. That area would be a likely candidate for a scout to investigate. According to one of the editors at O'Reilly Press, their philosophy is to identify areas of "information pain" and then to go there. A scout could employ much the same technique, looking to identify the frustrating elements of the information retrieval process, places where patrons are encountering problems.

A library could identify clusters of data that have formed a critical mass needing a librarian's assistance to ensure their rational distribution. For example, an academic land-grant institution's cooperative extension service might be seeking guidance on how to describe and organize its publications for electronic distribution.

A scout could look for areas where a library could make a difference, where a new audience has opened up for existing information. The following example illustrates how a library implemented a service that was made possible by commercial companies' responses to a developing market. With the proliferation of microcomputers in the mid-1980s, online database vendors such as Bibliographic Retrieval Services and Dialog sensed a new market in home computer users. These vendors began to make deeply discounted search services available after standard business hours, and in response some libraries instituted evening search services. Those libraries had been scouting and seized an early opportunity to provide low-cost searching services to scholars.

Another logical area for focus is where there is an assessment that a failure to plan and act could have unwanted consequences. The pricing models for electronic journals, currently in a state of flux, will have long-range effects on library budgets and services. Most libraries must scout in this direction, being attentive to developments and trends in that arena. Presently, most of this landscape is unmapped territory.

Finally, there is the wildcard option that has no logical justification. The scout, and the organization, should follow hunches, the evanescent clues and wisps of trends that may eventually become major developments in the information environment and important for the library. A current example of such a "wisp" is peer-to-peer file-sharing technology such as that used by Napster (which supported the sharing of music files across the Internet). A bioinformaticist at Cold Spring Harbor is exploring the potential of peer-to-peer technology for the identification and retrieval of information such as annotated DNA sequences. That same technology is very likely to have additional applications for information other than sequence data [4].

9. DELIVERING THE INFORMATION BACK INTO THE ORGANIZATION

The final step in this navigation process is the incorporation of information into the decision-making process. It is critical that the scouts report their findings back to the organization. If the information is not incorporated into the organization's decision-making process, there is no reason to gather it. It is best if the reporting is a structured analysis and presentation of the information that has been gathered. That presentation can be formal (as a white paper, or written report) or informal (a verbal presentation). The function of either process is to ensure that the library internalizes the information and the assessment at the necessary level, by the appropriate people: the department head, director, provost, or senior management group, for example. Generally, it is most fruitful if the information is delivered in a written document and then discussed and clarified in a meeting.

Then what? In some cases the scout will have sufficient information to make an assessment on how the library should proceed. In some cases the scout may not have enough information, so the assessment would be made after discussions with the management individuals or groups. In either situation an agreement on an assessment should be reached. There should be an agreement on the probable impact of a trend (e.g., for a library that collects whale vocalizations, streaming audio technologies will have an impact on how information central to its mission is delivered). There should also be a decision on what to do. There are several paths that can be determined: (1) Trend X is not an area to move into (the Gopher example); (2) wait and monitor trend Y examples until further movement puts it into a go or no-go situation (the example of peer-to-peer technology for information transfer); or (3) do something about trend Z (the GIS example).

In Chs. 2, 5, and 7 we discuss how those decisions can play out into projects—implemented by teams—that are eventually mainstreamed into the library's everyday work.

10. INDIVIDUAL AND ORGANIZATIONAL ELEMENTS: WHO DOES THE SCOUTING?

What elements are needed to make the scouting process work? Success comes from a combination of the proper individuals as scouts with a receptive organization.

In order to do well, a scout must have a mindset that enjoys a fast pace since the information environment is changing so quickly. Scouts must be comfortable with ambiguity and able to make overview assessments. They should like working in uncharted territory, be happy working alone, and have a modicum of intuition. There is an element of superficiality to this process, since the scout is identifying trends but not necessarily becoming an expert in a particular development.

The scout's role might be to make identifications and assessments, but then to bring that information back into the organization for discussion, requests for additional information, and a determination of action. The action might be for other staff to actually implement the library's response. Therefore, the scout should be able to hand off the work and move to the next frontier. The scout should not be possessive, or a maverick, and therefore unwilling or unable to return the information back into the organization.

On the other hand, sometimes a scout will see a project through and then remain central to that effort after mainstreaming. Alternatively, a scout might see trends through from scouting to project to mainstream, and then move on to the next frontier.

It is an enjoyable role for some people. There is low individual risk since the infrastructure and subsequent organizational assessments keep the effort from going too far afield. The scout has the positive feedback loop of seeing the successful initiation of services or collections, of patrons directly appreciating the projects as identified, and of other libraries eventually moving into the area.

Depending on the size of a library, it might have several scouts, or just one or two. A library might need to hire into the role if it needs to get the right personality match. However, institutions generally have potential scouts on staff and can begin by setting up the structure, formulating the process, and developing the skills in the appropriate staff. There are courses in trend analysis and forecasting. A library could hire "professional scouts" (e.g., futurist consultants). But it is better to have permanent staff working in this role so that knowledge can be kept in the organization.

The role of scouting should be distinguished from the role of leadership. Leaders assess the information scouts bring back and they make the actual decisions on what should be done. Leaders must factor in many variables (situational, economic, and political) and make choices as to execution, priority, and sequence of any actions. Leaders set the direction and make overall decisions, combining the scout's findings with other relevant information. For example, when GIS-related services were being discussed in the Mann Library, it was the assessment of the senior management team that the library's role in GIS should be to get data to its patrons in a useful format. Since there was no campus license for GIS software, library management decided to wait. GIS software and coursework would not be areas in which the library would take the initiative, because this library's role was to support content. Other groups on campus were responsible for providing the technologies that manipulate and present content. Enough groups on campus were interested in having affordable GIS software to keep the issue alive, and several of those groups were more suited to supporting the software than the library was. A year after that decision was made, a more appropriate unit on campus did become the site manager for GIS software.

Preparation is an important element in this activity. A library must look far enough ahead to be able to act "in time," because once a library decides to do something, it needs to assemble the financial and human resources to make a project happen. Existing budgets and staff might accommodate small projects, but larger projects are likely to require a reallocation, additional funding, or perhaps grant support, to be accomplished.

When external funding (either from the home institution or a granting source) is required for an innovation, it is best to anticipate it will take three cycles of funding requests to obtain the budget. The first year the budget request is made it will probably be too new, too strange, for the administration to understand it. The second year it will have progressed to being an understandable, but still unfundable, request. By the third year the administration will not only understand the value of the request, but it will also have had time to plan for its funding. In addition to a strong leadership within the library, it is helpful if the library is able to exercise a level of influence on its environment and is supported by the overall organization that it serves. It is easier to obtain needed resources if the home institution wants the library to make innovations and take a leadership role.

Timing is tricky. If a library plans too far ahead, it can run into several possible snags. Funding sources often do not share the vision and are unwilling to fund a project. If they do fund a project, a library may discover that available technology is inadequate, or that human and institutional factors are not merging with the technology as needed for the project to be a success. Even so, a library can still take away valuable experience and expertise from the process and apply it elsewhere. This timing assessment is like trying to assemble a jigsaw puzzle that is moving away from you as you work on it.

There are other challenges. A library may identify a trend but have insufficient resources, or skills, or influence to do anything about it. A frustration associated with technological solutions is they often require a large programming investment, something that an individual library may not be able to generate. In such cases a library has to wait for a commercial company to create a solution. A library faces another roadblock if the solution requires participation outside the organization, a wider agreement on the goals and "rightness" of the project. Projects requiring standardization are an example of this need for wider agreement.

11. RISKS AND BENEFITS

There are risks involved in scouting the frontier. A library can make a wrong assessment and focus on an arena that proves to be a minor one. This error results in a less-than-optimal use of resources and may divert resources from an area that was more deserving. The process is one of educated guesses with the possibility of great gains in services, or a needless use of resources and confusion for the patrons. However, even if a planned service is not implemented, or a particular project is not achieved, it is highly likely the library will have gained expertise that can be applied to future projects and services. Benefits to the individual library, as well as to the profession, usually outweigh the risks.

There are many of these benefits. By using scouting to guide progress, a library can be proactive, ahead of patrons' needs. It can have services ready when patrons need them, instead of having to scramble to respond to changing circumstances. In turn, this gives the library credibility with the community it serves. The library will earn a reputation as a quality organization. If its community includes funding sources—as is often the case—the library's scouting helps to maintain continuing support.

Staff also benefit from scouting. Potentially, many staff can engage in it. The whole library can be involved to one degree or another. The staff can develop unique expertise, which enhances their professionalism. Staff satisfaction increases, and they can take pride in their innovations (after all, lead dogs get the best view). Staff are given the chance to accomplish, to meet challenges, and to solve problems. Staff members have confidence in their organization and stay motivated and engaged.

For librarians working in a service operation, there is always the challenge of balancing their proactivity as information scientists while they maintain a user-driven service operation. Librarians are the information engineers, taking technologies and theories from diverse fields (such as computer science and cognitive psychology) and applying them to the real-world situation of the user needing information. But we cannot simply wait for those fields to provide us with packaged solutions. As professionals, we must be engaged in the production of systems.

In that role, we have the potential to affect the information environment so that our sphere of influence is expanded beyond our primary users. The innovations we create can help anyone working with information—including information producers and distributors. We can help to create better, more useful resources. That in turn helps other libraries, which in turn enhances our profession. Furthering our profession, in turn, benefits our society. As Jefferson said, "Enlighten the people generally, and tyranny and oppressions of body and mind will vanish like evil spirits at the dawn of day" [5].

REFERENCES

1. De Solla Price DJ. Little Science, Big Science and Beyond. New York: Columbia University Press, 1986.
2. Scobczak J. How Visionaries Lead Us Astray. Bus Comm Rev Oct 1998: 22–24.
3. Committee on Assessing Crop Yield—Site-Specific Farming, Information Systems, and Research Opportunities, Board on Agriculture, National Research Council. Precision agriculture in the 21st Century: Geospatial and information technologies in crop management. National Academy Press: Washington, DC, 1998;17.
4. Declan B. Music Software to Come to Genome Aid. Nature. April 13, 2000; 404:694.
5. Letter to Du Pont de Nemours. April 24, 1816.

Index